ELEMENTS OF JOURNALISM

ELEMENTS OF JOURNALISM

R. Choudhary

CENTRUM PRESS
NEW DELHI-110002 (INDIA)

CENTRUM PRESS
H.O.: 4360/4, Ansari Road, Daryaganj,
New Delhi-110002 (India)
Tel: 23278000, 23261597, 23255577, 23286875
B.O.: No. 1015, Ist Main Road, BSK IIIrd Stage,
IIIrd Phase, IIIrd Block, Bangalore-560085 (INDIA)
Tel: 080-41723429
Email: centrumpress@gmail.com
Visit us at: www.centrumpress.com

Elements of Journalism

First Edition, 2010

ISBN 978-93-80540-61-0

PRINTED IN INDIA

Printed at Mehra Offset Press, Delhi

Contents

Preface

The Elements of Journalism describes some of the problems, articulates the values, outlines the risks and offers understandable and practical ways to respond to the difficulties of the present state of journalism. It captures the shortcomings, subtleties, and possibilities of modern journalism. Others may say this list is nothing new. Journalists are constantly jockeying for the time and space necessary to tell their stories as they see fit. Only 47 percent of Americans even read a newspaper. And Time and Newsweek--news magazines, remember?--"were seven times more likely to have the same cover story as People magazine in 1997 than in 1977."

To the contrary, it is discovered that many ideas about the elements of journalism are wrapped in myth and misconception. The notion that journalists should be protected by a wall between business and news is one myth. That independence requires journalists to be neutral is another. The concept of objectivity has been so mangled it now is usually used to describe the very problem it was conceived to correct.

These are tough times for journalism. Newsroom executives' bonuses tend to be based on their company's profit margin. Unless we can grasp and reclaim the theory of a free press, journalists risk allowing their profession to disappear. The first principle is, "Journalism's first obligation is to the truth." The last: "Its practitioners must be allowed to exercise their personal conscience." In between come issues of loyalty, verification, independence, and power monitoring, among others.

If, as they set forth, "the purpose of journalism is to provide people with the information they need to be free and self-governing," it is believe that journalism has lost its credibility in the interest of the bottom line. One of the main reasons for this new emphasis on the bottom line, is that "technology is shaping a new economic organization of information companies, which is subsuming journalism inside it."

Chapter 1

Introduction

Many journalists like Jon Katz today feel that the boundaries between news and entertainment are blurring, particularly in the television medium. In this book, I examine these boundary concepts and attempt to answer a few complicated questions, such as: Why and how are journalism's boundaries socially constructed?

How are they negotiated by different groups of people with interests in mass communications? And—perhaps most importantly—how do journalists breach these boundaries and then respond to the breaches through boundary-maintenance exercises? I hope to recover some of the messiness of the boundaries through this inquiry.

The impetus for this study are the numerous observations and arguments that network television news and tabloid television entertainment programs are converging in style and content into a new genre called "reality-based programming."

This study will examine some of these arguments, looking for how this phenomenon is described, the explanations given for it, as well as the ex planations for why it has become an issue. As analyst, I will not be in a position to reach a definitive conclusion about the boundaries of these categories.

Rather, I will describe how interested players draw the boundaries. It is important to note that boundary work is committed within the day-to-day work of journalism as well as in the latter representations and reconstructions of journalism content and practice.

To accomplish these goals, I will examine three case studies—specific instances of boundary construction, negotiation, and maintenance in journalism. Most of the emphasis will be on how these boundaries affect television journalism, but other journalism media are also examined.

According to Justin Lewis, television is arguably the greatest culture-producing machinery on earth. For that reason, and because many conceive of television as primarily an entertainment medium, most of the attention in this study will be focused on television journalism boundaries.

SIGNIFICANCE OF THE PROJECT

As Peter Dahlgren says (perhaps understatedly), "Journalism's centrality in politics and culture, as well as its vested economic and occupational interests, make questions regarding its boundaries, uses and contingencies of more than idle concern".

Some of the questions along this vein that demand our attention include: How have journalists been able to demarcate their area of mass communication from other types of mass communication? What do they gain from such work? Do journalists maintain control over the production and evaluation of news?

How are journalists able to maintain the public perception that they are authoritative or credible? How do journalists convert cultural authority into other opportunities, such as jobs, political influence, and prestige? How do journalists respond to threats or challenges to their cultural authority? Admittedly, this study is just a start in this line of research. Journalists assert that they have the authority to perform an important function in our democratic society: to truthfully report the news and to inform the public.

This authority depends on the trust of the publics that the news media serve. American journalists say the defining characteristics of their work are that it is true, accurate, and in the interest of the audience—yet these are irrelevant unless audiences believe in the truthfulness and accuracy of journalistic accounts. If the public believes in the accuracy of journalism, then journalists gain authority—the authority to tell the news.

Other culture-producing mass media institutions, such as the advertising, public relations, and entertainment industries, also communicate to the masses. When these institutions and industries produce messages that appear similar to journalism, journalists interpret these events as threats to the boundaries and authority of journalism. The cultural authority of the institution of journalism depends on the ability of people to distinguish between it and other kinds of mass communication.

It is useful for us to examine what sociologists of science call *boundary-work rhetoric*: the rhetorical strategy of one group wishing to distinguish itself from another. For example, medical doctors draw a boundary—within their discourse and routine practices—between what they do and what faith healers do. Likewise, journalists who consider themselves mainstream draw boundaries between what they do and what other mass communicators do.

As I will show, these other communicators include people such as entertainment talk show hosts and tabloid journalists. When the public does not notice the difference between a faith healer and a doctor, either the doctor, the faith healer, or both will engage in boundary-work rhetoric; socially constructing a boundary in order to protect the authority to do their work.

Likewise, journalists engage in boundary-work rhetoric because they want the public to be aware of the differences between news work and entertainment work. The main questions I examine in this study are: How and why have television journalists and others defined "television news" and the goals, norms, and ideologies of television journalism as they have?

How have the boundaries between entertainment and news been constructed and negotiated as they have; and what rhetorical moves do journalists and others make to distinguish between the two? What are the differences in the uses of distinguishing characteristics between those within the journalism profession and those outside the profession? In effect: Who does boundary work, and how do different groups do it differently?

And finally, how do the interests and strategies of boundary-work rhetoric along the news/entertainment boundary compare to the interests and strategies of rhetoric uncovered along other boundaries, such as science/non-science; and what is it about the news/entertainment boundary that makes these strategies different—or similar?

To understand the significance of these questions, we must first examine some of the concepts that seem to be at stake here, such as authority, jurisdiction, and autonomy.

THE AUTHORITY AND SELF-DEFINITION OF JOURNALISM

The institution of American journalism has earned a mantle of authority in American society. The mere fact that many historians rely on newspaper and magazine accounts as primary source material indicates in a small way how journalism and the work of journalists become authoritative. As purveyors of facts and interpretation, journalists use this authority to describe events and everyday life to the public. Gieryn and Figert describe this kind of authority as social power: "'Cognitive authority' is the legitimate power (in designated contexts) to define, describe or explain bounded realms of reality".

The public entrusts journalists with this cognitive authority to the extent that they believe in journalists and their work. When the authority is threatened, journalists respond to consolidate their power. Paul Starr, in his studies of the medical profession, calls this power *cultural authority*. He says "cultural authority entails the construction of reality through definitions of fact and value".

Starr distinguishes cultural authority from social authority, which he says "involves the control of action through the giving of commands." Cultural authority, on the other hand, is derived from performing a service and from the ability to determine the *needs* of clients. If journalists perform the service of informing public debates, then they determine which cultural conversations people need to be aware of and engaged in.

The cultural authority of journalists, therefore. is based on the dependence of the public on the ability of journalists to present important information in a coherent and reliable fashion, or at least make it seem that way. This authority is reproduced in and through the everyday practices of journalists as well as later through boundarywork rhetoric. Starr says the cultural authority of medical doctors rests on three aspects of legitimacy: collegial, cognitive, and moral. For journalistic cultural authority, these same aspects of legitimacy are appropriate:

- The collegial legitimacy of the journalist—the acceptance by others in their profession;
- The cognitive legitimacy of the journalistic product—it is perceived to be based on rational, objective methods; and
- The moral legitimacy of the journalist—journalists' judgments are expected to be oriented toward altruism and public service.

Threats to cultural authority of an institution or profession do not always come from outside the institution or profession. A well-publicized case of fraud or fakery is perhaps the prime example of an internal threat to the cultural authority of a social institution or profession. Such turmoil is publicly discussed and thereby constructed as an issue or problem.

The discussion of the issue occurs as discourse within journalistic media by journalists who control the content and topics of the medium. For example, in 1980, *Washington* Post reporter Janet Cooke fabricated a news story about an imaginary eight-year-old heroin addict and was on the verge of accepting a Pulitzer Prize for it when the deception was revealed.

The *Post*'s subsequent analysis of the deception argued that the problem was not organizational, the problem was that Cooke was an aberration—a compulsive liar. As Dahlgren notes, one of the distinctive aspects of turmoil within the institution of journalism is that those within the institution "strive to maintain discursive control over such turmoil.

Among other things, this helps to consolidate and legitimate professional practices and identity (by). retain(ing) definitional control of the field, its problems and potential solutions".

Definitional control of the boundaries of journalism is also accomplished by journalists when they do things like formulate definitions of news and news work. It is also accomplished through the selection of news topics.

Defining news is not a simple task. A 1965 textbook for journalists admits, "To recognize news is easier than to define it". Yet the primary role of journalists is to determine what is newsworthy, that is, to define news. In defining news, journalists also define what it is they do. This study shows how journalists often define journalism in relation to its neighboring professions.

SOME BACKGROUND ABOUT "THE PROBLEM"

Many journalism critics have recently argued that American journalism is undergoing a profound change because it now regularly mixes entertainment with the news. Critics typically argue that this entertainment is in the form of sensationalistic celebrity-scandal. In fact, there is a long history of sensationalism in American journalism, a fact documented by several journalism historians.

But the main point of contemporary critics is that sensationalism and tabloid-style techniques, which were always present on the fringes of journalism, are now becoming the norm in American journalism, and are being adopted by so-called "mainstream" media as part of economic survival strategies in the cutthroat business climate of American mass media.

These contemporary critics typically argue that there should be a rigid boundary between mainstream journalism and other kinds of mass communication such as tabloid journalism. The critics imply that one kind of communication is more legitimate in certain contexts than the other, and even that tabloid journalism is not journalism at all but is instead entertainment. As noted above, one of the claims made by mass media critics is that journalism just recently got worse.

But this may be a perennial complaint. A quick review of journalism criticism reveals that the argument that journalism used to be better but just recently got worse is common throughout the history of journalism. The critiques usually say that journalism used to make bold distinctions between news and entertainment but now combines the two.

These critiques construct the logical conclusion that journalism has steadily decreased in quality over many years. Taken together, the criticisms add up to the conclusions that the people who used to do journalism were better and had higher standards than those of today and that the distinctions between news and entertainment used to be greater. Examples of this critique can be found in even the earliest discussions of American journalism.

For instance, critics panned Benjamin Day New York Sun of the early 1830s because it often contained humour and sensational news of suicides. Similarly, some critics hated James Gordon Bennett New York Herald of the mid- to late-1830s because it contained entertaining, satirically written police court reports, as well as in-depth crime stories.

Bennett pioneered the "human-interest story" or feature story, when he wrote in vivid detail in 1836 about the grisly murder of the prostitute Helen Jewett, quoting her madam and describing Jewett's apartment in minute detail. Bennett's day-by-day narrative of the ensuing sensational trial reminds us of how journalism and entertaining literature have been combined for many years to make newsworthy stories "more palatable for consumption."

Bennett was soundly criticized by his competitors and others for blurring the boundary between journalism and entertainment. His detractors, many of them his competitors, waged what they called a "Moral War" in the late 1830s against Bennett and his enjoyable but sensationalistic newspaper. They maintained that Bennett was a "deviant" journalist because he blurred the boundaries of journalism by making his newspaper entertaining and popular.

Those running the "Moral War" against Bennett were unsuccessful at running him out of the journalism business, but they did seriously wound his business. In the 1920s, many journalists were labeled "yellow journalists" because they sensationalized and twisted the news by appealing to prurient interests and base instincts.

In 1962, philosopher Jürgen Habermas argued that the boundaries between news and entertainment are blurring because people prefer "entertaining" news and its immediate rewards: Public affairs, social problems, economic matters, education and health. 'delayed reward news'—are not only pushed into the background by 'immediate reward news' (comics, corruption, accidents, disasters, sports, recreation, social events, and human interest) but, as the characteristic label already indicates, are already read less and more rarely.

In the end the news generally assumes some sort of guise and is made to resemble a narrative from its form down to stylistic detail (news stories); the rigorous distinction between fact and fiction is ever more frequently abandoned.

News and reports and even editorial opinions are dressed up with all the accouterments of entertainment literature, whereas on the other hand the belletrist contributions aim for the strictly 'realistic' reduplication of reality "as it is" on the level of clichès and thus, in turn, erase the line between fiction and report.

The integration of the once separate domains of journalism and literature. Brings about a peculiar shifting of reality—even a conflation of different levels of reality. Under the common denominator of so-called human interest emerges the mixtum compositum of a pleasant and at the same time convenient subject for entertainment that, instead of doing justice to reality, has a tendency to present a substitute more palatable for consumption and more likely to give rise to an impersonal indulgence in stimulating relaxation than to a public use by reason.

Habermas, in making the observation that literature and news were "once separate domains," is doing, in 1962, journalism/entertainment boundary work. An example of a similar critique of journalism boundary-degradation—but attributed to a different root cause—is the melodramatic opening paragraphs of Ron Powers' 1977 book *The Newscasters,* which says the sea-change in journalism happened in the 1970s:

The biggest heist of the 1970s never made it on the five o'clock news. The biggest heist of the 1970s *was* the five o'clock news.The salesmen took it. They took it away from the journalists, slowly, patiently, gradually, and with such finesse that nobody noticed until it was too late. By the 1970s, an extravagant proportion of television news—local news in particular—answered less to the description of "journalism" than to that of "show business."

This transformation, carried out by the sales-oriented station managers in an unbounded quest for profits, bore the profoundest implications in the way Americans were to receive information and perceive political choices. Many local newscasts ceased serving the public (at best, they served the public only incidentally) and bequeathed their primary allegiance to the advertisers.

Powers blames the quest for profits, instead of journalistic values, for the swing toward show business techniques and content. Similarly, Edwin Diamond, in 1975, notes that the potential for profits associated with high ratings points for news programs led to the downfall of journalistic control in local television newsrooms around the country.

The responsibility of controlling the news process was relinquished to news consultants who had no knowledge of journalism but who were well-versed in audience survey techniques and behavioural psychology.

In other words, they knew how to design a local news programme that would attract a mass audience but not one that would inform it: Up until a few years ago, television news was in the hands of professional news directors and producers, traditionally trained in newspaper or magazine work or broadcast journalism.

It still is at the networks. But local station management has not had the same professional approach, especially since the local stations began discovering that their news times could be highly salable, often cheaper to run than straight entertainment shows, and attractive to many advertisers. Not only has television news become longer. It has become too important to be left to the newspeople.

Audience research has been perceived as the key to ratings success. For Diamond, "professionals" are those trained in journalism, especially in newspaper and magazine journalism, areas where audience research has not been pursued as thoroughly as in television.

In taking control away from the professionals, journalism has taken a back seat to superficiality, and news judgments are now made by managers skilled in audience research. Powers' and Diamond's critiques of television journalism are quite similar to the critiques that were raised throughout the early history of the television medium.

They seem to argue for a monopolization of authority and protection of autonomy for journalists. In other words, Powers and Diamond would like to see journalists maintain control over all aspects of journalism and keep others from controlling any aspects of it. Recently, Steven Stark, a commentator on popular culture for National Public Radio, wrote that the root cause of increased sensationalism in radio and television news is the advent of all-news channels in the 1980s, such as CNN.

He says the increased demand for news around the clock has caused journalists to become irresponsible: Unlike the old days, when there were, at most, two news cycles a day, there is now a 24-hour demand for information. That means the network news and newspapers have to provide a different product than they once did, because they assume people get their headlines elsewhere.

The result has been a considerable broadening of what is considered reportable news and analysis—much of it far less objectively verifiable than in the past. We now have fields of news that didn't exist 15 years ago, such as entertainment reporting. News from the tabloids is considered fair game.

Call-in shows can put forward any "expert" they can drum up, while encouraging callers to speculate and gossip. Some TV commentary itself is close to staged: Crossfire and

The McLaughlin Group are to James Reston and Edward R. Murrow what pro wrestling is to sports.

Because of the incessant demand, news is also presented more quickly to the public, with the inevitable result that there's a far thinner line between fact and rumor—one reason why personal details about celebrities get reported more quickly, if not falsely—than before.

This is all part of a far larger cultural pattern—the babble of a postmodern age that has seen feeling gain pre-eminence over thought, while elites collapse. Stark's theory that journalists responded to the increased frequency of news "cycles" and an increased demand for news by lowering their standards for newsworthiness implies that journalists are not doing their jobs, and are, in fact, remiss in their responsibility to decide what counts as news.

This is not a new critique, though the root cause selected by Stark may be a new idea. Many other examples could be cited of journalists and others arguing that journalism is changing, moving toward more entertainment and less information. The critique is indeed perennial.

As shown above, examples of it can be shown from the very beginnings of American journalism right up to the present. Journalism professor and historian Mitchell Stephens (1988) puts this kind of criticism in context:

Some of the criticism television journalism inspires is. shortsighted. News and entertainment [did not] meet and mate for the first time on often giggly, often frivolous, local television newscasts in the United States; their affair dates back at least as far as criers and minstrels.

Television news, in other words, did not inject a foreign substance—playfulness—into the news; news has been enjoyed for as long as it has been exchanged.

Like the penny papers of the 1830s, the yellow journals of the 1880s and 1890s and the tabloids of the 1920s, television has succeeded in attracting a new audience to the news. Once television sets became affordable, news became available to audiences of many millions, including even those lacking the energy, skill or maturity to read a newspaper or concentrate on a radio narrative. If the critique is perennial, then there must be a reason for it being so persistent. Perhaps these critiques serve an important purpose. Instead of evaluating the legitimacy of these claims and critiques, the constructivist approach to this debate focuses on how self-interested stakeholders (relevant actors) construct a conception of journalism that makes sense to them and that helps to consolidate their power and prestige.

These stakeholders believe that the cultural authority of their institution depends on distinct boundaries, which, in turn, rest on concepts such as the perceived credibility and objectivity of their work. This constructivist approach to the issue helps us understand how the boundaries of journalism are constructed, negotiated, and maintained, giving us insights into what journalism means to people. To say that these boundaries are *constructed* implies that they have no firm, absolute contours.

Instead, they are contextually contingent, local, and episodic, with the *potential* to become stable and widespread. To give a brief example of boundary-work analysis, let us examine the words of the authors cited earlier in their arguments about the blurring of the news/entertainment boundary. They all imply that "real" journalism is something different from what we have now.

The characteristics of "real" journalism that the various authors mentioned earlier in this section cite include distinctions such as: News is meant to inform, not entertain; it presents facts, not fiction; it does not include speculation or gossip; and it is controlled by professionals who serve the public, not by advertisers who seek only profits.

These are demarcation criteria that help journalists "construct" their role in society—and help them understand the shape and contours of the *cultural space* in which journalism resides. Looking at the claims more closely, it appears that the authors mentioned earlier in this section cite the *functional* differences between news and entertainment: One informs, the other entertains.

They also note *epistemological* differences: One is a factual kind of knowledge, the other contains fiction. They also cite *methodological* and *organizational* differences: One uses gossip and speculation, the other does not; and one is controlled by professionals who serve the public, the other serves less-altruistic goals.

As an analyst, I am not in a position to "solve" the debates about these issues. Instead, I look at how others solve them. In particular, I examine the apparent goals of boundary debates; how interested parties pick out the essential elements of the boundaries; and whether and how their work achieves any results.

The goal of this project is to analyse how the boundaries between news and entertainment are "constructed" by relevant actors. To accomplish that goal, I look at several examples of constructions of monopoly, deviance, and autonomy as "social issues" with stakeholders in journalism. The constructivist approach to questions about what is journalism and what is not replaces the answer with the question as the thing to be studied.

In other words, I do not try to find a definitive-necessarily essentialist—answer to the question "What are the boundaries of journalism?" Instead, I analyse and examine how journalists and others have attempted to answer this perplexing question, particularly when they claim that certain acts and practices are not journalism but are entertainment.

In these kinds of claims, we gain valuable in sight into the ways journalists make sense of what they do, and about the role of journalism in society. Journalism, like all social institutions, is socially constructed. Questions about where journalism ends and entertainment begins are a viable field of study that up to this point, has been largely ignored. This project should begin to remedy this situation by examining what many call journalism ethics issues from a constructivist point of view.

The way journalists make distinctions about acceptable behaviours, intentions, and content says a lot about culture production and how society creates and defines itself. Throughout this study, cartographic metaphors—mapping images-are used as a way of thinking about the relationships between different institutions in American culture. Journalists map out the cultural space of journalism by specifying where the boundaries are located.

As Gieryn notes, cartographic metaphors are useful when discussing the idea of a cultural space—territorial markers that people use to make sense of the world around them. He says, "cartographic metaphors offer a robust language for thinking about relations among cultural phenomena," particularly the relations between adjacent phenomena.

In the cultural space of mass media, news and entertainment appear to be adjacent phenomena. Gieryn suggests thatwe consider using cartographic terms such as "contours, landmarks, scale, orientation, coordinates, points of interest, and legend". These terms compel us to examine how this cultural space was slowly carved out of the cultural landscape rather than privilege journalism-as-it-is as the only logical outcome.

Some of the boundaries of journalism may be moving and flexible or perhaps blurry and indistinct. In other places they may be uncontested and easy to see. In any case, it is the players on either side of the alleged boundary (or in the middle of it) who are the primary stakeholders in constitutive rhetoric that attempts to delineate borders.

That is why the primary site of this study is in the rhetoric of journalists: They have the most to gain or lose by such rhetoric about the boundaries of journalism.

Newspapers and periodicals often contain features written by journalists, many of whom specialize in this form of in-depth journalistic writing. Feature articles are usually longer forms of writing; more attention is paid to style than in straight news reports. They are often combined with photographs, drawings or other "art." They may also be highlighted by typographic effects or colors.

Writing features can be more demanding than writing straight news stories, because while a journalist must apply the same amount of effort to accurately gather and report the facts of the story, he or she must also find a creative and interesting way to *write* it. The *lead* must grab the reader's attention and yet accurately embody the ideas of the article.

In the last half of the 20th Century the line between straight news reporting and feature writing has blurred. Journalists and publications today experiment with different approaches to writing. Tom Wolfe, Gay Talese, Hunter S. Thompson are some of these examples. Urban and alternative weekly newspapers go even further in blurring the distinction, and many magazines include more features than straight news.

Some television news shows experimented with alternative formats, and many TV shows that claimed to be news shows were not considered as such by traditional critics, because their content and methods do not adhere to accepted journalistic standards.

National Public Radio, on the other hand, is considered a good example of mixing straight news reporting, features, and combinations of the two, usually meeting standards of high quality. Other US public radio news organizations have achieved similar results. A majority of newspapers still maintain a clear distinction between news and features, as do most television and radio news organizations.

Professional journalism is a form of news reporting which developed in the United States at the beginning of the 20th century, along with formal schools of journalism which arose at major universities. As documented by Robert McChesney, "[n]one of these schools existed in 1900; by 1915, all the major schools such as Columbia, Northwestern, Missouri, and Indiana were in full swing."

According to McChesney, professional journalism arose in the response to the capitalist imperative of consolidation. As the many independent newspapers which existed at the turn of the century, often with a radical agenda and with no presumption of balance or objectivity, were acquired and consolidated, the large resulting newspapers understood they needed to appear balanced and objective to their audience and advertisers. Thus, professional codes developed, as well as the academic programs to fill these positions.

Sports journalism covers many aspects of human athletic competition, and is an integral part of most journalism products, including newspapers, magazines, and radio and television news broadcasts.

While some critics don't consider sports journalism to be true journalism, the prominence of sports in Western culture has justified the attention of journalists to not just the competitive events in sports, but also to athletes and the business of sports.

Sports journalism in the United States has traditionally been written in a looser, more creative and more opinionated tone than traditional journalistic writing; the emphasis on accuracy and underlying fairness is still a part of sports journalism. An emphasis on the accurate description of the statistical performances of athletes is also an important part of sports journalism.

Science journalism is a relatively new branch of journalism, in which journalists' reporting conveys information on science topics to the public. Science journalists must understand and interpret very detailed, technical and sometimes jargon-laden information and render it into interesting reports that are comprehensible to consumers of news media.

Scientific journalists also must choose which developments in science merit news coverage, as well as cover disputes within the scientific community with a balance of fairness to both sides but also with a devotion to the facts. Science journalism has frequently been criticized for exaggerating the degree of dissent within the scientific community on topics such as global warming, and for conveying speculation as fact.

Investigative journalism, in which journalists investigate and expose unethical, immoral, and illegal behaviour by individuals, businesses and government agencies, can be complicated, time-consuming and expensive — requiring teams of journalists, months of research, interviews (sometimes repeated interviews) with numerous people, long-distance travel, computers to analyse public-record databases, or use of the company's legal staff to secure documents under freedom of information laws.

Because of its high costs and inherently confrontational nature, this kind of reporting is often the first to suffer from budget cutbacks or interference from outside the news department. Investigative reporting done poorly can also expose journalists and media organizations to negative reaction from the subjects of investigations and the public, and accusations of gotcha journalism.

When conducted correctly it can bring the attention of the public and government to problems and conditions that the public deem need to be addressed, and can win awards and recognition to the journalists involved and the media outlet that did the reporting.

New Journalism was the name given to a style of 1960s and 1970s news writing and journalism which used literary techniques deemed unconventional at the time. The term was codified with its current meaning by Tom Wolfe in a 1973 collection of journalism articles.

It is typified by using certain devices of literary fiction, such as conversational speech, first-person point of view, recording everyday details and telling the story using scenes. Though it seems undisciplined at first, new journalism maintains elements of reporting including strict adherence to factual accuracy and the writer being the primary source. To get "inside the head" of a character, the journalist asks the subject what they were thinking or how they felt.

Because of its unorthodox style, new journalism is typically employed in feature writing or book-length reporting projects. Many new journalists are also writers of fiction and prose. In addition to Wolfe, writers whose work has fallen under the title "new journalism" include Norman Mailer, Hunter S. Thompson, Joan Didion, Truman Capote, George Plimpton and Gay Talese.

Gonzo journalism is a type of journalism popularized by the American writer Hunter S. Thompson, author of *Fear and Loathing in Las Vegas, Fear and Loathing on the Campaign Trail '72* and *The Kentucky Derby is Decadent and Depraved,* among other stories and books. Gonzo journalism is characterized by its punchy style, rough language, and ostensible disregard for conventional journalistic writing forms and customs.

More importantly, the traditional objectivity of the journalist is given up through immersion into the story itself, as in New Journalism, and the reportage is taken from a first-hand, participatory perspective, sometimes using an author surrogate such as Thompson's Raoul Duke. Gonzo journalism attempts to present a multi-disciplinary perspective on a particular story, drawing from popular culture, sports, political, philosophical and literary sources. Gonzo journalism has been styled eclectic or untraditional.

It remains a feature of popular magazines such as *Rolling Stone* magazine. It has a good deal in common with new journalism and on-line journalism (see above). A modern example of gonzo journalism would be Robert Young Pelton in his "The World's Most Dangerous Places" series for ABCNews.com or Kevin Sites in the Yahoo sponsored series on war zones called "In The Hot Zone"

Another area of journalism that grew in stature in the 20th Century is 'celebrity' or 'people' journalism, which focuses on the personal lives of people, primarily celebrities, including movie and stage actors, musical artists, models and photographers, other notable people in the entertainment industry, as well as people who seek attention, such as politicians, and people thrust into the attention of the public, such as people who do something newsworthy.

Once the province of newspaper gossip columnists and gossip magazines, celebrity journalism has become the focus of national tabloid newspapers like the *National Enquirer*, magazines like *People* and *Us Weekly*, syndicated television shows like *Entertainment Tonight, Inside Edition, The Insider, Access Hollywood*, and *Extra*, cable networks like E!, A&E Network and The Biography Channel, and numerous other television productions and thousands of websites. Most other news media provide some coverage of celebrities and people.

Celebrity journalism differs from feature writing in that it focuses on people who are either already famous or are especially attractive, and in that it often covers celebrities obsessively, to the point of these journalists behaving unethically in order to provide coverage. Paparazzi, photographers who would follow celebrities incessantly to obtain potentially embarrassing photographs, have come to characterize celebrity journalism.

An emerging form of journalism, which combines different forms of journalism, such as print, photographic and video, into one piece or group of pieces. Convergence journalism can be found in the likes of CNN and many other news sites.

Ambush journalism refers to aggressive tactics practiced by journalists to suddenly confront and question people who otherwise do not wish to speak to a journalist. The practice has particularly been applied by television journalists, on news shows like The O'Reilly Factor and 60 Minutes and by Geraldo Rivera and other local television reporters conducting investigations.

The practice has been sharply criticized by journalists and others as being highly unethical and sensational, while others defend it as the only way to attempt to provide those subject to it an opportunity to comment for a report. This can usually be discerned by the level of physical aggression the journalist displays and in the time allowed for an uninterrupted answer.

In the 1920s, as modern journalism was just taking form, writer Walter Lippmann and American philosopher John Dewey debated over the role of journalism in a democracy. Their differing philosophies still characterize a debate about the role of journalism in society and the nation-state.

Lippmann understood that journalism's role at the time was to act as a mediator or translator between the public and policy making elites. The journalist became the middleman. When elites spoke, journalists listened and recorded the information, distilled it, and passed it on to the public for their consumption. His reasoning behind this was that the public was not in a position to deconstruct the growing and complex flurry of information present in modern society, and so an intermediary was needed to filter news for the masses.

Lippman put it this way: The public is not smart enough to understand complicated, political issues. Furthermore, the public was too consumed with their daily lives to care about complex public policy. Therefore the public needed someone to interpret the decisions or concerns of the elite to make the information plain and simple.

That was the role of journalists. Lippmann believed that the public would affect the decision-making of the elite with their vote. In the meantime, the elite (i.e. politicians, policy makers, bureaucrats, scientists, etc.) would keep the business of power running. In Lippman's world, the journalist's role was to inform the public of what the elites were doing. It was also to act as a watchdog over the elites, as the public had the final say with their votes.

Effectively that kept the public at the bottom of the power chain, catching the flow of information that is handed down from experts/elites.

Dewey, on the other hand, believed the public was not only capable of understanding the issues created or responded to by the elite, it was in the public forum that decisions should be made after discussion and debate. When issues were thoroughly vetted, then the best ideas would bubble to the surface.

Dewey believed journalists should do more than simply pass on information. He believed they should weigh the consequences of the policies being enacted. Over time, his idea has been implemented in various degrees, and is more commonly known as "community journalism."

This concept of *community journalism* is at the centre of new developments in journalism. In this new paradigm, journalists are able to engage citizens and the experts/elites in the proposition and generation of content. It's important to note that while there is an assumption of equality, Dewey still celebrates expertise.

Dewey believes the shared knowledge of many is far superior to a single individual's knowledge. Experts and scholars are welcome in Dewey's framework, but there is not the hierarchical structure present in Lippman's understanding of journalism and society. According to Dewey, conversation, debate, and dialogue lie at the heart of a democracy.

While Lippman's journalistic philosophy might be more acceptable to government leaders, Dewey's approach is a better description of how many journalists see their role in society, and, in turn, how much of society expects journalists to function. Americans, for example, may criticize some of the excesses committed by journalists, but they tend to expect journalists to serve as watchdogs on government, businesses and other actors, enabling people to make informed decisions on the issues of the time.

According to *The Elements of Journalism*, a book by Bill Kovach and Tom Rosenstiel, there are nine elements of journalism. In order for a journalist to fulfill their duty of providing the people with the information they need to be free and self-governing. They must follow these guidelines:

- Journalism's first obligation is to the truth.
- Its first loyalty is to the citizens.
- Its essence is discipline of verification.
- Its practitioners must maintain an independence from those they cover.
- It must serve as an independent monitor of power.
- It must provide a forum for public criticism and compromise.
- It must strive to make the significant interesting, and relevant.
- It must keep the news comprehensive and proportional.
- Its practitioners must be allowed to exercise their personal conscience.

In the April 2007 edition of the book, they have added one additional element, *the rights and responsibilities of citizens* to make it a total of ten elements of journalism.

In the UK, all newspapers are bound by the Code of Practice of the Press Complaints Commission. This includes points like respecting people's privacy and ensuring accuracy. However, the Media Standards Trust has criticised the PCC, claiming it needs to be radically changed to secure public trust of newspapers. This is in stark contrast to the media climate prior to the 20th Century, where the media market was dominated by smaller newspapers and pamphleteers who usually had an overt and often radical agenda, with no presumption of balance or objectivity.

There are several professional organizations, universities and foundations that recognize excellence in journalism in the USA. The Pulitzer Prize, administered by Columbia University in New York City, is awarded to newspapers, magazines and broadcast media for excellence in various kinds of journalism.

The Columbia University Graduate School of Journalism gives the Alfred I. duPont-Columbia University Awards for excellence in radio and television journalism, and the Scripps Howard Foundation gives the National Journalism Awards in 17 categories. The Society of Professional Journalists gives the Sigma Delta Chi Award for journalism excellence. In the television industry, the National Academy of Television Arts & Sciences gives awards for excellence in television journalism.

Such a code of conduct can, in the real world, be difficult to uphold consistently. Journalists who believe they are being fair or objective may give biased accounts—by reporting selectively, trusting too much to anecdote, or giving a partial explanation of actions. Even in routine reporting, bias can creep into a story through a reporter's choice of facts to summarize, or through failure to check enough sources, hear and report dissenting voices, or seek fresh perspectives.

A news organization's budget inevitably reflects decision-making about what news to cover, for what audience, and in what depth. Those decisions may reflect conscious or unconscious bias. When budgets are cut, editors may sacrifice reporters in distant news bureaus, reduce the number of staff assigned to low-income areas, or wipe entire communities from the publication's zone of interest.

Publishers, owners and other corporate executives, especially advertising sales executives, can try to use their powers over journalists to influence how news is reported and published. Journalists usually rely on top management to create and maintain a "firewall" between the news and other departments in a news organization to prevent undue influence on the news department.

One journalism magazine, Columbia Journalism Review, has made it a practice to reveal examples of executives who try to influence news coverage, of executives who do not abuse their powers over journalists, and of journalists who resist such pressures.

Self-censorship is a growing problem in journalism, particularly in covering countries that sharply restrict press freedom. As commercial pressure in the media marketplace grows, media organizations are loath to lose access to high-profile countries by producing unflattering stories. For example, CNN admitted that it had practiced self-censorship in covering the Saddam Hussein regime in Iraq in order to ensure continued access after the regime had thrown out other media.

CNN correspondent Christiane Amanpour also complained of self-censorship during the invasion of Iraq due to the fear of alienating key audiences in the US. There are claims that the media are also avoiding covering stories about repression and human rights violations by the Israeli and Iranian regimes in order to maintain a presence in those countries.

Chapter 2

The Cultural Authority of Journalism

This chapter is an ethnographic analysis of the process whereby anomalous journalists who are perceived to be a threat to the institution are ritually "relocated" to the outer edges of the boundaries of journalism. It is an examination of a case of journalistic misconduct that was discussed in great detail within the institution of journalism.

Dateline NBC, a network news division-produced weekly newsmagazine, broadcast a story in 1992 about General Motors pickup trucks; it contained a fiery simulated crash scene, which was staged by the program's producers. This staging was not disclosed to the audience.

Michael Gartner, then president of NBC News, was held responsible for the misconduct, which was labeled an act of journalistic fraud. The rhetoric by journalists that followed this example of journalistic deviance resembles what Harold Garfinkel calls a successful status degradation ceremony, whereby deviant members are expelled from an institution (in this case, the institution of journalism) in order to minimize harm to the institution as a whole.

Garfinkel has had a profound impact on sociological theory. As the founder of the ethnomethodology movement, his social constructivist emphasis on the way members of a group "make sense of, find their way about in, and act on the circumstances in which they find themselves" has opened up a vast new territory within sociology.

This chapter utilizes Garfinkel's theory and methods to

examine one way in which journalists demarcate the realm of journalism within the cultural landscape.

This rhetorical analysis scrutinizes the naturally occuring discourse among journalists following the *Dateline* broadcast, focusing attention on the elements of status degradation ceremonies described by Garfinkel. This is an examination of the rhetorical strategies of journalists reacting to accusations that the NBC News division used fraudulent methods in presenting the news and that Michael Gartner failed his profession by allowing it to happen.

Deviance in American journalism is defined and confronted by the official agents and apologists of the institution of journalism—namely, other journalists who discuss the practices of journalism as an *interpretive community*. This chapter is an examination of how members of a public institution produce cultural meaning and reproduce social structures by engaging in rhetorical discourse designed to map out the cultural space of a social institution.

The "universe" sample for this chapter included all the articles listed in the NEXIS database containing the words "Dateline NBC" and "General Motors" appearing in major American newspapers, magazines, and wire services between November 1, 1992, and June 30, 1993.

Dateline NBC was a weekly network newsmagazine programme that began in April 1992. On November 17, 1992, *Dateline NBC* broadcast a report entitled, "Waiting to Explode?," which criticized the design of General Motors full-size pickup trucks built between 1973 and 1987, alleging that they were more susceptible to dangerous explosions when involved in side-impact vehicle collisions.

The news report included a powerful visual demonstration of the problem: footage described as an "unscientific crash demonstration," which included a fiery explosion. General Motors Corporation investigated the charges made in the story and then filed a defamation lawsuit against NBC.

GM took the unprecedented step of announcing their lawsuit via a two-hour globally televised press conference on

February 8, 1993. During the press conference, GM lawyers alleged that *Dateline*'s producers allowed "incendiary" or "sparking devices" (model rocket engines) to be attached to the underside of the trucks to ensure that any gasoline spilled during the simulated accident would ignite—and that *Dateline* then failed to publicly disclose this fact in the programme.

NBC responded with an on-the-air apology the next night, read by *Dateline* anchors Jane Pauley and Stone Phillips. GM dropped its lawsuit shortly after the apology. Michael Gartner resigned on March 2, 1993. Three producers responsible for the GM pickup story segment were forced to resign on March 19, 1993.

NBC President and CEO Robert Wright publicly apologized to viewers and to GM on March 22, 1993.The news media covered the story of NBC's fraud in detail, and many journalism critics discussed it in various newspapers, magazines, professional journals, and on television programs.

The Poynter Institute for Media Studies in St. Petersburg, Florida, sponsored a conference entitled "When Good Journalists Do Bad Things: Truthtelling and the Public Trust." The conference included a twohour discussion of the *Dateline* scandal by professional journalists and journalism professors, which was televised live on C-SPAN on April 15, 1993, recordings of which Poynter now sells on videocassette.

RESPONDING TO DEVIANCE

The very public outcry by journalists and journalism critics in this case—people who believed they were part of the "mainstream" American journalism institution—was a signal that a boundary line was crossed by *Dateline NBC*.

The line was described as an epistemological boundary between different kinds of knowledge (truth and fiction), as a functional boundary between news and entertainment, and as a methodological boundary between disinterestedness and agency. The *Dateline* story was portrayed as a violation of professional norms that threatened the distinction between mainstream and tabloid journalism, or between news and entertainment.

This public discourse served several purposes:

- To distance the methodology, content, and apparent function of the *Dateline* episode from commonly accepted journalism standards and to signal that this kind of behaviour is deviant.
- To reassure the public that professional journalists are able to police their ranks.
- To maintain the social boundaries between journalism and entertainment (or between mainstream and tabloid television news) by showing that deviant behaviour that results in products that resemble these other genres of communication will not go unpunished.

To demonstrate the contours of the boundaries of journalism, Gartner and his associates were labeled as deviant journalists. There are both costs and benefits to revealing deviant behaviour: "the basic dilemma of social control: to publicize or not to publicize deviant behaviour".

Such publicity is negative and can serve to undermine public confidence in the institution—especially in the short term. A pattern of unpunished violations of norms, however, could be more damaging to the perceived integrity of the profession in the long run.

Durkheim says the public sanction of deviance is a healthy exercise for a group or institution because it helps to show group members how to recognize the area between acceptable and unacceptable behaviour.

In his study on the sociology of deviance among the Puritan settlers of America, Kai Erickson notes that "the interactions which do the most effective job of locating and publicizing the group's outer edges would seem to be those which take place between deviant persons on the one side and official agents of the community on the other".

The official agents of the journalistic community are fellow journalists, who operate together as an interpretive community, "united through their collective interpretations of key public events. The shared discourse that they produce is thus a marker of how they see themselves as journalists".

One of the distinctive aspects of turmoil within the institution of journalism (probably much like turmoil in other institutions) is that those within the institution "strive to maintain discursive control over such turmoil. Among other things, this helps to consolidate and legitimate professional practices and identity (by). retain(ing) definitional control of the field, its problems and potential solutions".

The site of this chapter is in the symbolic actions of journalists-their communicative acts—as they respond to threats to the cultural authority and boundaries of the institution of journalism in America. These rhetorical actions are interpreted and evaluated as components of a successful status degradation ceremony. Such a ceremony consists of "communicative work directed to transforming an individual's total identity into an identity lower in the group's scheme of social types".

The individual in this case is Michael Gartner, former president of NBC News. The other three *Dateline* workers who were fired over the controversy—executive producer Jeff Diamond, senior producer David Rummel, and field segment producer Robert Read—were also denigrated somewhat by their peers, but Gartner received the major blame for the controversy because he was ultimately responsible as head of the NBC news division.

Because he served as a lightning rod for criticism, most of the attention here will be given to Gartner and the rhetoric directed at him. It is clear that—to his detractors—Gartner symbolized everything that was wrong with NBC News and everything that was wrong with American television journalism.

SOME BIOGRAPHICAL NOTES ON GARTNER

Throughout the 1980s and 1990s, Michael Gartner was one of the most well-known and outspoken personalities in the journalism profession. Gartner—with his trademark bow tie—was an icon for First Amendment absolutism. A third generation journalist, his father and grandfather both worked at newspapers in Iowa.

Some of his previous accomplishments include: page one editor, Wall Street Journal; editor and co-owner, Ames Iowa, Daily Tribune; general news executive, Gannett Co.; president, Des Moines Register and Tribune Co.; editor, *Louisville Courier-Journal* and *Louisville Times*; member, Pulitzer Prize board; and president, American Society of Newspaper Editors. For instance, Gartner once argued that "there is no right to privacy—except from the government".

This stance led to some controversial decisions, such as NBC's decision to identify the alleged rape victim in the William Kennedy Smith trial. Gartner is also known among journalists for his strict stand on the use of anonymous sources. He says it is wrong for reporters to use anonymous sources "in all but the most delicate of stories," because it damages the credibility of all journalism.

Gartner is also known for his business and financial expertise. In 1984, he managed to get the Gannett Co. into a bidding war for control of *The Des Moines Register*, and reportedly pocketed more than $3 million from the deal.

THE STATUS DEGRADATION CEREMONY

Garfinkel theorized that there are eight sequential stages of a successful status degradation ceremony, consisting of specific "effects that the communicative tactics of the denouncer must be designed to accomplish". These eight types of arguments must be put forward by people within a community or institution that wants to banish deviants and at the same time, minimize harm to the institution itself. The eight stages of this rhetorical ceremony are

- Both the event and the perpetrators are made to look unusual.
- The perpetrators are compared to bad stereotypes—implying that they are not just accidentally bad.
- The denouncers show that they belong to the community and that they are speaking for the community or institution, not just as private individuals.
- The denouncers show that the values of the

community are salient, and that they are correct and justified.

- The denouncers show that they speak for these values.
- The denouncers show that they have support from the community.
- The deviants are banished.
- The deviants are ritually separated from the community so that the community may go on as before.

Next is a detailed examination of each of the steps in the status degradation ceremony. Journalists made arguments before, during, and after the *Dateline* fiasco that seem to resemble each of the stages described by Garfinkel 40 years ago.

Stage 1: Both the Event and the Perpetrators Are Made to Look Unusual

The charges against NBC first came to light when GM staged its global press conference to announce its lawsuit. Harry Pearce, executive vice president and general counsel of General Motors Corp., said: "We now face a poisoned environment spawned by the cheap, dishonest, sensationalism of NBC's programme 'Waiting to Explode?' and its aftermath." GM's attack was quickly reported by journalists who seemed shocked that NBC had apparently used "other than standard" newsgathering techniques.

Journalists argued that *Dateline* used methods journalists don't normally use—they hired a biased subcontractor who staged a news story. NBC had hired The Institute for Safety Analysis (TISA) as a subcontractor to conduct the "unscientific crash demonstration." TISA is commonly hired to provide evidence for plaintiffs in personal injury lawsuits. GM argued that the Institute had an agenda to promote, and *Dateline* did not disclose this fact, nor did it attempt to balance TISA's views with those of disinterested sources.

It appeared that *Dateline* had crossed an epistemological and methodological boundary into the realm of agency, fiction, and entertainment. The information was gathered using entertainment-style methods, so it was fictional—designed to shock or entertain.

NBC was also charged with stonewalling—for not quickly admitting guilt but instead trying to rationalize its methods and its story. Stonewalling is one thing journalists particularly despise—but love to publicize. Eventually, Gartner realized that he should come clean: "I realized that we were just plain wrong. We were stonewalling them, using all kinds of excuses and rationalizations.

What we had done was just plain dumb, and wrong. And I was raised to admit you're wrong when you're wrong". Gartner did not come to this realization, however, until after GM initiated its multimillion dollar lawsuit. Michael Gartner, *Dateline NBC,* and NBC News were made to appear strange, and their offenses were made to look like elementary violations of common sense.

Howard Rosenberg of the *Los Angeles Times* delivered a potent insult: "A high school journalism student knows that staging or faking or fabricating or falsifying news is, under any circumstances, absolutely forbidden. The big lie, the ultimate corruption. Sweep that ethic under the rug, and a news organization becomes morally barren".

Rosenberg's rhetoric implies that *Dateline*'s producers were not journalists at all because they apparently did not receive (and do not reproduce) the methodological training common to all journalists (even high school journalists); they were made to seem unusual.

Even before the *Dateline NBC*/ GM event, critics charged that NBC was unable to launch a successful newsmagazine or other types of news programming, implying that NBC had an inferior network news division. NBC News was also criticized for inadequate checks on accuracy and journalistic standards. Peter Herford, a 26-year veteran broadcast journalist from CBS, said the *Dateline NBC*/ GM event would have never happened at ABC, where someone is in charge of standards.

Herford, who now heads the broadcasting programme

at Columbia University Graduate School of Journalism, said, At ABC, they had a full-time person, a vice president for news standards, who had a staff, who did nothing but review every investigative piece that went on the air, every major magazine piece that went on the air. He read all the scripts, etc., etc., etc. At ABC, that ['Dateline'] piece never would have gotten past him.

Thus, the NBC News division was portrayed as an unusually inferior organization, with no one doing the normal task of enforcing journalistic standards. In some of the rhetoric following the event, Gartner was portrayed as an outsider to broadcast journalism. For instance, Jonathan Alter noted that a few years before he went to work in broadcast journalism Gartner once told some ABC News producers that he thought

TV News is nothing more than a "shallow comic book". a superficial medium incapable of complex ideas. Today Gartner is in danger of being fired as president of NBC News, in essence for living down to his low expectations for the medium in which he works. Ultimately he looked down his nose a bit at what he did for a living—and it showed. That both loosened his own standards and left him without allies below him.

Alter thus argues that Gartner's outsider attitude toward television journalism carried on during his tenure at NBC News and could be one of the causes for this scandal. Alter also criticized Gartner for being more of a money manager than a journalist.

This is a familiar charge among journalists who bristle at the thought of money managers—"bean counters"—invading their ranks (penetrating their jurisdictional boundaries) and controlling journalistic output. It is an attempt by journalists to equate the journalist/manager organizational boundary with a "good" journalism/"bad" journalism boundary.

In the rhetoric examined here, Gartner, NBC News, and Dateline, were all made to seem unusual—as deviants who lacked knowledge of basic journalistic standards and thus operated outside the realm—the boundaries—of journalism.

Stage 2: The Perpetrators Are Compared to Bad Stereotypes-Implying That They Are Not Just Accidentally Bad

One of the ways journalists made sense of the *Dateline NBC*/ GM event was to stereotype it as similar to other well-publicized instances of journalistic deviance. The 1980 Janet Cooke/ *Washington Post* scandal and the 1989 scandal following ABC News's re-enactment of the Felix Bloch suspected spy case were mentioned by several journalists as examples of similar lapses in journalistic standards.

In the infamous Janet Cooke case, a *Washington Post* reporter fabricated a story about an eight-year-old heroin addict and then passed the fiction off as reality. In the Felix Bloch case, ABC's World News Tonight showed a tape that it identified as suspected spy Felix Bloch, passing a briefcase of secrets to a Soviet spy. The people in the video were actually actors hired by ABC, and the video was doctored to make it look like a surveillance tape.

By stereotyping the practices of *Dateline NBC* as similar to those of other well-known journalistic scandals, journalists were able to quickly make sense of the event, understand its significance, and formulate responses to it. Four authors mentioned the Cooke scandal and one mentioned the Bloch scandal as stereotypical examples of the same kind of fraud.

Another author implies that the *Dateline NBC*/ GM event is stereotypical of news values used in other countries where simulations, staging, and nondisclosure are not taboo in journalism: If NBC is looking for some consolation, it can find plenty of company in Japan. Staging the news is so commonplace that the Japanese have a word for it: *yarase.*

"In America, it's the exception rather than the rule," says *Newsweek*'s Tokyo Bureau Chief Bill Powell. "Here, it's just standard operating procedure. There is much greater latitude given to producers to set things up if it doesn't work out." Adds Dorian Benkoil, an Associated Press editor who researched Japanese media on a Fulbright journalism fellowship: "In the U. S. the lines between entertainment and news are blurring recently.

In Japan they never developed." The implication of this rhetorical claim is that the way *Dateline NBC* operates is completely foreign (literally and figuratively) to American journalists. Another of the rhetorical claims made by journalists following the *Dateline NBC*/GM event was that the "unscientific crash demonstration" was methodologically similar to things done on tabloid television programs, and that there were organizational similarities between *Dateline* and the tabloids.

Others noted that some of the people who worked on the *Dateline NBC* programme had previously worked at the tabloids. Ironically, tabloid producers used the *Dateline NBC* event as an opportunity to argue that their standards were higher—if anything-than NBC's network news standards. John Terenzio, executive producer of A Current Affair, was quoted in a *New York Times* article: "We would not have re-enacted a car crash using little rockets to blow up the car. We would have felt that was not correct, and our legal department would not have allowed it".

Terenzio thus delivers the fatal rhetorical blow to *Dateline NBC*: Its standards are even lower than those of tabloid television programs.

Rosenberg makes a similar point about NBC News's standards when he notes that none of the tabloid shows identified the alleged rape victim of William Kennedy Smith, though NBC's Nightly News did.

Stereotyped as anomalous, Gartner, NBC News, and *Dateline NBC* are rhetorically "moved" outside the realm of journalism to the cultural space where tabloid television, "reality-based programming," and entertainment television programs reside.

Stage 3: The Denouncers Show that They Belong to the Community and that They Are Speaking for the Community or Institution, Not Just as Private Individuals

Journalists demonstrated that judgment on Gartner and the *Dateline* scandal was only to be passed by fellow journalists—who understood the nuances of journalism—and who alone had the jurisdiction to police their ranks and control the boundaries of their profession.

The Poynter Institute conference in which the actions of NBC in the GM truck incident were debated was filled almost exclusively with members of the journalism community—reporters, editors, producers, and journalism professors. Lawyers were notably absent from the field of invited participants.

Lawyers did get involved when NBC hired "outside" counsel, Robert Warren of Gibson, Dunn & Crutcher in Los Angeles, and Lewis Kaden of Davis, Polk & Wardwell in New York, to conduct an investigation of how the exploding truck story came to be broadcast.

This concerned some journalists who felt threatened by the fact that people from outside the institution of journalism were going to judge the performance of journalists: Some NBC News staffers have questioned why the network hired lawyers to investigate the case rather than. asking a respected journalist to conduct an internal inquiry.

NBC's [spokeswoman Peggy] Hubble said that management felt outsiders would provide the most impartial investigation. [But]. one source speculated that hiring attorneys may be in part to protect lawyer-client confidentiality and to protect the network [from] lawsuits.

In the final analysis, journalists quickly assumed the role of jury in this case, undercutting any attempts by General Motors to have the trial go to a real court. Later, at the Poynter conference, Michael Gartner said that he wanted to settle the case quickly and get it behind them, and this is why the on-air apology was broadcast the day after GM filed its lawsuit. He also said that he had complete authority on the wording of the apology, and whether to accept the conditions of it or not.

Gartner's rhetoric was a reassurance to the journalists present at the conference that journalists were in control of the outcome of this case, and were thereby maintaining cultural authority—and jurisdictional control— over the settlement. GM's swift acceptance of the apology and dropping the suit indicates that the lawsuit was probably intended as a public relations move designed to provoke media criticism and the embarrassing public apology from NBC.

Stage 4: The Denouncers Show that the Values of the Community Are Salient, and that They Are Correct and Justified

For many years, television news was accepted as a money-losing venture for the networks, who accepted the burden of news as a part of the "public service" requirements required by the FCC. By the late 1980s, television newsmagazines like 60 Minutes had proven to be quite profitable for the networks, so they all launched new newsmagazine programs designed to make money and to win ratings periods.

Several broadcast news critics sounded alarms when they heard that John F. Welch, Jr., the president of General Electric (which bought RCA and its subsidiary NBC in 1985), wanted to make the NBC News division profitable. After all, they argued, NBC's entertainment division was way ahead of the other networks in prime-time ratings points, so NBC had a comfortable profit margin; and besides, they argued, News was traditionally an unprofitable division.

In August 1988, former news division president Lawrence Grossman was fired for not cooperating in GE's quest to make the division profitable; and Michael Gartner was hired in his place, partly because of his devotion to the idea that news businesses should make money. In a 1992 interview, Gartner said, "You can't be journalistically vigorous unless you're financially strong.

You just don't want to lose money-you don't want to be walking around with a tin cup. It is a news business and you want to be successful in both worlds, news and business". The altruistic mission of journalism to inform the citizenry does not always mesh well with the business mission to make money and profits for stockholders.

This is a perennial dilemma for journalism organizations,

which must remain in business if they are to serve the public. To be true to the social mission of journalism means that one must appear to be suspicious of profit-centreed motives.

Gartner was not clearly on the side of altruistic motives, and his critics used this as ammunition in their arguments portraying him as an outsider who was not completely devoted to the social functions of journalism.

Stage 5: The Denouncers Show that They Speak for These Values

In 1989, television journalism critic Jonathan Alter attacked the bottom line ethic of NBC: Instead of feeling liberated by their entertainment success to spend more of their riches on serious journalism, G.E.'s managers have downgraded the news division. Lacking the ratings benchmarks of hits like "L.A. Law" and "Cosby," the other networks don't expect as much ratings success from news, and have more air time to devote to it.

At CBS, news is still the jewel in the crown. At ABC, now loaded with talent, news is practically the crown itself. At NBC, it's a fancy belt buckle. What really matters is proving (NBC is) a company with a commitment to something beyond the bottom line.

Alter was echoing a familiar theme in newsrooms: Journalism is a public service that should not be concerned with profits. Clearly, the profit motives of Gartner, the NBC network, and its parent GE seemed foreign to some journalists.

Evidence also surfaced that NBC allowed its Entertainment Division to have control over news promotions—deciding which programs and segments would be mentioned during self-promotion advertisements. This connection between entertainment and news is not a healthy one, according to Reuven Frank, former president of NBC News. Frank notes that as news has become profitable, and as news employees—journalists—become concerned with profit, they naturally want these kinds of self-promotions to help increase the ratings for their programs:

Since TV magazines have achieved the status conferred by profit, they. get promos now. But the nabobs of entertainment continue to determine what will be hyped. This gives them veto power over the choice of topics in news division programs. A smart executive [news] producer will pick up topics likely to appeal to West Coast show business executives.

Entertainment executives were probably thrilled when they saw the sensational crash footage from the "Waiting to Explode?" segment. Frank's argument shows a concern that the boundary between news and entertainment divisions became blurred at NBC, raising questions about the authority and independence of journalism at the network. Journalists seemed dismayed that NBC News did not maintain strict boundary separation and autonomy from the other branches of the network.

Once the guilt of Dateline NBC had become a foregone conclusion, journalists came up with a variety of explanations of personnel and structural problems and other factors that pressured Dateline and Gartner into the climate that would allow such behaviour. One of these explanations was that business pressures were affecting the journalistic product. Diamond argued:

NBC News has been in disarray. because (1) GE has been trying to sell the network, thus contributing to a "Who cares?" atmosphere, and (2) the severe staff layoffs of the past few years, ordered by GE and executed by Gartner, have cut into the quality of the newsgathering.

Further, it's said, Dateline NBC has pushed the boundaries of accepted journalism because of the unrelenting need to create a successful magazine show like CBS's 60 Minutes and ABC's 20/20.

One unidentified NBC News producer said profit motives and competitive pressures were the keys to why the event occurred: "The tenor of the creation of 'Dateline' was that the profit of the news division rested on this show. In an atmosphere where there is such intense pressure for ratings, something like the 'Dateline' incident was bound to happen".

Gartner had approved massive cost-cutting measures at the news division, including layoffs of seasoned journalists. "There is a feeling among many here that the thrust of the present management is on ratings and that many of the people who have been pushed out had higher standards than some of those who are now in charge of these prime-time shows".

The denouncers of Gartner and NBC showed that they were suspicious of values that were other than purely journalistic.

Stage 6: The Denouncers Show that They Have Support from the Community

Although Gartner's detractors did not claim to be speaking for the journalism community, the preponderance of rhetoric critical of Gartner-the-individual indicates that they did. Only one or two came to his defence, signaling that his denouncers were supported by the journalistic community.

Another way Dateline's and Gartner's critics demonstrated their support from the institution of journalism was by building an "us versus them" mentality between the institution of journalism and the NBC News organization, accomplished primarily through professional solidarity.

Gartner was portrayed in many articles as a "prickly" manager who was easy to dislike, signifying that his position was probably not permanent, and Gartner himself seemed to acknowledge as much. Being known as unlikable certainly made him easier to banish from television news, but not all television critics thought that his personality was relevant.

Some seemed to indicate that it was an unfair attribute upon which to base his expulsion: Pressure for Gartner's ouster had been fueled by criticism from editorialists and columnists. "Gartner has become a bit of a sacrificial lamb for the media, the fall guy for all of television's problems," said Jon Katz, a media critic and former CBS producer.

"Michael has an uncanny ability to [anger] any audience of two people he encounters; he projects arrogance," said Eric Bremner, former head of King Broadcasting in Seattle and former chairman of the NBC affiliates. But, he said, "You have to respect some of his accomplishments." The banishment of Gartner and the three Dateline producers was supported by all those who engaged in published discussions of the event. Their unanimity proves that, perhaps unwittingly, they discovered that the way to fix the problem was through professional solidarity and ritual banishment.

Stage 7: The Deviants Are Banished

Gartner and individual journalists responsible for the Dateline story on GM were ritually banished from journalism through rhetoric designed to remove them from the cultural space of journalism. They were also banished by the company, NBC, which made a clean sweep—signaling that it was going to recover from this setback by upgrading the quality of its personnel.

Michael Gartner resigned from NBC—under pressure—on March 2, 1993. Three other producers, executive producer Jeff Diamond, senior producer David Rummel, and field segment producer Robert Read were forced to resign March 18, 1993. The accused were "made strange" compared to the rest of the institution of journalism—so that the institution would survive. And survive it did.

Stage 8: The Deviants Are Ritually Separated from the Community So that the Community May Go on as Before

Statements from NBC after the incident reflected the idea that the way to fix the news division was to sweep out the old and to find a good replacement for ousted president Michael Gartner. An NBC News executive said the ideal candidate would be a "top TV journalist who is a terrific communicator and has a squeaky-clean reputation for integrity".

Diamond notes that one of the conditions for Gartner's replacement was that the person had to come from within the television industry: "Newspaper people need not apply," he said.

The implication of this rhetoric is that one of Gartner's problems was that he lacked broadcasting experience, his lack of experience may have been a contributing cause of the event, and he was always considered an outsider to broadcast journalism.

A few months after the event, Gartner's replacement declared that all was better at NBC News: Andy Lack, president of NBC news said it took just three weeks for the news magazine Dateline NBC to bounce back in the ratings after the fiasco of a doctored test on General Motors pickup trucks.

Lack said those who produced the questionable report "risked their credibility." But he said he believed the show bounced back so quickly and was again accepted by viewers because NBC "handled the issue professionally, straightforwardly, as openly and honestly as you would expect. and the audience said 'OK, we get it, let's move forward.'"

Others within the company also made arguments that the setbacks from the event were temporary. NBC Nightly News anchor Tom Brokaw described the temporary nature of the damage:

The incident on 'Dateline' was a mistake. I don't think it's fair to say we've been permanently scarred, any more than CBS was permanently scarred by the [lawsuit filed by Gen. William Westmoreland over a 1982 "CBS Reports" documentary] or the *Washington Post* was permanently scarred by Janet Cooke.

By emphasizing the temporary nature of the setback and by citing some classic examples of other journalism outlets surviving scandals, NBC executives showed they were confident that NBC News would survive the mistakes of a few deviant individuals.

Others within the NBC News division expressed a positive attitude about the effects of the event. Knight-Ridder entertainment columnist Gail Shister wrote that Stone Phillips, a co-anchor of Dateline NBC, believed the consequences of the event would be good for the profession and the NBC News institution:

NBC's strength will come from the news division's newly

instituted system of internal checks and balances, Phillips says. That system is the silver lining in the Dateline cloud.

"Industrywide, there has been a re-examination of how newsmagazines go about doing their work. That's always healthy. Nobody wants to be the broad cast that hurts the over-all credibility of the whole medium. When there's a mistake of this magnitude, it hurts us all. Hopefully, some good will come out of it."

Again, expressions of optimistic rhetoric within NBC News in the aftermath of the ceremony reflect the attitude that the institution will fix itself and become stronger because of the negative experience. More than just a public relations ploy for outsiders, this kind of rhetoric also helps boost employee morale--making it a self-fulfilling prophecy.

NBC News used the Dateline fiasco as a justification to make changes and fix problems, hoping that the experience would strengthen them. As Hemingway wrote in *A Farewell to Arms,* "The world breaks everyone and afterward many are strong at the broken places."

Definitions of journalism matter to those working in the profession and institution of journalism. These definitions are a way for journalists to make sense of what they do and who they are. Definitions help them determine who belongs in journalism and helps to delineate the contours of the cultural space of journalism.

The status degradation ceremony serves as a warning to journalists to follow the rules and stay within the boundaries of journalism or be cast out as a deviant. In this case, journalists defined their profession/institution as one that does not permit fabrications or fictions.

In an act of social control, journalists ritually removed Gartner and several other deviants from the institution. Sociological "strain" and "interest" theories help explain how and why the journalism institution produces boundary-work rhetoric like this status degradation ceremony.

Clifford Geertz says in strain theories, people "flee anxiety," and in interest theories, they.pursue power," and they probably will do both at the same time, or do one as a result of the other. It could be argued that in the rhetoric surrounding this event, journalists attempted to flee the anxiety of the public disgrace of a well-publicized example of fraudulent practices; and at the same time they attempted to pursue the power of the authority of journalism—accomplishing both by sanctioning the perpetrators.

Perhaps they were fleeing from Gartner himself, a man who, with his strange ideas about privacy and profitability, had often been a source of anxiety for journalists. More than three years later, Gartner was still considered an outcast by many journalists. After the Society of Professional Journalists announced that Gartner would be the keynote speaker for its Fall 1995 annual convention, several members argued against his selection.

"Making someone the keynote speaker is an honour. And Gartner, for all his journalism accomplishments, forfeited the right to that honour because of his ethical lapses at NBC," wrote SPJ member Jonathan Salant. "[We] must hold ourselves accountable and ferret out ethical violations within our profession".

Although the rhetoric in this status degradation ceremony did not precisely match all the stages itemized by Garfinkel 40 years ago, it is obvious that the responses to this threat to the authority of journalism demonstrate how the boundaries of a social institution are drawn by those who consider themselves inside the institution, and that it is up to the members of a social institution to enforce its boundaries.

Garfinkel theorized that the status degradation ceremony is accomplished in order to deflect attention away from the structural or organizational defects of an institution. That did not happen throughout this case. For instance, conflict over the business/journalism boundary was mentioned by Gartner's accusers as an underlying motive for the misconduct, which tends to move the blame from the individual—Gartner—onto the organization—NBC.

In Stages 1 and 2, the NBC News organization was frequently blamed as the underlying cause of the scandal. By March 1993, however, criticism of the organization as the cause of the scandal had virtually disappeared, and the blame was set squarely on Gartner's shoulders. Most of the later articles about the Dateline scandal (in Stage 8) focused on how Gartner and the producers responsible for the episode were banished from the organization.

This tended to shift attention away from the structural and organizational flaws that made the scandal possible, and implied that the real problem was a few individuals, most notably Gartner. One reason for this discrepancy is that many of the denouncers in Stage 8 were people within the NBC News organization who clearly had a motive for shifting blame to the banished individuals and for seeing that the organization was again trusted as credible and able to produce quality, truthful journalism.

The concept that truth (and, implicitly, a social institution that practices full disclosure) will prevail in times of controversy descends from the seventeenth-century self-righting principle expressed by John Milton: "Let [Truth] and falsehood grapple; who ever knew Truth put to the wors[e], in a free and open encounter?"

Clearly, in the rhetoric critical of NBC, Gartner, and Dateline, the critics believed that their criticism would sensitize journalists to these issues and, therefore, prevent this from happening again. This rhetoric is also designed to stake out a cultural space in mass communications—programs produced by network news divisions.

In the cultural space between journalism and other things like entertainment, some boundaries are sharper than others. In this instance, journalists sought to sharpen a boundary by expelling one of its prominent members who they perceived had an ambivalent attitude toward questionable behaviour. The strength of their rebuke demonstrates how seriously they took the threat.

Chapter 3

Refining the Core Elements

Research into the managerial role of communication/ public relations practitioners represents a major strand in public relations research and theory development. However, much of this research has focused either on how female gender discrimination affects career advancement, salary, and status, or on arguments about practitioner involvement or exclusion from participation in management decision making and strategic planning, rather than focusing on questioning what is understood by the concept of "management" in the communication/public relations context.

Although public relations researchers have advanced a number of role typologies to help explicate the key dimensions of practitioners' roles within organizations, most notably, Broom and Smith's1 four role-typology framework and Dozier's manager-technician dichotomy, neither conceptual framework explains effectively what it is that public relations managers actually do.

The manager-technician role dichotomy has been the most widely used framework in roles research over the past two decades, but this typology has come under both ideological and methodological criticism. The former centres primarily around the vociferous liberal feminist critique of the manager-technician dichotomy which maintains that this typology tends to trivialize the technical dimension of the practitioner's role that tends to be performed more frequently by female than male practitioners.

However, it is the methodological criticisms of how the manager's role has been conceptualized and measured in the public relations context that is this chapter's focus. These criticisms, focused on the limitations of the role measures used to identify manager role enactment, and on the argument that the manager-technician dichotomy oversimplifies the complexities of role enactment, are drawn from work by Leichty and Springston, and by Moss, Warnaby, and Newman.

This chapter responds to these methodological criticisms by presenting results drawn from an ongoing international collaborative research programme into the nature of communications/public relations management and managerial work.

The principal aim of this research, begun with an earlier phase of qualitative research into work patterns of practitioners operating at managerial levels in U.K. and U.S. organizations, is to develop a more comprehensive and empirically-based understanding of management and managerial work performed by communication/public relations practitioners-one that reflects what it is that public relations practitioners actually do.

By extending the research across a range of countries, the aim is to eventually establish whether any generic elements or components of managerial work can be identified in the communication/public relations context that might transcend national and cultural boundaries.

PUBLIC RELATIONS MANAGEMENT PERSPECTIVES

Broom and Dozier's pioneering work in practitioner roles research and in advancing the principal role typologies widely used by other roles researchers is well documented. In addition to the emphasis on identifying and classifying the main elements of work activity associated with the enactment of different role typologies, research has examined the relationship between roles and a number of other variables, including gender and role enactment, gender salary inequalities, and practitioner career advancement.

Other themes emerging from roles research include the

relationship between role enactment and the status and power of public relations units in organizations;" practitioner involvement in strategic decision making; practitioner use of and involvement in evaluation research and environmental scanning; and practitioner involvement in issues management.

Roles research has come under increasing criticism during the past five to ten years on ideological and methodological grounds, including the strong feminist critique of roles research highlighted earlier. Other criticisms have focused on the rather static perspective of role enactment often provided by roles research, which has tended to treat roles as static categories into which practitioners are "pigeon-holed." One of the most significant criticisms has been the call for a re-examination of how the managerial dimension of practitioners' work is understood.

Leichty and Springston challenged the value of the manager-technician typology, suggesting that meaningful information may be lost by categorizing practitioners as either simply managers or technicians. They suggest that the public relations manager scale "lacks a coherent theoretical justification," and the eighteen items comprising the management role scale might be labeled "the everything other than technical activities scale."

Moss, Warnaby, and Newman also questioned the appropriateness of the way the managerial dimension of practitioners' work has been defined, pointing to the failure of most roles studies to distinguish between "managerial tasks and responsibilities" and "managerial behaviours."

Although roles researchers have developed some alternative role measurement scales, in most cases these are variations on Broom's original role inventory derived mainly from reviews of the public relations consulting and/or boundary spanning literatures, rather than being empirically based.

Wright's research is one of the few studies that focused on more senior communication practitioner roles, using survey, interview, and focus group research to identify a "communication executive" role comprising corporate senior vice presidents who appeared to report directly to CEOs. Reviewing these research and role measurement strategies, Grunig, Grunig, and Dozier pointed out there is no simple answer to the question of which approach to measuring practitioner roles is best, since roles are essentially abstractions of reality, making their measurement inherently problematic.

They acknowledged that the ongoing evolution of the communication profession suggests that Broom's ".original twenty-four item role set needs constant reinvention through intensive observation of what communicators do." It is here that some comparison with the work of management scholars who investigated the nature of managerial work and behaviour may prove informative.

THEORETICAL PERSPECTIVES ON MANAGEMENT

Our previous research pointed to the contrast between the broad consensus view of "management" and the practitioner's managerial role found in the public relations literature, and the ongoing and often-contested debate about the nature and practice of management found within the management literature. From the management theory perspective, two main schools of thought about the nature of managerial work emerge.

On one hand, the classical view of management, normally associated with the seminal work of Fayol, is of a rational profession in which managers perform a set of activities designed to enable them to plan, organize, command, coordinate, and control.

This technocratic model of management as a rational profession has been challenged by a series of studies conducted during the past thirty to forty years that sought to identify what managers actually do. The general picture suggests that the image of managers as rational analytical planners, decision makers, and issuers of commands does not stand up to scrutiny.

Rather, as Stewart has suggested, a manager appears to be someone who often: lives in a whirl of activity, in which attention must be switched every few minutes from one subject, problem, and person to another. It is a picture not of a manager who sits quietly controlling but who is dependent on many people, other than subordinates, with whom reciprocating relationships should be created; who need to learn how to trade, bargain and compromise.

Although on the surface these two views of management may appear irreconcilable, as Hales and others have suggested, these differing management perspectives can be attributed, in part, to the different foci and methods adopted by management researchers.

While some studies have examined the substantive "elements" of managerial work (what managers do), others have examined the distribution of managerial time between work elements (how managers work), managerial interactions with others at work, or the informal elements of managerial work (what else do managers do).

Perhaps the most significant distinction that emerges across these studies is how scholars have conceptualized the constituent features of managerial work in terms of the difference between the "observable activities that constitute the performance of the job, and the implied or reported tasks, which represent expected or intended outcomes."

This distinction has not been reçognized in public relations roles research, where the focus appears be placed primarily on identifying the reported tasks that constitute the "manager's role" rather than investigating how managers work-in terms of observing or recording what activities they undertake.

As Culbertson and others highlighted, most roles studies essentially offer a "snapshot view" of practitioner role enactment, rather than attempting to reflect the dynamism of role behaviour, particularly in terms of capturing the fluidity of managerial work in its different guises. Two further observations about the work of managers emerging from management research might also be relevant to understanding the manager's role in the public relations context.

First, management scholars broadly agree that managerial work is contingent upon inter alia function, level, organization (type, structure, size) and environment. second, managerial jobs appear to be sufficiently loosely defined to be highly negotiable and susceptible to choice in terms of style and content.

Not only do managers appear to make choices about the job content (which aspects of a job a manager chooses to emphasize), but also about the methods (how the work is done). Dalton suggested that negotiation over job content is not only part of what managers do, but also a motif running through all managerial activity.

Turning to the treatment of the manager's role in public relations roles research, with one or two exceptions, there appears little explicit recognition that the content of the manager's job might vary with functional level as well as from organization to organization.

Despite the fact that roles theory suggests an individual's role is determined through an interactive process of "role sending and role taking," there seems to be little explicit acknowledgment that practitioners might "negotiate" their role's content other than in terms of demonstrating a preference for the retention of a craft or creative element in their work.

There are clearly some significant differences between management and public relations scholars in terms of their understanding of the potential complexity and variation in managerial work and practice. Public relations roles research has offered a relatively simplistic onedimensional view of management, focusing largely on the reported "tasks" performed by public relations managers, and largely ignoring the "how" and "why" dimensions of management.

Even in examining what public relations managers reportedly do, questions arise about the adequacy of the role inventory measures used to try to capture what it is that public relations managers actually do.

Only in more recent research have public relations scholars begun to consider how management work and management expertise might vary in scope both within and across organizations. Grunig, Grunig, and Dozier suggested managerial expertise can be usefully segmented into two empirically and conceptually distinct components-strategic and administrative managerial expertise.

However, even here there appears to be some incongruity in terms of the elements of expertise that the authors designate as "administrative," and "strategic," tying the latter to elements of stakeholder environmental and evaluation research-what they suggest are the strategic tools a communication department needs to use with the two symmetrical and asymmetrical models.

More controversially, Grunig, Grunig, and Dozier suggested activities such as "developing strategies," "managing issues," and "developing goals and objectives" should be recognized as elements of "administrative" rather that "strategic" managerial expertise. Such questions about what constitutes "strategic" or "administrative expertise" in the communication/public relations context represent a further example of the lack of integration of management and public relations theory building with respect to the concept of management and managerial work.

These limitations in the understanding and treatment of "management" within the public relations context surfaced clearly in our earlier qualitative study of senior practitioner role enactment. We recognized that a comprehensive reconceptualization of management in the communication/ public relations context would require a re-examination of not only the key elements of managerial work (what communication/ public relations managers do), but also of managerial processes (how practitioners perform their managerial roles), and the influences on managerial role enactment (why they behave in the way they do).

To conduct such a single multi-dimensional study would prove highly complex and difficult, so for this study the emphasis was placed on identifying the key elements of managerial work performed by communication/ public relations practitioners to develop a more effective and empirically grounded conceptualization of the communication/public relations manager's role.

METHOD

The literature reveals a variety of qualitative and quantitative approaches and methods used to measure constructs such as management roles. In the case of public relations roles research, the majority of studies take a quantitative approach, primarily using surveys based on Broom and Smith's traditional twenty-four-item role inventory.

This study also uses a survey instrument focusing on the type of work activities performed by practitioners operating at a managerial level, but rather than drawing on Broom and Smith's role inventory, it uses an inventory of practitioner managerial work activities derived from the public relations' practitioner role literature, management literature, and our previous research.

This exploratory research is unique, as it departs theoretically from Broom's role inventories to measure practitioner role enactment, and instead develops a survey design that explores empirically the public relations practitioners' work activities. Survey items were constructed and measured using a series of seven-point semantic differential scales, common in studies of this kind.

These are used to rate a specific variable depending on the relative importance it possesses. The instrument was a self-administered mailed questionnaire, with fifty-seven items covering eight operational dimensions of managerial responsibility or work:

- Counseling and advisory responsibilities;
- Issues management;
- Policy and strategy making;
- Trouble shooting and problem solving;
- Administration;
- Monitoring and evaluation;
- Negotiation; and
- Technical responsibilities.

A later section of the instrument contained the classification and demographic sections.

At item level, question development drew on the content

analyses of the managerial public relations practitioners' narratives from earlier qualitative work. In this phase, the elicitation of statements drew substantially on the analyses of subjects' accounts of their daily tasks and work activities across eight dimensions.

This stage focused on identifying the core elements and relative importance of the work performed by managerial-level practitioners, rather than attempting to investigate how they might perform their roles and the distribution of time spent on activities.

To improve reliability and eliminate reverse coded items, the questionnaire was pilot tested with a small sample of public relations practitioners accustomed to specifying role definitions. The characteristics of this study's sampling frame embraced two important criteria: (1) respondents reflected as many industry sectors as possible, including government, corporate, and not-for profit practice; and (2) all respondents held managerial-level positions within their respective departments or organizations.

The authors first developed a comprehensive typology of U.K. sectors and then, using these sampling criteria, randomly drew more than 1,000 names and address of suitable candidates from the U.K.'s Institute of Public Relations (IPR) online database. From this initial trawl, relocated members and educators or student categories were eliminated from the sample, which comprised 900 surveyed respondents.

To boost response rates a postal survey with a return envelope was chosen in place of e-mail and electronic attachments. The mail survey, which took place in March and April 2004, achieved a 25% response rate. After adjustments for spoiled questionnaires, 218 cases were analysed.

FINDINGS

Factor analysis has been widely employed within roles research as a method of reduction to simplify data and facilitate analysis of variables, as exemplified in studies such as Kelleher and Dozier and Broom. However, exploratory factor analysis was the chosen approach for this study rather than confirmatory factor analysis, as this work sought to uncover knowledge beyond the established two-factor (manager-technician) theoretical dichotomy.

Exploratory factor analysis explores the field to uncover new dimensions and constructs, and was therefore suited to this exploration of what might constitute the managerial dimension of practitioners' work, particularly given the relatively large number of variables that needed to be analysed.

The ultimate objective of the analysis was to reduce and summarize these variables with minimum loss of information, while a relatively small number of latent factors represented relationships among interrelated variables. The forty work activity scales were subjected to Principal Components Factor Analysis, with the remaining variables retained for later analysis.

This revealed the presence of nine components, all of which achieved eigenvalues greater than one. These nine components explained a total of 66% of the variance, which suggested the salience of these components. However, it was recognized that PCA can overestimate the number of factors to draw on and that the variance accounted for is also a function of the instrument's scale item wording.

As this exploratory research design necessitated the isolation of a relatively small number of dimensions on which relevant items loaded, two further methods were chosen as confirmation of the number of factors to rotate: the computation of total variance explained and a Scree test as verification of this cut-off point (the point at which the slope of the line changes).

Based on these observations, a five-factor model was identified. An orthogonal Varimax rotation facilitated the identification of a simplified factor structure. The five key factors that emerged suggest the core dimensions of the role performed by communication/public relations practitioners operating at the managerial level and, by implication, represent the core dimensions of what can be termed the communication/public relations manager's role. These five dimensions or core areas of practitioner work comprise four areas of what is identified as being essentially managerial responsibility: monitor and evaluator; key policy and strategy advisor, trouble shooter/problem solver: and issues management expert; as well as a further technical dimension labeled communication technician dimension.

The second stage of the analysis, an Oblimin or oblique rotation procedure, provided the theoretically important underlying dimensions and, because factors were correlated, represented the relatively large number of variables more accurately. Basing initial judgements on Hair et al., and given the sample size (n=218), it was determined that a factor loading of.32 and below was poor.40 was significant, and loadings of or greater were very significant.

Items with secondary loading lower than.40 were disregarded. Factor loadings on the monitor and evaluator, key policy and strategy advisor, trouble shooter/problem solver, issues management expert, and communication technician dimensions ranged from.41 to.89.

Cronbach alpha scores were computed on the items to indicate the level of internal consistency and reliability. The five key factors (with alpha scores) or core dimensions of the communication/public relations manager's role are now discussed within the context of factor loadings by drawing on the pattern matrix.

The first dimension (Factor 1), labeled the Monitor and Evaluator dimension, consisted of ten items, seven (primary) and one (secondary) (alpha =.87), and two secondary loadings on Key Policy and Strategy Advisor dimension.

This dimension captures the important managerial responsibility managerial-level practitioners often have for "organizing, controlling, and monitoring" the work of communication/public relations departments from both an internal and external standpoint; in the former case, being responsible for setting targets, operating within budget, monitoring performance against targets, and preparing departmental reports. In the latter case, the manager's role involves coordinating with other organizational management units, including top management, to set targets for the public relations function, negotiating for organizational resources, and commissioning external agencies.

The secondary loadings on items in the Key Policy and Strategy Advisor dimension suggest how the work of target and goal setting along with reporting on results embraces elements of close working with senior management in planning communication strategies and ensuring senior management appreciate the communication implications of their decisions.

The second factor (Factor 2), the Key Policy and Strategy Advisor dimension, focuses on the relationship public relations practitioners have with the senior management function (dominant coalition) within organizations, and comprised eight items, five primary (alpha =.83), and one secondary item that loaded on the Issues Management Expert dimension.

Items here were indicative of the type and level of policy advice and contribution that at least normatively public relations practitioners operating at a managerial might expect to offer to senior management. The negative loading on this factor's items suggests that for most of the U.K. practitioners surveyed, this type of involvement in the work of senior management teams (dominant coalitions) within their organizations remains largely the exception rather than the rule.

The third factor, the Issues Management Expert dimension (alpha =.78), consisted of six primary and three secondary items related to the public relations practitioner's role in diagnosing and responding to external threats from major or minor issues.

Working in this issues management mode sees practitioners acting not only as the organization's "eyes and ears," but also as an information processor and interpreter adding meaning to information. The primary and secondary loadings on the Trouble-Shooter/Problem-Solver dimension suggest a degree of ambiguity experienced by practitioners in terms of how they might distinguish between what is "trouble shooting" and what is "issues management."

This dimension also embraced some degree of involvement in providing support for other organizational departments, although the relatively low secondary loadings of less than 0.50 for some activities suggest that such involvement may be infrequent or at least not a regular job element.

The Trouble-Shooting/Problem-Solver dimension focuses on the practitioner's role in responding to and dealing with a range of internal or external challenges, threats, and/or crises confronting the organization. In this sense, public relations/communication practitioners are generally acknowledged to be the organization's designated "fire-fighters." The dimension encompassed six primary items, three of which loaded on the Issues Management Expert dimension and three on the Trouble-Shooting/Problem-Solver dimension.

Two secondary items also loaded on the Issues Management Expert dimension. The existence of the primary loadings across two dimensions again suggests there may be a degree of ambiguity in the minds of U.K. practitioners about their understanding of what constitutes "trouble-shooting/problem solving" as opposed to "issues management."

The negative loading on three of the primary items relating to practitioners' involvement in regular intelligence gathering and analysis, monitoring external trends, and making recommendations about handling a range of internal and external challenges that might potentially threaten the organization suggests that the majority of U.K. practitioners surveyed did not engage in this type of work.

While the previous four dimensions of the senior practitioner's role in organizations relate to what can be defined as managerial elements of their work, this study found a further fifth factor or dimension of the senior practitioner's role, labeled the Communication Technician dimension.

Although it produced the lowest alpha scores (alpha =.60) on three primary items, this dimension was retained because this research is exploratory and thus an alpha of.60 is acceptable.56 The strong loadings on two of these items relating to the handling and/or overseeing of technical work suggests many of the U.K. practitioners surveyed retain responsibility for at least overseeing technical communication within their departments, which may also include some direct involvement in this type of work.

One interesting finding is the media relations variable negative and positive loading of -.46 and.41. This dual loading has been interpreted as suggesting that, although operating at a managerial level, some practitioners appear to continue to engage in media relations work, while others do not.

The retention of some media relations work by some of the practitioners surveyed might reflect differences in department size and resources available to delegate such work, but equally, may reflect a preference on the part of some practitioners to retain a degree of involvement in media relations even though they may have moved up the organizational hierarchy.

In this sense, the findings here reflect those of previous roles research that has pointed to the tendency for practitioners to enact elements of both the manager and technician roles.

The sample's characteristics helped ensure that the study captured the dimensions of the public relations manager's role across a range of the U.K. sectors (e.g. government, corporate, not-for-profit).

On the surface, this interpretation of the key dimensions of the role performed by public relations practitioners operating at a managerial level in organizations might appear to display some similarities to the main elements comprising Dozier's manager-technician role typology.58 However, we believe the five-dimensional model advanced here offers a more robust and empirically grounded representation of the key responsibilities that practitioners have identified as of central importance in their managerial jobs.

This study focuses only on the U.K. phase of an international programme of comparative research into management and managerial work performed by communication/public relations practitioners.

It is suggested that this five-dimensional model of the managerial level communication/public relations practitioner's role will provide a useful framework for explicating the managerial dimension of the role performed by communication professionals in organizations operating in other national, regional, and/or cultural settings across the world.

By focusing on communication/public relations professionals identified as holding managerial-level positions within U.K.-based organizations, this study uncovered what appeared to be the major elements of "managerial responsibility" and "managerial tasks" performed by practitioners operating at managerial levels.

Moreover, the five-dimensional model advanced here offers a more comprehensive and empirically grounded explication of the managerial dimension of practitioner role enactment in organizations than is provided by the traditional definition of the "manager-technician" role dichotomy used by public relations roles researchers.

The authors believe this five-dimensional model of practitioner role enactment provides a more effective representation of the increasing complexity and sophistication of the work performed by communication/public relations professionals in many of today's organizations.

In one respect, however, this study does appear to confirm the findings of previous roles research in that even practitioners operating at relatively senior levels within their organizations appeared to retain some elements of technical work alongside their "managerial" responsibilities.

Albeit true for many of the more senior-level practitioners in the United Kingdom, this involvement in technical work appeared to be confined to overseeing the work of more junior colleagues.

It is important to acknowledge this research has focused on identifying the reported tasks or responsibilities that comprise the main elements of the "manager's role" in the communication/public relations context; the study did not attempt to investigate how managers work-in terms of recording the day-to-day pattern of practitioner activities.

Uncovering the latter would have required a far more intensive, essentially qualitative investigation using observation or diary techniques similar to the approach taken by management scholars such as Kotter, or in the public relations field, by Moss, Warnaby, and Newman, and DeSanto and Moss.

It is also important to re-emphasize that this present study is based on responses from a U.K. sample of practitioners only, so it would be inappropriate to attempt to generalize about the wider applicability of the five-dimensional model until further research has been completed in other regions/ countries of the world to test the validity and reliability of the dimensions of communication/public relations management advanced here.

This study found that although elements of the work performed by those practitioners studied such as monitoring and evaluation, issues management, policy and strategy advice, and trouble shooting/problem-solving might figure more prominently, most practitioners acknowledged that they continued to retain personal responsibility for what they saw as those more important elements of technical work. In some sense, this finding reaffirms the findings of other roles researchers who argued that, in practice, all practitioners "enact activities of both the manager and technician roles."

Our earlier qualitative research phase also found evidence of many managerial-level practitioners continuing to engage to some degree in elements of technical/ craft work, particularly those elements deemed to be highly important or sensitive.

The retention of some technical/ craft responsibilities by public relations/ communications practitioners might also simply reflect the relatively small size of the communication departments found increasingly in organizations today. Toth et al. noted the impact of this trend toward smaller-sized communication/public relations departments in the United

States and suggested that this trend resulted in many experienced managerial-level practitioners spending more time looking after day-to-day operational matters at the expense of performing more significant "managerial tasks" such as advising and counselling.

The expectation and even preference of some practitioners to retain some involvement in technical work irrespective of their seniority was noted by Dozier and Broom who acknowledged that for many practitioners the task of "creating and disseminating communication, especially mediated communication, is core to the public relations function."

Reflecting on what have been identified as the other core dimensions of the communication/public relations manager's role, two further important observations warrant consideration. First, one obvious inference is that practitioners operating at a managerial level appear to have a strong external focus in their work, emphasizing the importance of issues management, policy and strategy advice, trouble-shooting/problem solving, and the evaluatory elements of the manager's role.

Much less emphasis was placed on day-to-day administrative and organizing tasks as well as on human resource/team management responsibilities. This particular characteristic of the managerial dimension of practitioner work might be explained in terms of Hales's observation that: ".managerial work is contingent on inter alia: function, level, organization (type, structure size) and environment."

For the public relations function, the expectation may well be that practitioners will focus their efforts on maintaining effective organizational-stakeholder relationships, particularly with external stakeholders, and handling events and issues that might impinge on or threaten such relationships.

This is not to suggest that dayto-day team management and administration tasks are or can be ignored; rather, it may be a matter of priorities and the relative importance assigned to them. Thus, we believe the five-dimensional model of communication/ public relations practitioner responsibilities/

work described here represents a significant advance in terms of developing a more comprehensive framework for analyzing and understanding what can be identified as the "managerial dimension" of the work performed by communication/public relations practitioners and the contribution they can make to the overall strategic management of organizations.

This remains an essentially exploratory model and is based only on data collected from a cross section of U.K.-based practitioners. However, further international comparative studies in collaboration with researchers from other countries are being conducted, which should not only enable the robustness and reliability of the dimensions of public relations management identified here to be tested further, but will allow the generalizability of these dimensions of communication/public relations management to be tested across different cultural settings.

Chapter 4

Function of Journalism in Coverage

Print journalists at first halfheartedly played the celebrated role of "watchdog," in some cases urging readers to be tolerant of Japanese-Americans. But their tolerance, and their time in the "watchdog" role, lasted only until the government put the finishing touches on its policy to deal with alleged fifth column activity, a policy which culminated in the internment. From that point on, print journalists assumed the role of "guard dog," acting as the government's sentry, patrolling for threats to the official version of events that unfolded after Pearl Harbor.

Donohue, Tichenor, and Olien outlined the "guard dog" function as it relates to political reporting, but I argue that it is of particular relevance here. "Guard dog" journalists act as "sentries" for groups who hold power and who have the ability to create their own security systems - in this instance, the federal government, local and state officials, and the military.

Guard dog reporting takes place "when external forces present a threat to local leadership". In writing favorably about dominant groups, journalists tend to "concentrate on individuals while accepting the structure," a tendency seen clearly (and discussed in more detail later) in reporting on the alleged Japanese-American threat to national security. Through their interaction with and dependence on local leaders for information, journalists are trained to suspect potential intruders, and sometimes, as is the case here, "sound the alarm" for reasons that the dominant group may initially be unable to understand.

This inability arises when the authority within the power structure is divided or when part of the power structure is made uncertain by an organized challenge. Along the way, groups who lack power and influence receive little attention from "guard dog" journalists. How a journalist gathers information and writes stories is shaped by the nature of the structure being served and by whom the dominant groups label a threat.

When there is consensus in a community, the guard dog "sleeps," stirring only when an external threat to local leadership materializes. Conflict is reported "in a constrained way and only on certain issues and under certain structural conditions" - in short, when there is conflict between "dominant powers or power blocs". Further, "where different local groups have conflicting interests," Donohue, Tichenor, and Olien argue, "the media are more likely to reflect the views of the more powerful groups".

Such protection highlights "the functions of externally based conflict for reinforcement of local cohesion". Coverage emphasizes the role of dominant groups in addressing issues and correcting problems faced by the community. The guard dog function rejects as "unrealistic" the "watchdog" role of the press taught in so many university journalism classes as a guiding principle for journalistic practice.

The media are not autonomous; they operate as part of the power structure; as such, they "have neither the inclination nor the power to challenge those dominant groups, unless they are already under challenge by other forces". Unable to develop social policy or motivate political action, the media are left to report on actions taken by dominant groups.

If, as in the case of alleged "fifth column" activity explored in this monograph, "these groups and agencies are concerned primarily with an external threat, that will be the agenda of the media.". Questions from reporters that seem to challenge the official view of an event or issue amount to "role playing" driven more by attacks from "contending powers" than by a journalist's desire to expose corruption or challenge action taken by a corporation or agency.

The "guard dog" theory of reporting also runs counter to the view that reporters are little more than "lapdogs," - submissive, dependent, and oblivious to all interests except those of powerful groups. While a "guard dog" journalist does defer to authority, he or she is not completely subservient to dominant interests.

In times of conflict, the work of a "lapdog" journalist would amount to little more than a "defence of the powerful against outside intruders," while the "guard dog" reporter would look for opportunities to report conflict between dominant groups. How deferent a journalist is "depends upon the nature of the community structure as well as on the concentration of power in the larger society".

Finally, the guard dog theory rejects the notion that the media are "equal co-actors" in society's power structure, able to motivate support for policies created by the government, their influence so palpable "that only unusually strong institutions and leaders can counter it". In actuality, reporters are "dependent on the dominant powers" and act to protect "the local power establishment".

Reporters pay a great deal of attention to "nation and society - their persistence, cohesion, and the conflicts and divisions threatening their cohesion". The "tug of war" between the media and dominant powers seen by some is in reality "a result of reporting and reflecting the conflicting views among divided political or economic bodies".

A secondary theoretical strand for this chapter comes from Fiske's work on news as text. Fiske argues for the study of news as a form of discourse - "a set of conventions that strive to control and limit the meanings of the events it conveys". A string of events like those that unfolded after Pearl Harbor are, to use Fiske's term, "unruly." Journalists struggled to make sense of events and to gather information on which to build coverage.

This analysis also explores how journalists applied some of the "strategies of containment" discussed by Fiske to try and routinize coverage of the issues. It is argued, for example, that the government's take on the Japanese American threat became the dominant narrative strand in news coverage of this period; that is, it was "nominated," to use Barthes' term.

Coverage that promoted fairness and tolerance in dealing with Japanese-Americans was "exnominated" once the government took steps to implement its policy for dealing with the Japanese-American issue. For an event to be newsworthy, Fiske argues, it must pertain to "elite" people; it must also be "negative" and "surprising". Of the Japanese-Americans quoted in early coverage, many were prominent business owners and organization officials-the "elite," it could be argued, of the Japanese-American community.

Not only did this reliance on elite sources make it easier for journalists to manage early coverage of the crisis, it also gave them the means to begin marginalizing Japanese-Americans. When journalists began paying more attention to the government's version of events, they all but stopped using Japanese-Americans as sources. Instead, they looked only to prominent government and military officials for the lion's share of their information.

As Fiske notes, "the socially powerful tend to be familiar to us as individuals, the powerless or the voices of opposition are familiar mainly as social roles, which are filled by a variety of forgettable individuals". Donohue, Tichenor, and Olien conclude their discussion of the "guard dog" function with a series of hypotheses formulated to guide further exploration of journalistic practice:

In any structure, the intensity of press reporting and editorializing about a public issue is directly proportional to the degree to which top power positions are uncertain as a result of organized challenge.

Media are more likely to report attacks on individuals in power roles than attacks on power structures. Guard dog media reporting is less intense when the strategies of powerful actors are confined to the traditional roles of political conflict. Media coverage tends to be evaluated as more favorable among groups and occupations occupying more established and dominant power positions, compared with groups and organizations having less established power.

Questioning of the guard dog role is more likely in a highly pluralistic structure than a less pluralistic one. The balance of the monograph will be a test of these hypotheses built on coverage by journalists at three of the nation's most important newspapers of alleged "fifth column" activity by Japanese-Americans.

This case study of the "guard dog" function of the press is built on a textual analysis of the New York Times, San Francisco Chronicle, and Los Angeles Times from December 8, 1941-the day after the attack on Pearl Harbor - to February 19, 1942, the day FDR issued Executive Order 9066.

In all, the main news sections of seventy-two issues of each newspaper were reviewed. The New York Times was selected because of its reputation as the nation's "newspaper of record." The Los Angeles Times and Chronicle were included because they were, and continue to be, two of the most widely read newspapers on the West Coast.

Articles, columns, and letters to the editor that discussed Japanese-Americans, alleged fifth column activity, or calls for or against evacuation of Japanese-Americans were analysed for recurring thematic elements and thematic changes. The goal of the analysis was to chart the emergence of the "guard dog" function, and to show how journalists framed coverage of the alleged Japanese-American threat to national security.

President Franklin D. Roosevelt's decision in 1942 to intern more than 140,000 Japanese-American citizens is one of the darkest chapters in the nation's history. Constitutional rights were trampled; possessions were seized, lives destroyed - all in the name of eliminating a nonexistent threat to national security. Justification for Roosevelt's action came from fabricated reports of potential "fifth column" activity by Japanese-Americans from military officials bent on marshaling support for the United States' entry into World War II.

Issued by Roosevelt on February 19, 1942, Executive Order 9066 empowered the Secretary of War to "exclude any and all persons, citizens, and aliens, from designated areas in order to provide security against sabotage, espionage, and fifth column activity". Immigrants born in Japan (Issei) and second generation Japanese-Americans (Nisei) were not allowed to work or travel anywhere on the West Coast.

They were rounded up and sent first to "assembly centres," and then to one of ten relocation centres run by the civilian-staffed War Relocation Authority. On December 7, Roosevelt empowered Attorney General Francis Biddle to have the FBI arrest a set number of enemy aliens. On December 8, the Department of justice closed the borders of the United States both to enemy aliens and to "all persons of Japanese ancestry, whether citizen or alien".

By December 11, nearly 1,400 Japanese-Americans, by then classified as "dangerous enemy aliens," had been taken into custody. The Aliens Division of the Department of Justice, created by Congress in 1940, maintained lists of aliens who would be interned once war began. The Aliens Division was run by John Franklin Carter, a former journalist.

It was Carter who sent FDR a report from West Coast businessman Curtis Munson in which Munson claimed that while most Issei and Nisei were loyal to the United States, "there are still Japanese.who will tie dynamite around their waist and make a human bomb out of themselves".

Despite Munson's report, military officials at first concluded that "widespread sabotage by Japanese is not expected" and that "identification of dangerous Japanese in the west coast is reasonably complete". Nevertheless, 3,000 enemy aliens-half of them Japanese -were interned during the week following Pearl Harbor; the Treasury Department soon froze their bank accounts.

On December 19, 1941, General John DeWitt made the first military proposal for internment. The strongest advocates for internment would include then California Attorney General Earl Warren, later a revered champion of civil rights during his time on the Supreme Court, and DeWitt, who, along with Secretary of War Henry Stimson, encouraged Roosevelt to pursue evacuation as a viable means of ending the Japanese-American "threat" to national security.

Warren told a Congressional committee in February 1942 that Japanese-American sabotage and treachery would inevitably surface: "I believe that we are being lulled into a false sense of security.our day of reckoning is bound to come". In fact, DeWitt lied in his report to Roosevelt about the existence of the threat, a lie left unchallenged for more than four decades, until a federal appeals court ruled that the statute of limitations did not cancel the claims of Japanese-American evacuees whose property was seized before they were interned.

The Supreme Court relied on incomplete evidence when it held that possible subversive activities justified the evacuation of Japanese-Americans, the appeals court ruled. A key purveyor of this "incomplete evidence," according to a number of historians and institutions acting on behalf of Japanese-Americans, was the print media.

Acting far more pliant than the "guard dog" described by Donohue, Tichenor, and Olien, journalists were willing pawns in the government's attempts to paint Japanese-Americans as a threat to national security. Anecdotal evidence cited in accounts written by these historians offers some support for this claim. The Los Angeles Times, for example, announced on December 8 that California was "a zone of danger".

"We have thousands of Japanese here," a Times reporter wrote, "some, perhaps many are good Americans. What the rest may be we do not know, nor can we take a chance in the light of yesterday's demonstration that treachery and double-dealing are major Japanese weapons". After Pearl Harbor, Daniels contends, the Los Angeles Times called on "alert keen-eyed citizens" to finger what were surely "spies, saboteurs, and fifth columnists in their midsts". And it was not the first time that newspapers on the West Coast had attacked Asian-Americans.

In 1905, the San Francisco Chronicle lashed out at Asian immigrants in a series of articles supporting attempts by California's political parties and the American Federation of Labour to end immigration from China and Japan. Stories from the Chronicle carried headlines like "Crime and Poverty Go Hand in Hand with Asiatic Labour" and "Japanese a Menace to American Women".

Four decades later, an immediate call came from a number of journalists to deal decisively with the potential Japanese-American threat; according to Hosokawa, "other voices took up the cry as the days passed, until newspaper and radio commentators were baying like a pack of wolves on a hot trail."

West Coast newspapers "abandoned [their] tradition of supporting the underdog, seeking the truth, unmasking the demagogues, and demanding fair play". Syndicated columnist Henry McLemore brashly called for internment: "herd `em up, pack `em off, and give `em the inside room in the badlands". No journalist was more ardent about evacuation than Scripps-Howard columnist Westbrook Pegler, who advocated putting all Japanese-Americans under surveillance and suspending their habeas corpus rights.

For every hostage killed by the Axis powers, Pegler argued, the United States should kill "100 victims out of [American] concentration camps". At the time, however, the federal government was not actively considering evacuation. In a memo to Roosevelt, Attorney General Nicholas Biddle said that an attack on the West Coast by the Japanese was not imminent.

Hysteria, "and, in some instances, the comments of the press and radio announcers have resulted in a tremendous amount of pressure being brought to bear" on Warren and California Governor Culbert Olson, Hoover said in a memo to Biddle.

But joining Pegler in warning readers about the potential for a Japanese attack on the West Coast was revered columnist Walter Lippmann. At DeWitt's request, Lippmann, in his February 20, 1942 column, told his readers that he agreed with Warren, who argued that because the Japanese and Japanese-Americans were all the more dangerous since they had not yet engaged in any surreptitious activity. Inactivity, Lippmann wrote, was "a sign that the blow is well-organized and that it is held back until it can be struck with maximum effect".

More than twenty years later, Lippmann stood by his work: "There is no doubt that the rights of the [Japanese-American] citizens were abridged by the measure, but I felt then, and still do, that the temper of the times made the measure justified". Lippmann's quick assent to DeWitt's wishes contradicts his standing in the eyes of many scholars as "the most wise and forceful spokesman for objectivity" in journalism.

Indeed it was Lippmann who wrote that "men who have lost their grip upon the relevant facts of their environment are the inevitable victims of agitation and propaganda. The quack, the charlatan, the jingo, and the terrorist can flourish only where the audience is deprived of independent access to information".

The government and the military capably filled the role of charlatan as the period between Pearl Harbor and Executive Order 9066 unfolded, encouraging stories of decisiveness even as they wavered about the correct course of action. But for their part, reporters did not, to use Hosokawa's words, begin "baying like a pack of wolves on a hot trail."

They gradually fell into the role of "guard dog" discussed by Donohue, Tichenor, and Olien, focusing for at least a short time on the patriotism shown by Japanese-Americans. Only as the crisis unfolded - and the government deployed a policy to deal with it - did print reporters shift coverage to the fifth column threat fabricated by officials. We turn now to a detailed textual analysis of how this coverage unfolded.

AN ORGANIZED CHALLENGE

Two seemingly paradoxical strands of news coverage emerge immediately after Pearl Harbor: the first focused on efforts by Japanese-Americans to show their patriotism and loyalty to the United States and their support of the U.S war effort; the second revolved around glowing reports by journalists on efforts by law enforcement officials to detain Japanese nationals and Japanese-Americans.

Fiske might argue that the competing strands of coverage were a by-product of the "unruly" nature of a story that was still taking shape. Like the law enforcement officials working to develop a policy for dealing with Japanese-Americans, print journalists were trying to make enough sense of events to provide adequate coverage for their readers.

By writing at great length about efforts to detain Japanese-Americans, reporters reminded their readers that local, state, and federal officials still had the ability to "create security systems" - in short, to protect American citizens. Donohue, Tichenor, and Olien note that reporters "are on guard against all intruders so long as the authorities are acting in unison and the power relationships among them are stable".

A cynic might argue that law enforcement officials wanted to create the illusion of instability in order to muster support for their containment efforts. While the threat to national security never existed, there probably was a sincere belief on the part of law enforcement officials that the nation was in danger.

But instead of trying to stem the "confusion about who is running things,", officials, still trying to craft a policy in the wake of Pearl Harbor, decided to put a bit of manufactured "confusion" to work for them in order to sustain their version of stability.

And instead of examining the validity of the government's claims, journalists, who themselves were trying to manage coverage of the story, accepted and disseminated the information. Thus, on December 8, 1941, a page one story in the Los Angeles Times was headlined "Japanese Aliens Roundup Starts." The story, placed next to a story on the reaction of Los Angeles residents to the attack on Pearl Harbor, told of how "a great man hunt was underway," as the FBI sought "300 alien Japanese suspected of subversive activities".

In this story, like many of the others reviewed here, journalists quoted only federal and local law enforcement officials. The reporter described how FBI agents "grabbed" eighteen Japanese-Americans in West Los Angeles and how the "roundup" was the culmination of "months of investigation by FBI agents" led by Special Agent Richard Hood, who had been busy preparing "an index file of suspicious Japanese."

Federal officials, the story said, "planned to hold persons rounded up at various outlying police stations.until a concentration camp is decided upon." Here, the federal government's policy was still forming; nevertheless, journalists showed an early tendency to "sound the alarm" about the as yet unknown threat.

As Donohue, Tichenor, and Olien argue, "[m]aximum uncertainty in the structure occurs when countervailing groups have the capacity to challenge the established power, and thereby raise a realistic possibility that the power relationships may be altered".

But as noted earlier, this threat was manufactured; by reporting what would become an ongoing tally of arrests, reporters allowed federal and state officials to convey the false sense that the nation's position of power was uncertain - that Japanese-Americans living on the West Coast would inevitably alter the nation's power structure.

Thus, even as law enforcement officials were coming to grips with the ramifications of Pearl Harbor, reporters seemed to be creating conditions conducive to an "official version" of events. As we will see, the "intensity" of reporting about the incarceration of Japanese-Americans would increase as days passed.

In addition, the December 8 Times story focused on how the problem of Japanese-Americans living in the area impacted local officials, not JapaneseAmericans themselves or the system of government in place. As Donohue, Tichenor, and Olien note, "guard dog media display a tendency to concentrate on individuals while accepting the structure".

But the December 8 issue of the Times included a page two story that exemplifies the second theme seen in the newspapers reviewed here after the attack on Pearl Harbor: the loyalty and patriotism shown by Japanese American citizens. Under the two-column headline "Japanese-Americans Pledge Loyalty to United States," the story told of how the Japanese American Citizens League (JACL) pledged its "fullest cooperation and its facilities to the United States Government".

In a statement, the JACL deplored the attack, and urged FDR to declare war on Japan. The story quoted Shuji Fujii, editor and publisher of Doho, a Japanese newspaper, as saying that Japanese-Americans would be loyal to the United States. Fujii made his feelings known in a telegram to FDR. Also quoted was Yasuchi Sakimoto, an official with the Japanese Fishermen's Association.

Sakimoto said that his members, many of whom would come under fire as the government began manufacturing a fifth column threat, would "turn to agriculture as a means of support during the present conflict". On the same page, the Times ran a story about an apology from the Japanese consul to Los Angeles, Kenji Nakauchi, for Japan's actions. The reporter referred to Nakauchi as "slight" and "bespectacled" in the second paragraph of the story.

In response to the reporter's question, Nakauchi said 20,000 "Japanese nationals" and the same number of Nisei lived in the Los Angeles area. Under a two-column photo of Nakauchi in the centre of the page reading a copy of the Times with an enormous headline reading "War! Japs Bomb U.S. Base" was a caption that told readers Nakauchi was "surprised and shocked" about the attack.

Internment camps were not necessary, he said, especially since German and Italian Americans living in Vancouver were not interned when war with Germany began. Nakauchi was the subject of a shorter story in the December 9 Times which reported that he was "probably the calmest Japanese in Los Angeles."

A third loyalty-related Times story on December 8 told readers that it was "business as usual" in the Little Tokyo section of Los Angeles. "[T]he Japanese populace went about its ordinary Sunday business with an air of resigned calm" despite a steady, daylong flow of curious sightseers, the reporter wrote. News of the attack "failed-on the surface at least-to create much of a stir," according to the reporter. Japanese-Americans "were discussing the news in little knots on street corners." The story concluded with the news that a Committee of Eleven had formed "to maintain loyalty to the United States on the part of the Japanese population here". Local law enforcement officials did not take Japanese American citizens at their word.

The next day, federal, state, and local officials closed all Japanese-owned businesses in the district. The pejorative language used by Times reporters carried over from the previous day's coverage: "little clusters of Japanese gathered to discuss the wholesale display of American authority". Page five of the December 9 Times featured a five-column photo of seven JACL members and Los Angeles Mayor Bowron.

Ken Matsumoto of the JACL is seen holding the American flag; the photo's heading reads "Citizens Offer Loyalty Pledge to Flag." The accompanying story, headlined "Japanese-Americans Ready to Aid Nation," included a statement from the JACL's Anti-Axis Committee which read in part: "the enemy will try to sabotage our usefulness by inciting race hysteria. Let us be vigilant".

A story on the same page told of efforts by Los Angeles school officials to deal with the antiJapanese sentiment shown by many students. Their plan was a response to rumors circulating about everything from school closures to bombing raids. In a particularly ironic statement, Los Angeles School Superintendent Kersey said "the spreading of inflammatory rumors is a powerful weapon of the adversary to undermine morale".

The article talked about everything but easing the strain felt by Japanese-American students, other than a closing quote from Kersey that a "continuing spirit of tolerance should be shown to all who actively support the ideals we are defending".

It is tempting to applaud journalists for creating a tenor of tolerance in their coverage of events in the days after Pearl Harbor. However, their approach serves an important "guard dog" function: it tries to inspire readers to feel the sense of "local cohesion" that Donohue, Tichenor, and Olien discuss.

Thus, stories about loyalty and patriotism shown by Japanese Americans were in fact a tool used by print journalists to help officials keep order until a policy emerged. As they tried to make sense of Pearl Harbor, officials simply did not need the commotion or controversy-at least not yet.

Like the Times, the Chronicle on December 8 gave a prominent position (the bottom of page one) to a bylined story about Japanese-American attempts to prove loyalty to the United States. The Chronicle article went to greater lengths to show how strenuously Japanese-Americans would back the United States - and how far they had to go to do it. The three-deck headline read: "We Are Loyal Americans - We Must Prove It to All of You".

Ironically, the photo accompanying the story showed Hangiro Fujii, a Japanese national and a local business owner, being led away by San Francisco police officers. Chronicle reporter Milton Silverman led the story with a quote (a rarity in news stories) from JACL President Saburo Kido: "The hour is here.

We are Americans!" After delivering his message of patriotism to the fifty-six JACL chapters around the county, Kido "walked away from the radio. He smiled - as he and his people have always smiled when they are tense and worried. He thought of the Japan has never seen".

Kido thought of "the new Japanese-Americans, now, who were born in this country, who are American citizens, who have a new loyalty to face." Silverman assumes, of course, that Japanese-American citizens had to prove their allegiance to the United States.

But he quoted Kido as saying just that: Japanese-Americans "have been proclaiming their loyalty - the time to prove their true feelings has arrived." Eight paragraphs into the story, Silverman underscored the distinction made by the photo of Fujii; Kido, he said, "speaks for most of the 150,000 Japanese in this country.

Most of them - 70 per cent of them - are American, born

in this country." As if reassuring his readers that their Japanese-American neighbors were not a threat, Silverman made clear that "most of them have never seen Japan, can't read or speak Japanese".

Older Japanese, including Toyoji Abe, publisher of the New World-Daily Sun, a Japanese-language newspaper, know "that their children owe no loyalty to Japan: They are Americans." Silverman quoted Abe as saying that he hoped "to remain in this country as a law-abiding resident, co-operating wherever possible with the American authorities," an attitude he claimed was shared by other Japanese-Americans.

Upon hearing of Pearl Harbor, Silverman wrote, "these men swallowed the most bitter pill they could imagine. They discovered their new country was attacked by their old country, and they made their decisions. They went American". Patriotism and loyalty were also the themes of a four-column San Francisco Chronicle photo of a group of Japanese-American soldiers huddled around a car, listening to war reports on the radio.

The banner above the photo read "Japanese Would Fight Japan," even though the soldiers were correctly identified in the caption as Japanese-Americans. "In a few months," the caption read, "they may be fighting on, and against, the soil their parents left." But like Kido and Abe, quoted in Silverman's story, "there was no hesitancy in this group," the caption read. "The attack was treacherous. The counter-attack should be relentless."

For the moment, Japanese-Americans were still a significant part of the news frame constructed by journalists covering the impact of Pearl Harbor. They had been given the chance to show their patriotism, even if journalists had in effect deployed their loyalty in order to help officials maintain order and cohesion. In addition, these early stories served a more destructive purpose: they marginalized - or, as Gitlin might argue, "domesticated"- Japanese-Americans, even though they posed no threat, and were, for the most part, loyal citizens.

In their coverage, journalists created two groups of Japanese-Americans: the officials and the masses; only official, high-ranking Japanese-American officials were quoted, a finding consonant with Donohue, Tichenor, and Olien's claim that conflict is reported only when it involves "dominant powers or power blocs".

If there was any anti-American sentiment on the part of Japanese-Americans, it was not covered. Moreover, the average Japanese-American citizen appeared in stories as a cartoon-like, flag waving caricature. With this part of the story established, journalists were now primed to "sound the alarm" about the threat allegedly posed by Japanese nationals.

They soon moved beyond Japanese-American patriotism, beyond what Barthes (1973) calls "inoculation." Reporters allowed Japanese-Americans - for Barthes, "radical voices" - "a controlled moment of speech," one which ensured that "the social body [was] strengthened and not threatened by the contrast between it and the radical".

The guard dog function also offers a possible explanation for journalists' willingness to cover this angle: reporters often act as "fair weather friends for those with marginal positions of power". Journalists shed light on Japanese-American patriotism only until the government developed a policy for dealing with them.

Further, even in stories with a patriotic themes, reporters cited "official" Japanese-American sources in order to better manage the story, a practice that would continue, even when Japanese-Americans were nearly absent from the pages of these newspapers.

Eventually, the lives of Japanese-Americans would be "exnominated," to use Barthes' term. Homages to Japanese-American loyalty would end abruptly as coverage focused on the government's effort to win the war. Journalists continued their extensive coverage of roundup efforts. A page one headline in the December 8 Chronicle announced "Japanese in the U.S.: S.R Joins the Nation in Rounding Up Suspicious Characters and Some Business Men".

The reporter gave the local roundup a sense of national

context, leading with "federal agents and troops moved into Japanese communities from San Francisco to Norfolk, Virginia, [and] Alaska to the Panama Canal shortly after noon yesterday and took into custody an undisclosed number of Japanese nationals."

The Chronicle story touched on incarceration efforts in San Diego, Sacramento, and New York. Police blocked off little Tokyo in Los Angeles, referred to in the story as "headquarters for 60,000 Japanese in Southern California. The Times reporter noted that "traffic was halted on First Street" in Little Tokyo in order to "prevent incidents". The Chronicle reported that "a number of people were picked up" by law enforcement officials, a fact missed or not included in the Little Tokyo story by the Times reporter.

The focus here is still on individual law enforcement officials exerting power, as Donohue, Tichenor, and Olien would argue. Nowhere is the structure from which their power emanates examined or challenged. Moreover, reporters were writing less about Japanese-Americans as individuals; Japanese-Americans were reduced to the number of people rounded up during a raid.

This suggests a corollary to the "guard dog" function: while conflict is reported to the extent that it affects individuals, those creating the conflict - even if that conflict is imagined or unrealized - are represented by journalists as a group of faceless, nameless individuals.

As law enforcement officials rounded up Japanese nationals, journalists began to engage in what Fiske calls "claw back"; they attempted to mediate this turn of events "into the dominant value system without losing [its] authenticity". The language used by the Chronicle reporter in the story cited earlier, for example, reinforces a positive image of law enforcement officials. The reporter wrote that a Japanese man "was hustled" into the local immigration station; FBI agents "swooped down" on a predominantly Japanese part of San Francisco.

Agents also arrested a man who was the "head man" of the local Japanese "colony" and who was also the editor of a

Japanese newspaper. The article also gives a glowing description of how law enforcement officials "threw a blockade around the big Japanese fishing villages" on Terminal Island in Los Angeles Harbor.

Japanese fishermen coming home from the day's work "were herded into wire enclosures" by soldiers. To be sure, government officials were acting outside their traditional roles by rounding up Japanese-Americans, which in part explains the extensive coverage by journalists, the guard dog theory argues. Reporting would become even more intense when the federal government moved into the uncharted territory of internment.

STEPPING OUTSIDE TRADITIONAL ROLES

For the moment, the loyalty theme had simply outlived its usefulness. Officials now prepared to step outside of their traditional roles - a key condition for the emergence of "guard dog" reporting. In addition, government officials now supplied journalists with a steady stream of information about the arrests, which enabled journalists to more effectively manage the story.

In the Los Angeles Times, there was an unmistakable end to its recognition of Japanese-American patriotism. On December 9, it ran a lengthy page-nine article on the State Council of Defense's rejection of Governor Culbert Olson's plan to stave off potential riots by restricting Japanese nationals and Japanese-Americans to their homes.

The council was motivated more by pragmatism than by tolerance. Olson's restriction, the story noted, "might endanger the supply of vegetables and fruits to the public". Olson was quoted as saying that citizens "can expect anything since the occurrences of yesterday." It was the council's duty, he said, "to watch that no part of the civilian population be caught unaware or unprotected from any possible attack from the air or invasion."

Olson also outlined "action that should be taken to alleviate any tension in the situation crated by the 10,000 Japanese living in this area". Here, Olson sounds almost rancorous, perhaps because taken as a whole, the Times article is balanced. For example, the reporter emphasized the economic ramifications of detaining Japanese nationals and Japanese-Americans.

A December 13 Times photo showed JACL Anti-Axis Committee headquarters with a sign in its window reading "America - We Are Ready."

The photo's caption told readers that the organization would "turn over to authorities all `consorts of enemy."' But after publication of the photo, which appeared under the heading "Japanese-Americans Ready to Fight Enemies," the Times fell silent on the loyalty issue.

Its readers began seeing stories about Japan and its people with charged headlines like "Japan Fanaticism Began in 559 B.C." and "Japan Pictured as Nation of Spies". In that first wave of photos, reporters allowed Japanese-Americans to reach out to the reader and show their loyalty; in the last Times photo, Japanese-American loyalty was reduced to a sign on a storefront.

It is worth noting that only one person appeared in the photo - a sudden change from the groups of Japanese-Americans professing loyalty in earlier photos. An accompanying article told readers that 500 Japanese and Japanese-Americans attended a meeting in which a state official told the farmers in the crowd to keep "tilling their fields and bringing their produce to market".

The New York Times' December 9 story on Japanese-American loyalty ran under a two-deck, one-column headline in the back of the issue's first section - a much less prominent position than those occupied by the Chronicle and Los Angeles Times stories. The chair of the American Committee for Protection of the Foreign Born said that "the foreign-born people of the United States will rally to the national cause with full loyalty in the present crisis" .

The story talked about guarantees of loyalty from German, Italian, and Japanese-Americans in the form of telegrams to FDR. The Times' pedestrian approach to the story is attributable to a comparatively small Japanese-American population in the eastern United States and in New York City. A day earlier, the Times ran a photo essay titled "The New War in the Pacific: Japanese and Chinese Reactions."

Reactions captured in the photos came from a group of Chinese diplomats giving the thumbs up sign in front of the Japanese Consulate, from a Japanese official burning boxes of papers outside the Japanese embassy in Washington, D.C. (with the caption "Japanese waste no time in burning State papers on the grounds of their embassy"), and in two photos of Japanese officials representatives of the "dominant power" allegedly threatening our safety - leaving the Japanese consulate in New York, one with a police escort.

Japanese Americans still appeared in news stories and photos, but their marginalization by journalists continued. Reporters failed to explore why Japanese-Americans were in a position to have to .profess their loyalty. Loyalty was embodied by patriotic Japanese-Americans gathered around a radio, and, later, by Japanese officials being escorted from the consulate.

In a subsequent story, Los Angeles Times writer Thomas Hamilton quoted First Lady Eleanor Roosevelt as saying she saw no reason "why Japanese with `good' records meaning `no criminal or anti-American record' - had anything to fear, whether they were long-time residents or had only just arrived." In the same article, Hamilton detailed Nicholas Biddle's order to the FBI to arrest "a selected group of Japanese aliens", but also quoted him as saying that mass arrests would be "unwise".

Hamilton does frame the issue as a discussion of the system-the structure -in place to deal with questions of loyalty, but builds the story on quotes from powerful individuals. Hamilton's story, along with a shorter December 10 Times story about the number of Japanese-American arrests in the United States to that point, details the "organized challenge," albeit an imaginary one, that Donohue, Tichenor, and Olien discuss as being at the heart of the guard dog function.

In fact, the government made extensive and successful use of the manufactured challenge; journalists responded to the uncertainty with more intense coverage of the "alien" issue. When government officials stepped even further outside their "traditional roles" and began to discuss internment, the guard dog barked even louder. We see this in a Times story in the December 10 issue. An adjoining two-column photo shows a group of Japanese Americans being taken into custody by sailors in Norfolk, Virginia.

In the story, the Times reported that an order from FDR that German and ItalianAmericans be caught in "the FBI dragnet" along with Japanese-Americans since "an invasion or predatory incursion is threatened upon the territory of the United States" by the other two Axis powers. FDR had to make this proclamation in order to invoke a federal law that allowed him to order the arrest of enemy aliens on sight.

Officials were now threatening the rights of innocent people - clear movement, Donohue, Tichenor, and Olien would argue, outside "the traditional roles of political conflict." The New York Times joined the Chronicle and Los Angeles Times in intensifying coverage of the issue.

On December 9, a New York Mmes story described the government's first sweep, telling readers that the arrests "of disloyal Nipponese still are being made as part of protective moves against any possible fifth column action". The December 10 New York Times story talked of "roundups" and the FBI's "sudden swoops" and resulting arrests.

A second December 9 story in the New York Times told of civilian officials "striking swiftly throughout Los Angeles and Southern California" to take 500 "alien Japanese" into custody. True to the guard dog function, the story told of individuals in power roles struggling to deal with the problem: "Deputy sheriffs, led by Undersheriff Jack Ross, and California highway patrolmen, combed the farm houses and Japanese vegetable growers dormitories through the Santa Maria, Guadalupe, and Lompoc valleys".

On December 13, a two-deck headline in the New York Times announced: "2,541 Axis Aliens Now in Custody." The first eight paragraphs of the accompanying story focused on Biddle, the official source, including his reminder to citizens that aliens were "dangerous to the peace and safety of the nation".

Thus, in less than a week, print reporters had raised the issue of Japanese-American patriotism, removed it from the news frame, and diminished Japanese-Americans by quoting only official sources, and by focusing on efforts of law enforcement officials and the federal government to control a problem that didn't exist.

By reporting on what Donohue, Tichenor, and Olien might call an "externally based conflict," journalists cleared the way for the government to take its nascent Japanese-American policy to the next level. As discussed in the next section, journalists would continue to encourage the "reinforcement of local cohesion" discussed by Donohue, Tichenor, and Olien.

Readers of these newspapers soon began seeing inaccurate and inflammatory reports of fifth column activity along with the arrest summaries. Having to deal with this threat was portrayed by reporters as beyond the government's traditional role - beyond its control, as Donohue, Tichenor, and Olien discuss. It was as if these "guard dog" reporters were offering a bit of breathing room to a government struggling to get its act together.

Coverage of the threat soon intensified, and was clearly biased in favour of government officials. The Los Angeles Times reported that Charles Ishii, president of the Regional American Japanese Public Service Association, had been arrested despite his earlier statement that Japanese-Americans were loyal. The story's subhead diminished Ishii: "Asiatic, who had pledged loyalty, found with guns".

In the same issue, the Times had laid the groundwork for reports of fifth column activity in the United States by running a story on Japanese troops landing in the Philippines "with the probable help of `fishermen' fifth columnists" near the entrance to Manila Bay.

The level of sourcing deemed acceptable by journalists working at the time is seen in the story's third paragraph: "the report of the landing on Lubang, some sixty miles southwest of the big American naval base of Cavite, was not confirmed officially, but enough credence was placed in it that defence officers were trying urgently to contact the provincial Governor."

The reporter here fails to define "credence," and does not inform readers who supported the account. For the Chronicle, the ensuing days were marked by the continuing count of detained aliens. On December 9, a page eight headline read: "The Alien Roundup: 200 S.F. Policemen Begin Looking for Germans and Italians". Subheads inserted in the story included "The Big Take" and "Fresno Arrests."

The reporter imbued the story with a decidedly misanthropic flavour: The arrests netted Japanese nationals, as well as some Japanese citizens of the United States, in Los Angeles, Seattle, San Diego, Sacramento, Fresno, Stockton, various other Pacific Coast and inland points, and on the Eastern Seaboard. Hawaii jailed 391 Japanese.

The word "netted" gives the impression that Japanese-Americans were little more than animals. The reporter also wrote that "guards were stationed in front of 100 Japanese business houses, throttling their operations." An agent from the Department of the Treasury was quoted by the reporter as saying he and his colleagues had thwarted numerous attempts to remove financial documents from Japanese-owned businesses.

It should be noted, however, that the call for tolerance and recognition of loyalty did not completely disappear; it moved for a time to the Chronicle's editorial pages. A December 9 Chronicle editorial acknowledged that "some Japanese-born, legally barred from naturalization, are at heart strong for American ideals.

However, in the same editorial, the paper argued that "some American-born Japanese, hence citizens (written as if this was a sudden development), are reasonably suspect for alien sympathy." The paper warned its readers that "there is no excuse to wound the sensibilities of any persons in America by showing suspicion or prejudice" ("This is a Tough Time," 1941).

Doing so, the editorial continued, "is a help to the fifth column spirit." Moving the loyalty argument to a different section of the paper allowed reporters and editors to manage and at the same time marginalize it. The issue was no longer important enough to be covered regularly, or to occupy space on the news pages.

Reporters were now occupied with fifth column activity, and with the government's movement outside of its traditional role to deal with it, as Donohue, Tichenor and Olien would argue. In his seminal work on news media portrayal of the left, Gitlin argues that the news media often "limit the terms of effective opposition".

Here, reporters were, to apply Gitlin's term, slowly "defining away" Japanese-Americans, and were doing so based on a false characterization the threat to national security - that they had a role in creating. Reporters had first placed Japanese-Americans in the position of having to defend themselves, and were now marginalizing their attempts to do so.

In the same issue, a letter to the editor detailed its writer's relationship with a fiercely loyal Japanese-American family. The writer urged tolerance: We Americans of European descent, we so-called whites, must choose. We can give the lead to the ill-willed, the stupid and the prejudiced intelligent among us, and so hurt and bewilder 100,000 fellow citizens. Or, repudiating our ugly intolerances, we can by mere quiet decency toward superficially "different" Americans, strengthen both army and navy with the equivalent of $100,000,000 worth of equipment.

Two days later, the Chronicle published a letter from Nori Ikeda of San Francisco. Ikeda pledged his support to Roosevelt's war policy and condemned the attack on Pearl Harbor. He said he spoke for all Japanese Americans "in saying that we are ready to do our share in the defence of the United States. We ask you to have faith in our loyalty to America, our country, and to believe in our desire to do what we can to promote unity of will and action in this national emergency".

Some readers were moved by these expressions of devotion. In a letter to the Chronicle, San Francisco resident Sylvia Brown asked: "Isn't there something that can be done about those feeble-minded `patriots' who go about venting their childish emotions upon our good and loyal Japanese citizens?"

But by the time these letters were published, journalists had successfully minimized reaction to the official stance on Japanese-Americans. Soon, even fewer voices rose to defend Japanese-Americans.

DOMINANT POWER POSITIONS

The federal government soon accelerated dissemination of fifth column reports. A page one story in the December 11 Chronicle said that the Army "had ringed the Nation with men and steel sufficient to `meet any threat' of invasion." As before, reporters told readers that the threat was directed at law enforcement officials, not the power structure, as Donohue, Tichenor, and Olien would argue.

It was reported that a group of unknown individuals had set a series of brush fires that resembled arrows, one pointing to the Bremerton Navy Yard in Washington, the other to Seattle. As a result, the story said, "the Fifth columnist search was on in the region of Post Angeles, Washington". The New York Times on December 11 ran a six-paragraph story on the alleged incident on page 25.

Two days earlier, the Los Angeles Times ran a page one story reporting the Army's announcement that two groups of enemy aircraft had been spotted near San Francisco Bay. An army general told the Chronicle that the planes "were turned back at the Golden Gate". DeWitt was quoted in the New York Times story on alleged incident as saying that those who believed there was no danger were "inane, idiotic, and foolish".

"Remember that San Francisco is so full of military objectives that the whole city is a military objective," DeWitt said, suggesting later that "it might have been `a good thing' if the visitors dropped some bombs". Such an event, DeWitt said, attacking opposition to the American war effort, "might have awakened some of the fools in this community who refuse to realise this is a war".

On December 13, the New York Times discussed reports of "unidentified planes" near San Diego and speculated about a possible air base "in sparsely settled Lower California, where border rumors have placed large concentrations of large Japanese". Nowhere in these articles do reporters describe their attempts to confirm the military's reports; they rely solely on military and government sources, or, in the case of the New York Times, or what were referred to by the reporter as "local Mexican sources."

In Chronicle stories published on December 11, reporters, having established a dominant narrative about Japanese-Americans for their readers, now took a more misanthropic tone; it is at this point that references to "Japs" and "Nips" begin appearing in their stories.

A turning point in the coverage was a press conference held by Secretary of the Navy Frank Knox on December 15, 1941 upon his return from examining the carnage at Pearl Harbor. Referring to Japanese-Americans living in Hawaii, he told reporters that "the most effective fifth column work of the war was done there". Some have argued that Knox lied to reporters about fifth column activity in order to convince Americans that getting involved in the war was the wisest course of action.

But as 1941 ended, journalists continued to intensify their reporting of alleged fifth column activity. There were even fewer signs of even-handedness; gone were accounts of Japanese-American loyalty; the use of Japanese-Americans as sources for stories waned.

The Chronicle on December 22 published an editorial in which it recognized a "proof of loyalty" offered by a group of Japanese-Americans in San Francisco who had organized a special chapter auxiliary to the Red Cross. Nisei, the editorial said, "are not to blame for defects of any persons in their groups."

According to the editorial, "it is actions, not antecedents

that count." Hypocrisy teems from this statement. Acting in their guard dog role, these newspapers had been propagating false and exaggerated reports from the government of the kind of "actions" alluded to in the Chronicle editorial. Japanese-Americans should not have felt the need to create their own Red Cross chapter, the editorial's writer claimed.

"If it seems to distinguish them by their own action as a unit apart, it is a distinction already forced upon them by the hysterical judgment of many Americans." Such a sentiment must have been little comfort to Japanese-Americans in the Bay Area, especially since the effort by reporters to frame the crisis in a way that supported the government was probably at the root of much of the "hysterical judgment" referred to by the author.

The next day, Chronicle columnist Dorothy Thompson repeated the warning uttered by Knox at his December 15 press conference: "There is a monstrous fifth column in the United States - just as there was a fifth column in Hawaii, which contributed to the disaster at Pearl Harbor.". Thompson asked: "Have those people been found, and are they still not operating?"

Thompson later gave vivid evidence of the news media's guard dog role when she wrote, "one of the greatest weapons that can be used against them is the press publicity, clarification of their methods, so that the people themselves can see what's going on". Thompson laid bare the news media's work as sentry - saying, in effect, that reporters were now part of the war effort, and that the government could count on their unstinting support.

As Donohue, Tichenor, and Olien note, "media coverage tends to be evaluated as favorable among groups.occupying more established and dominant power positions". Officials would have no cause to evaluate press coverage of their efforts as anything other than favorable. The successful marginalization of Japanese-Americans by the press, done to galvanize support for the war, had left no room for "questioning the guard dog role" played by reporters.

In an article published the same day, the New York Times

offered apparent confirmation of Thompson's claims, reporting on page four the arrest of 273 alleged fifth columnists in Hawaii. As had become common practice, the Times article cited only government officials. The reporter referenced the Knox press conference, but reassured readers that "there were no Fifth Columnists among the members of the armed services in Hawaii".

Our institutions, thanks to the presence of "great persons" like DeWitt and Knox were safe. But the threat still loomed; while most of the Japanese-Americans in Hawaii were loyal, the article reported, some had "provided the enemy with valuable military information".

As the year ended, the Chronicle continued to publish stories about successful containment of the threat. On December 27, Biddle ordered all aliens to turn over all cameras and radios or face internment in what the Chronicle referred to as "concentration camps."

A short page one article on December 28 was headlined "Aliens Must Surrender Their Radios"; the next day, the newspaper ran a detailed article about the nearly 5,000 radios turned over by "axis aliens" to San Francisco police. In the middle of the article, the reporter cited a government report that "enemy fifth columnists" had contacted enemy forces from Washington - "presumably Pacific raiders and undersea boats which have been attacking West Coast ships".

The New York Times on December 29 ran a two-column photo showing two elderly Japanese-American residents turning over a radio to a San Francisco police officer under the heading "Japanese Aliens Comply with U.S. Order." The rest of the Chronicle article read like a how-to guide for marginalized Japanese-Americans: "if an alien is in doubt about what he should do to comply with the order, he should turn in his camera or radio at once.

Resolve all doubts in favour of the Government." Reporters had allowed the government to organize and give life to the challenge, and were now content to report the success the government enjoyed in managing the challenge. The sentry was still at its post.

In a year-end article appearing in the New York Times, United Press reporter Wallace Carroll provided vivid evidence that journalists continued to act as "sentries" for the government even after Japanese-Americans had been completely marginalized. In a story headlined "Japanese Spies Showed the Way for Raid on Vital Areas in Hawaii," Carroll gave the most detailed account of the alleged fifth column activity.

Recall again that there was absolutely no evidence of such activity. Carroll's main contentions, based on a visit to Honolulu, were (1) that large arrows were cut in sugar cane fields to pinpoint military objectives; (2) that a Japanese man arrested for operating a short-wave radio during the attack on Pearl Harbor was a frequent visitor to a U.S. Army post; (3) that Japanese vegetable sellers were aware of movements in and out of port by the U.S. Navy; and (4) that ads, "innocent looking and accepted by newspapers in good faith, may have contained code messages to the fifth columnists".

Carroll's reports were never corroborated. Carroll did tell his readers that the article "was not intended as an indictment of all Japanese in Honolulu." For the most part, he wrote, "they were industrious and well-behaved. But enough of them were fifth columnists to make the attack successful."

Carroll showed the lack of any boundary between reporter and sentry when he wrote: "The facts, if presented to the American people now, may help put them on alert in other potential areas of danger". Carroll's article is noteworthy in at least one other respect: it was written in the first person. Journalists tend not to write stories using this voice because it damages their credibility by creating the appearance of bias.

Carroll carried the approach through to the end of the piece, when he warned readers that there was still work to be done: "When I left Honolulu ten days ago, I was informed that Japanese members of the Territorial Guard still were stationed at reservoirs, power plants and other public utilities. Japanese-Americans still held positions in the post office and telephone service."

Coverage of fifth column activity by all three papers in

January and February 1942 became even more inflammatory as calls began to come for internment - a larger step clearly outside the "traditional roles of political conflict" discussed by Donohue, Tichenor, and Olien. Stories continued to dehumanize Japanese-Americans. The Los Angeles Times reported on January 14 that a Japanese-American gardener was denied his chance to sue his landlord because he was unable to prove his citizenship.

The next day, a California Superior Court judged ruled that "foreignborn Japanese" lacked legal standing. The January 18 Times reported that Koshiro Endo, a teacher, had been arrested by the FBI. The three-paragraph story ran under the headline, "Jap Educator Seized by the FBI." The FBI refused comment on the reason for the arrest, a point apparently not challenged by the reporter who wrote the story.

On January 22, the Times ran an Associated Press story in which California Congressman Leland Ford called for immediate internment of all Japanese-Americans. Ford acknowledged that the issue was "rather touchy in some quarters due to the fact many Japanese are native-born,"- which, of course, would make them American citizens, a distinction lost on Ford and omitted by the AP reporter, who was content to run portions of Ford's statement verbatim.

The reporter made little or no effort to contextualize Ford's statement, listing Ford's opinions without challenge: "He feels that these native-born Japanese may not be any more loyal than are the foreign born," the story says. "He develops the fact that other loyal Americans are enlisting in the Army and Navy and Air Force."

The writer continued. Since so many other Americans are making sacrifices, "he believes is it not asking too much of the Japanese to make theirs in the form of permitting themselves to be placed in concentration camps, although they may be loyal." Once again acting as "guard dog," the reporter is framing the purported threat as it affects a single "great person" - in this case, Ford.

As support grew for our involvement in the war,

reporters continued to intensify the language they used in their stories to refer to the efforts underway to detain Japanese-Americans. On January 30, the Chronicle began what became an almost daily page one report under some variation of the heading "Alien Restrictions."

The newspaper reported that Biddle had ordered that San Francisco's "strategic waterfront districts" be "swept clean" of enemy aliens. Japanese-Americans would be banned from twenty-nine "forbidden zones" along the West Coast. Biddle warned local officials to let the federal government handle the removal of aliens, since it was "in possession of all the facts" regarding their threat to national security.

A follow-up story the next day on demands by members of Congress to give the War Department authority to clear "strategic areas" carried the massive headline "Rigid Rules Hit S.F. Aliens". A three-deck subhead told readers that "Subversive Elements Will Be Crushed." The Chronicle reporter proudly wrote that "America's long— ridiculed attitude of sweetness and light to enemy aliens has been forever blasted out of existence". For the first time, enemy aliens saw: the grim spectre of concentration camps, mass evacuation of families, revocation of business licenses, doctors and dentists thrown out of work, a savage hunt to crush secret organizations.

Government measures were grouped together by the Chronicle reporter and referred to for the first time as an "anti-alien programme." A page one story from the Los Angeles Times on January 28 shows a more reserved tone, despite its inflammatory headline - "Eviction of Jap Aliens Sought":

Southland authorities yesterday urged upon President Roosevelt and governmental agencies that all Japanese aliens be evicted immediately from Los Angeles Harbor and from the vicinity of defence plants and aircraft factories,

Much later in the article, the reporter, discussing the forced removal of Japanese-Americans from city jobs, makes a significant change in the news frame. To this point, reporters had at least sporadically acknowledged the possibility that some Japanese-Americans were loyal to the United States.

Quoting Los Angeles County Manager Wayne Allen, the reporter eliminates any vestiges of tolerance: "It is difficult if not impossible to distinguish loyal from disloyal Japanese." Citing this response is the work of a guard dog now in complete support of the official version of the Japanese-American issue.

Remaining signs of the balance seen in earlier stories were now gone. Under a two-deck headline that read "Speedy Moving of Japs Urged," Times reporter Kyle Palmer on December 31 described a call by local members of Congress on the Justice Department to take a stronger stance on evacuation.

In the lead, Palmer told readers that local members of Congress had taken "sharp issue with the leisurely programme" set up by Justice "for evacuating enemy aliens and possible sympathizers".

Waiting until the middle of February to evacuate Japanese-Americans, Palmer wrote, "might precipitate rather than prevent serious acts of sabotage". Local members of Congress urged Roosevelt to turn over control of all enemy aliens to the War Department.

At first glance, the guard dog seems to be wandering from its post. In actuality, however, only the master has changed. Here, the reporter focuses on the concern of local officials that the federal government was not acting quickly enough to deal with the problem.

The reporter frames the story as a disagreement among "power blocs" - a tendency of guard dog reporting posited by Donohue, Tichenor, and Olien. Nowhere do reporters cite reaction from the JACL or from Japanese-Americans in the area.

Thus, as officials accelerated their efforts to create a plan of evacuation, the people directly affected by that plan - Japanese-Americans - had been all but eliminated from the news frame, their presence lost to extensive coverage of squabbling among dominant institutions still at odds over the correct course of action.

Rather than explore the competing versions of the plan,

or probe their potential impact, journalists in effect looked on while the conflict among power blocs simmered.

THE "CONTENDING POWERS" GIVE IN

When federal officials completed their plans for dealing with JapaneseAmericans, journalists, who had long since abandoned objective portrayals of Japanese-Americans, embraced the return to stability. Criticisms of the plan from local and state officials - "contending powers," as Donohue, Tichenor and Olien call them - would continue, but federal officials soon moved decisively toward internment.

One of the first newspapers to fully endorse evacuation was the San Diego Union. On January 20, 1942, the paper started a series of editorials attacking the Japanese for Pearl Harbor. Later, Union editorial writers concluded that there was no way to determine the loyalty of Japanese-Americans. A Sacramento Bee reader argued that the Japanese "were forcing other races off the land, including whites from pioneer families".

In the Santa Rosa Press Democrat, a reader asked "Biologically and economically, is the Jap fitted (sic) to mingle in American life?" Los Angeles newspaper columnist Lee Shippey, prophetically advocated creating "a number of big, closely watched truck farms on which Japanese-Americans could earn a living and assure us a steady supply of vegetables".

In a February 1 front-page editorial (like the article written in the first person, a rarity for most newspapers), the Chronicle provided clear evidence that its reporters were ready to endorse whatever measures the government would implement: "In time of war, the way to escape politics and hysteria is to leave it to the constituted authorities. And that means, in this case, the Federal authorities".

Now that the threat had been identified, it was up to the government, buttressed by nearly two months of staunch support from print journalists, to deal with the problem. Journalists had seen the government through its indecision, as Donohue, Tichenor, and Olien argue, and now believed it was ready to act. Ironically, however, the Chronicle stopped far short of endorsing internment.

While it supported removal of Japanese-Americans from "designated strategic areas," the newspaper stressed that "it was not necessary to imitate Hitler by herding whole populations, the guilty and the innocent together, into even humane concentration camps" State and local officials should not adopt such a policy, nor should citizens "take `the law' - or, rather the absence of it- into their own hands." Instead, the editorial concluded, everyone should "leave it to the Government".

The Chronicle's zealotry continued to show in its headlines; the newspaper began almost every story on evacuation with a headline that included the words "aliens," "enemy aliens," or "alien roundup." The Los Angeles Times mixed reports of successful evacuation with stories of fifth column activity. On February 3, the Times ran two photos of Japanese-Americans on page six.

The first, under the banner, "Nipponese Get Free Trip to Immigration Stations" pictured a group of Japanese-Americans being transported to a detention station on Los Angeles' Terminal Island "on one of Uncle Sam's free bus rides." Gone were the happy pictures of loyal Japanese-Americans listening to the radio for war news.

Instead, readers of the Times saw an FBI agent questioning a Japanese-American man (in the other February 3 Times photo). The agent, the caption read, "instructed the man to go to his home." In an adjoining Associated Press story, Earl Warren was quoted as saying that the West Coast was "wide open to any kind of sabotage or fifth column activity".

Warren told a meeting of California law enforcement officials that there had already been "numerous violations" of California's Alien Land Act. Ventura County officials were soon joining in the call for evacuation, the Times reported the next day. "Our gravest danger," according to a county official quoted in the story, "is from native-born Japs who still worship the Emperor".

According to county officials, "it is impossible to know those Japanese who are loyal to the United States." On February 6, the Times reported that H.A. Van Norman, the chief engineer of Los Angeles' Bureau of Water Works and Supply in 1934 had received a request from the Japanese consulate for information on the city's water supply.

This was convincing evidence, the Times reporter wrote, of a plot to do damage to the water system. The letter, reproduced across three columns, would be part of the evidence gathered by Martin Dies, a member of Congress, of fifth column activity dating back before Pearl Harbor.

The story reported "growing dissatisfaction" with the federal government for failing to: take more drastic action in connection with not only the Japanese espionage activities in prewar times but in the seeming lack of speed and effectiveness with regard to the current handling of the alien problem on the Coast. Dies, who chaired the House Un-American Activities Committee, would release a report on "the extent of Nipponese espionage in this country," the Times reported on page six of the same issue.

The report, which included information gathered before Pearl Harbor, supported charges "that Federal authorities failed to take necessary precautions and prevented his group from disclosing the extent of the Japanese spy ring". Quoting only Dies, the story reported that Japanese citizens allowed to enter this country for business reasons - so-called "treaty traders" - had "energetically collected information which would have been of tremendous value to an enemy nation," the Times reported.

Further, the Dies report revealed that Nisei were allegedly forced to belong to organizations called "Kens" which demanded that they send money to Japan. Another Times evacuation story reported Mayor Bowron's concern that "if there is intrigue going on, and it is reasonably certain that there is, right here is the hotbed, the nerve centre, of the spy system, of planning for sabotage".

Local officials had no idea what the federal government was going to do to address the problem, Bowron said. City officials wanted to cooperate with their federal counterparts, "but it appears to us that no one in authority in the federal government knows what to do."

Here, at least part of the "organized challenge" to dominant institutions was coming from local officials. Coverage of the challenge intensified because these individuals clearly were acting outside their traditional roles. Later, the Times reporter underscored the changing definition of loyalty; under the subheading "Country First," the reporter asked "How to tell them apart?"

According to Bowron, "the answer is locked in the hearts of the Japanese-Americans in our midst." The Times would later quote Bowron as saying that he believed Abraham Lincoln would have ordered internment of Japanese-Americans.

As journalists continued to report the conflict between these "power blocs,", their treatment of JapaneseAmericans worsened. On February 6, the New York Times described a meeting between Olson and Japanese-American officials. The story also highlighted the claim by petroleum industry officials that a "sabotage plot" was in place, one that "awaits only the `zero hour' before being put into effect".

Times reporter Davies quoted Bowron as saying that "they should be put to work." Olson said that while he didn't endorse Bowron's plan, he thought there was "no middle ground for Japanese citizens."

If they weren't prepared to show complete loyalty, he said, they "ought to be concentrated." Later in the Times story, Olson is quoted as saying that he would appoint a committee of Japanese-Americans "to cooperate in drafting plans for an evacuation programme of lesser proportions."

JACL President Saburo Kido said his organization was willing to help, but "appealed against any denial of constitutional rights" to Nisei.

The use of Kido as a source and the inclusion of the JACL were rare in coverage of the evacuation issue. During the period leading up to Executive Order 9066, journalists for all three newspapers typically used only JACL officials to represent the Japanese-American side of the story. In its story detailing reaction to the order, the New York Times used only a prepared statement from JACL officials Kido and Mike Masoaka which pledged cooperation with the government and which urged calm among its members.

Japanese-American citizens were not asked for their reaction. By February 7, both the Los Angeles Times (page six) and the Chronicle (page four) ran an AP story in which Olson told a conference of Japanese-American leaders that the only way they could help themselves was by working to help the United States to defeat Japan.

"The government of Japan will be made to surrender and disarm and will be wiped out," Olson said. "There isn't any middle ground for Japanese citizens". While Chronicle reporters moved through February 1942 writing glowing reports about successful "alien roundups," its editorial writers mixed a bit of tolerance with caution, and even a bit of self-examination. In a February 6 editorial, the Chronicle said that there was little hysteria over alleged fifth column activity.

"Perhaps there is even too little of it," the editorial noted. It was government officials and journalists who were "seeking to capitalize on the supposed excitement of others, which is mostly a figment of their own imaginations." Donohue, Tichenor, and Olien note that placing blame on the media often occurs as a controversy develops.

But these expressions are "simply instrumental for keeping the media under control, to prevent damage". Chronicle columnist Chester Rowell said evacuation was necessary, but added that state and local officials may have been acting too zealously. "In war, the presumption of innocence shifts, and it is for the non-citizen resident to establish his loyalty, rather than for the authorities to prove his lack of it," he wrote.

State and local officials must cooperate with the federal government, he said, with federal officials deciding on the appropriate course of action. As before, coverage focused on the competing "power blocs" discussed by Donohue, Tichenor and Olien. "When it gets into local hands, pressure group politics and personal headline seeking also get in," Rowell said. Rowell's comment echoes the sentiment felt by local officials who had tired of waiting for the federal government to act.

As Donohue, Tichenor, and Olien contend, groups with less power tend to look less favorably at media coverage of their efforts. But despite these warnings, Rowell reminded his readers that "the danger, of course, is real. If German and Japanese consulates in California were not engaged in fifth column activities, they were the only exceptions in the world."

With a sound structure for addressing the threat issue finally in place, journalists soon began preparing readers for internment. On February 12, the Chronicle reported that imposition of martial law was imminent. As law enforcement officials continued their successful "raids on enemy aliens," legislators in Washington, D.C., were drafting legislation for a compulsory licensing system, to be administered by the U.S. Army.

The Times ran a page-one story on a renewed call by legislators from the west for immediate evacuation of "all persons of Japanese lineage". The licensing system had been scrapped in favour of an exercise of Presidential authority that would "dispose of the problem with less cumbersome machinery". A February 13 story in the Chronicle revealed that nearly 35,000 enemy aliens had not registered with the federal government. True to its guard dog function, the Chronicle reporter placed the onus on the backs of the unregistered aliens.

No mention was made of inefficiencies in the registration process. The Chronicle reporter wrote that citizens groups in southern California were not taking the news of the discrepancy well: they were "planning reprisals against all enemy aliens and against many citizens of Japanese parentage". Less than a week later, Roosevelt issued Executive Order 9066. More than 120,000 Japanese-Americans were rounded up and sent to 10 internment camps.

Print journalists from the New York Times, the Los Angeles Times, and the San Francisco Chronicle had in effect helped the government work through its period of indecision by marginalizing Japanese-Americans, by focusing on the acts of officials as individuals rather than as part of a larger structure, by accepting without question the government's manufactured challenge, by focusing on disagreement among "power blocs," and, finally, by offering their endorsement of the policy that, once finalized, would eventually lead to the internment.

The guard dog function of the press developed by Donohue, Tichenor, and Olien provides a strong theoretical foundation for understanding the work of journalists in the period between Pearl Harbor and the internment of Japanese-Americans and offers support for the hypotheses posed by the authors at the end of their article.

Reporters at the newspapers studied here did not, as Daniels and others have argued, fall in line behind government officials and leap to the conclusion that Japanese-Americans on the West Coast represented a threat to national security.

A more complex picture emerges: newspaper reporters initially gave Japanese-American citizens the chance to show their loyalty to the United States. Soon, however, the government began disseminating unsubstantiated reports of fifth column activity. Print reporters then assumed the role of "sentry" discussed by Donohue, Tichenor, and Olien and began changing the news frame to support the actions and policies of officials who had fabricated the Japanese-American threat in order to mobilize support for our involvement in the war.

After showing some tolerance for Japanese-Americans, print reporters began "working not for the entire community, but for "those particular groups who have the power and influence to create and control their own security systems". Reporters were soon conditioned by officials to suspect "all potential intruders" and "sound the alarm for reasons that individuals in the master household.can neither understand nor prevent".

The "master household" (government officials) clearly

understood the "reasons" for the alarm; it had in fact created them. Reporters at these newspapers soon encouraged suspicion of JapaneseAmericans. Some, like the columnist Westbrook Pegler, brashly took up the fifth-column cause; most journalists simply acted as sentries.

As the federal government moved closer to enacting an internment plan, journalists began framing Japanese-Americans as a threat to national security. It is this threat. purely manufactured, that became the "organized challenge" to which officials soon responded.

Attacks by local and state lawmakers on the federal government's plans for dealing with JapaneseAmericans were framed as dominant groups, or "power blocs," as Donohue, Tichenor and Olien call them, looking for a way to show that their plans to control the situation would be the most effective. Reporters helped manufacture the uncertainty that leads to intensified coverage in support of dominant institutions, as Donohue, Tichenor and Olien argue.

Reporters also framed stories about the fifth column threat as an attack on individuals - citizens, law enforcement officials, and government officials. Figures like FDR, Eleanor Roosevelt, Biddle, Bowron, Dies, DeWitt, and Olson - "great persons," as Donohue, Tichenor and Olien call them dominated the coverage.

Rarely did reporters give readers a context against which to judge the actions and motives of officials. These individuals embodied a structure that was never called into question. The real victims Japanese-American citizens on the West Coast - were marginalized by reporters; they Lost their voice as stories of loyalty gave way to hysteria, calls for evacuation, and reports of the "running tab" of alien arrests.

Their opposition to internment was imbued with a distinct "sideshow" flavour so that the distinction between supporters and opponents of evacuation was made to seem "natural" - a matter of "common sense," as Gitlin would argue.

Reporters used few Japanese-American citizens as sources. The JACL became their official voice - often the only entity cited by reporters in stories published in the days leading up to the internment.

On those rare occasions when reporters cited Japanese-Americans, they were diminished and marginalized; pejorative terms were often used to describe their physical characteristics. Intensity of reporting increased as the government contemplated moving outside what Donohue, Tichenor and Olien would call "the traditional roles of political conflict." Thankfully, attempting to strip citizens of their Constitutional rights is not an everyday occurrence.

Thus, as local, state, and federal officials crafted, discarded and revised evacuation plans, reporting, at least on the West Coast, picked up in intensity. The Chronicle, for example, offered readers its almost daily digest of "alien" arrests. The guard dog's strongest presence is in the inequity of coverage reviewed here. Japanese-Americans, reporters told their readers, represented a threat to our dominant institutions. In fact, the threat - the "organized challenge" discussed by Donohue, Tichenor, and Olien-was a complete fabrication. Reporting clearly framed the crisis (and defined the enemy) in a way that supported the official version of events.

Sadly, such conduct by journalists in times of crisis seems to be the rule, not the exception, even as reporters bask in the glow of their work during the Watergate crisis and the Vietnam War. Journalists routinely endorse official versions of events - they seem to play the role of "guard dog" once a story is under control, when it is no longer "unruly," even if that unruliness is manufactured by official sources.

The glow of Watergate obscures the fact that most news - including news produced through investigative reporting - is the product of routines built on a few key elements: journalists have values, but conceal them by adhering to the ideal of objectivity; journalists favour "statements of fact which are observable and unambiguous"; and they construct a view of reality "which reinforces official viewpoints", Thus, print reporters covering the aftermath of Pearl Harbor may simply have been waiting for the government to come up with an "observable" and "unambiguous" version of the Japanese-American threat.

Further, Protess, Cook, Doppelt, Ettema, Gordon, Leff, and Miller note that FDR had an amicable relationship with the press - much like Ronald Reagan's - and that this might have caused journalists to look the other way when the call first came for internment.

Thus, there is little evidence print journalists acted as "watchdogs" until the government came up with that policy-there were no investigations of how Japanese-Americans were treated by government officials, for example. Instead, the period between Pearl Harbor and Executive Order 9066 was a journalistic holding pattern.

Journalists waited until they could resume dependence on official sources of information. Herman and Chomsky explain that journalists "are drawn into a symbiotic relationship with powerful sources of information by economic necessity and reciprocity of interest". Here, the story was still forming; the Japanese-American issue arose while journalists were still trying to make sense of the attack on Pearl Harbor, and of the American response to it.

If we accept the "guard dog" theory of reporting, it made sense for them to seek out official sources of information - journalists knew these sources, and believed them to be credible. As Fishman notes, "[r]eporters operate with the attitude that officials ought to know it is their job to know.a newsworker will recognize an official's claim to knowledge not merely as a claim, but as a credible, competent piece of knowledge".

But Herman and Chomsky see this as something journalists do as a matter of routine; it does not happen only as a reaction to crisis. "The media need a steady, reliable flow of the raw material of news," they argue. Any tolerance shown for Japanese-Americans was more a product of the absence of an "official line" and the need to meet deadlines than a desire to portray events in an unbiased fashion.

As Donohue, Tichenor, and Olien explain, the "[m]edia do not have the capacity to innovate in devising social policy or political action, but must necessarily deal with ideas and actions generated among the powerful groups." If, as here, the dominant groups "are concerned with an external threat, that will be the agenda of the media.".

The guard dog theory leaves little, if any, room for the investigative reporting "binges" Schudson describes. Nevertheless, journalists point to their work in the Vietnam War as an example of strong investigative reporting, claiming that it triggered an adversarial relationship between journalists and the government.

But reports from Vietnam served only to galvanize burgeoning opposition to the war, opposition that was beginning to attract a great deal of coverage. Hallin argues, for example, that "political divisions at home," not the horrific images of the war reported by the news media, caused "the collapse of America's will" to continue fighting in Vietnam. Applying the guard dog theory, it could be argued that the military simply did a poor job of conveying its assumptions about Vietnam - its version of the war - to the public through the news media.

The military failed to contain reporters, as it would less then a decade later in Grenada and then in the Persian Gulf. But even if writers like Schudson, Bagdikian, and Chomsky are correct, and the news media are "primarily an establishment institution with few ambitions to rock establishment boats,", the Watergate myth of the zealous investigative reporter empowered by the "watchdog" role still carries a great deal of power in the field and with news consumers.

The news media have come under fire for their willingness to accept the restrictions on coverage imposed by the military in the various stages of conflict in the Persian Gulf. Such restrictions by the military would have been wasted on reporters covering the Japanese-American issue; they intensified their "guard dog" coverage once the government had crafted its policy.

Journalists responded to the Persian Gulf restrictions with perfunctory attacks, acting almost as if they did not want to anger military officials. By addressing the problem in this fashion, reporters underscored the military's success in moving the debate away from questions about the government's Persian Gulf policy.

This is not to say that today's journalists invoke Watergate with any consistency. As Rosenstiel explains, journalists "trot out" the myth of investigative reporting "on occasions when it's triggered, when it's appropriate, when we think it's safe, when we're not leading public opinion too much, when all the conditions and all the stars line up".

Even the term "muckraker" came from an official source. Most of the time, journalists are quite willing to rely on established sources of information - especially today, when so many news organizations are part of conglomerates. Journalists did not simply decide en masse to endorse the government's policy tóward Japanese-Americans; this analysis reveals that reporters initially gave Japanese-Americans the opportunity to profess loyalty to the United States.

But these stories amounted to little more than a "holding pattern;" journalists abandoned stories of loyalty and patriotism once officials made more sense of the tragedy and put into place a strategy- one built on bigotry and rumor - to deal with the issue. Once a coherent strategy emerged, journalists settled into the role of sentry.

As Donohue, Tichenor, and Olien note, the "occasional tendency to turn on one of the masters in a pluralistic power structure and yet protect their house is fundamental to the guard dog conception of media".

Chapter 5

The Law and Practice of Journalism

In the fall of 1995, at the same time that The Washington Post and New York Times were struggling with the decision to publish the Unibomber's manifesto, the Royal Canadian Mounted Police and local authorities were in the midst of a thirty-one-day confrontation with an armed group of natives at Gustafsen Lake, British Columbia. CBC Radio interrupted its afternoon programming in British Columbia four times on 13 September with a brief message, broadcast in English and in the language of Shuswap Indians. The message was written by RCMP officials, who told CBC that it was what the renegades had demanded to hear.

CBC senior management in Toronto endorsed the request by the RCMP to air the message, and defended their decision to accede to such demands "if the public interest is at stake." CBC's decision to cooperate with the RCMP during this confrontation was generally accepted in Canada as being the responsible thing to do.

In fact, following the standoff, political columnist Jeffrey Simpson summarized the episode in a column in The Globe and Mail under the headline: "Thanks to RCMP, the Gustafsen Lake standoff ended quietly." The column made no mention of CBC's participation.

Across the border, however, the decision by the Post and Times to publish the Unibomber's manifesto drew strong criticism from leading media professionals as being a serious violation of the canons of American journalism. William

Serrin, in a special to The Post, complained that the newspapers had violated those canons by giving in to the government and by turning their news columns over to a killer. Others, however, like commentator Daniel Schorr, agreed with the publishers that "This centres on the role of a newspaper as part of a community" and argued that the public increasingly views the press as shielding itself behind the First Amendment to exempt itself from its responsibilities to the broader community.

These contrasting illustrations and Schorr's summary observation help frame the issues discussed in this chapter by calling attention to: the relationship between media law and journalistic practice; the conflict between constitutional freedoms and civic responsibility; the importance of defining the role of the media in society; and the inherent conflict between the approaches of individualism and communitarianism.

Building upon these issues, this chapter examines the ways and the extent to which the law, the courts, and the media in Canada tend toward perspectives that either favour the rights of individual journalists and media operations or emphasize the values of community and the place of the media within the broader context of communities.

The first part examines the way courts in Canada compare to those in the United States in their interpretations of the respective constitutional provisions for freedom of expression by looking at themes in those judgments that appear to promote individual rights of the mass media on one hand, or community and societal interests on the other.

The second part begins an examination of the influence of English and French traditions on journalism and journalistic practice in Canada in ways that are similar to or different from those in the United States, particularly with respect to how these approaches encourage community or promote individualism.

COMMUNITY AND INDIVIDUALISM IN THE LAW

While the legal systems in Canada and the United States

share a similar tradition in English Common Law, their judicial and political approaches are different in important ways. For example, while their founding documents have some similarities, they reflect important differences in values and priorities. The American Declaration of Independence and its commitment to "Life, Liberty and the pursuit of Happiness" is contrasted to the British North America Act with its emphasis on the "Peace, Order and Good Government" of Canada.

The former reflects an individualistic, antigovernment theme, while the latter reflects a trust in government and ambivalence toward personal freedom. Lipset and Pool explain that while both nations seek to protect the rights of the individual while promoting and protecting the general welfare of the community, they "strike different balances, with Canada tipping toward the interests of the community, and the United States toward the individual."

Similarly, the formal statement of the constitutional guarantees for freedom of expression in Canada differs from that found in the American Bill of Rights. In the United States, these guarantees are found in the speech-press clause of the First Amendment to the Constitution. The language is quite specific in stating that "Congress shall make no law. abridging freedom of speech, or of the press."

U.S. court interpretations have largely held in favour of promoting individual rights, both of citizens and of the press, against directly promoting interests of community or the broader societal good.

In Canada, on the other hand, Section 2(b) of the Charter of Rights and Freedoms provides that everyone "has the fundamental freedoms of thought, belief, opinion and expression, including freedom of the press and other media of communication."This more positive affirmation is qualified in a manner that supports the broader community or societal interests through Section 1, which guarantees these freedoms but "subject only to such reasonable limits prescribed by law as can be demonstrably justified in a free and democratic society."

Despite these fundamental differences in the form and approach to press freedom and other basic rights in the two countries, an important emerging similarity is the expanding role the courts in Canada must play in defining and applying these protections. While this has long been the case in the United States, it is increasingly the case in Canada since enactment of the new Constitution in 1982 with its entrenched Charter of Rights and Freedoms.

Even in light of the Charter's provisions for parliamentary or legislative exceptions to these guarantees, it is ultimately left to the courts to determine what are "reasonable limits prescribed by law" that can be "justified in a free and democratic society". Just as the Supreme Court in the United States long ago established that the determination of what constitutes appropriate government limitations on freedoms "is clearly a judicial responsibility, not a legislative one" the new Charter has given to judges, and ultimately the Supreme Court of Canada, "the responsibility for weighing the merits of the conduct of elected bodies and governmental officials, both legislative and administrative, against the constitutionally protected elements of liberty."

BALANCING THE INTERESTS OF GOVERNMENT AND THE MEDIA

Several important provisions in the Canadian Charter of Rights and Freedoms give legislative bodies, both federal and provincial, authority to define the scope of these and other fundamental rights and freedoms specified in Sections 2-15. In particular, Sections 1 and 33(1) define the role of federal and provincial governments in balancing these fundamental rights against the broader needs and interests of society. The language of Section 1 requires that any legislative action limiting the basic rights and freedoms guaranteed in the Charter must satisfy three general requirements.

First, it must be a reasonable limit on the right or freedom being affected. Second, it must be demonstrably justifiable. And third, it must reflect the values of a free and democratic society. In 1986 the Supreme Court of Canada identified two central criteria that must be satisfied in order to establish that a limit is allowable under Section 1.

First, the objective must be "of sufficient importance to warrant overriding a constitutionally protected right or freedom." Second, once such an objective is recognized, "the party invoking must show that the means chosen are reasonable and demonstrably justified." The Court elaborated on this second criterion in R. v Whyte by explaining that a "proportionality test" must be met to show that the measures are reasonable and demonstrably justified.

The three parts of this test are: first, the measures must be carefully designed to achieve the objective of the legislation, with a rational connection to the objective; second, the measure should impair the right or freedom as little as possible; and, third, there must be proportionality between the effects of the impugned measures on the protected right and the attainment of the objective.

In the United States, balancing the protections of press freedom against the needs of government and society are played out differently because of different constitutional language and traditions. Despite the absolutist language of the First Amendment ("Congress shall make no law."), few justices or legal scholars have taken a firm absolutist position in defining the limits of protected speech.

In attempting to clarify the poles of the debate between those arguing that First Amendment rights are absolute and those advocating a balancing of competing interests, Supreme Court Justice William Brennan developed a two-tiered approach to media issues and the free press clause of the First Amendment that takes the form of "two distinct models of the role of the press in our society that claim the protection of the First Amendment."

The first, the "speech" model, protects the acts of speaking, publishing, or broadcasting and "readily lends itself to the heady rhetoric of absolutism." This model fosters the values of democratic self-government. The second model, the "structural" model, protects the press "when it performs all the myriad tasks necessary for it to gather and disseminate the news." Under this model, Brennan explained, "the court must weigh the effects of the imposition inhibiting press access against the social interests served by the imposition." Justice Brennan felt compelled to offer this clarification in response to considerable press criticism over several recent Supreme Court decisions. In particular, he focused on then-recent Court decisions that failed to provide reporters with a constitutional protection from having to testify, that upheld a third-party search of a campus newspaper's newsroom, and that required a media libel defendant to answer questions about his state of mind during the editorial process.

These activities, Justice Brennan explained, are among "the myriad tasks necessary for [the press] to gather and disseminate the news." They come under the "structural" model and are deserving of qualified protection when balanced against other rights and needs.

They must be distinguished from the more specific acts of publishing, included under the "speech" model, which are deserving of more absolute protection under the First Amendment.

QUALIFYING MEDIA RIGHTS

Both Canada and the United States have landmark decisions issued earlier in this century expressing a strong commitment to the principle of a free press, even though "freedom of the press" was not formally part of any constitutional document in Canada prior to the Charter of Rights and Freedoms in 1982.

This section, however, looks at cases in three areas that would come under Justice Brennan's "structural" model requiring the court to balance individual concerns about free press against the broader rights of the community. The three areas are libel, journalist's privilege, and covering the courts.

The Supreme Court of the United States has constitutionalized a major part of defamation law. Before 1964 and the Court's decision in New York Times v Sullivan, the Supreme Court had considered defamatory publication to be outside protection of the First Amendment. With that decision, however, the Court ruled that the principle of "strict liability" would not apply to elected public officials seeking to recover damages for civil libel.

Instead, they would have to meet a new national, uniform standard of fault by having to prove "actual malice", which Justice Brennan, writing for the Court, defined as publication "with knowledge that it was false or with reckless disregard of whether it was false or not."

Canadian courts have not adopted this approach to the civil defamation. In a recent case, Hill v Church of Scientology, the Supreme Court of Canada was asked in arguments by the appellants to adopt the actual malice rule from the United States, but the Court declined.

Justice Cory, writing for the majority, reviewed the development of this standard in the United States, including critiques of the actual malice rule, and explained how the courts in England and Australia had refused to adopt it. He concluded that "None of the factors which prompted the United States Supreme Court to rewrite the law of defamation in America are present in the case at bar."

His conclusion was that "the common law of defamation complies with the underlying values of the Charter and there is no need to amend or alter it." Earlier in his opinion, he refused to separate an individual's public and private rights to recover damage to reputation.

"The fact that persons are employed by the government does not mean that their reputation is automatically divided into two parts, one related to their personal life and the other to their employment status. To accept the appellants' position would mean that identical defamatory comments would be subject to two different laws, one applicable to government employees, the other to the rest of society.

Government employment cannot be a basis for such a distinction. Reputation is an integral and fundamentally important aspect of every individual. It exists for everyone quite apart from employment." In the end, by continuing intact the English common law tradition in civil defamation, the Canadian Supreme Court keeps Canada more in line with other Western democracies, which set themselves apart from the American tradition that grants considerable protection to the news media to comment on government and criticize public officials and public figures with less fear of being successfully challenged under libel law.

When the Canadian Court specifically rejected the American approach in its decision in Scientology, it did so out of respect for the tradition of common law, the proper role of the legislature in these matters, and the fundamental right to reputation over freedom of expression.

JOURNALIST'S PRIVILEGE

Neither Canadian nor American courts have been willing to grant journalists the same common law privilege from having to testify as is provided for doctor-patient, lawyer-client, and priest-penitent communications. In both countries, the general rule is that journalists will not be offered absolute protection from having to disclose the identity of a source or confidential information if it is considered relevant and necessary.

The U.S. Supreme Court's 1972 decision in Branzburg v Hayes dealt specifically with the application of a First Amendment protection for journalists from having to testify when confidential sources or information is involved. Most significant was the dissenting opinion by Justice Stewart who offered a three-part test that is used in state and federal courts in applying federal or state common law protection or statutory protection under a state "shield" law.

The test requires: first, there is probable cause to believe the journalist has relevant information; second, that the information sought cannot be obtained in another way less injurious of the First Amendment; and, third, that there is a compelling and overriding interest in the information.

In Canada, the issue of journalist's privilege had not been dealt with by the Supreme Court until 1989, when it decided a case similar in many ways to Branzburg v Hayes. In Moysa v Alberta a reporter for the Edmonton Journal refused to identify her sources of information, claiming confidential privilege protection under common law and the Canadian Charter.

The Court affirmed the decision of the two lower courts that the reporter in this case had no special privilege to refuse to testify before the labour board. While the Court did not feel compelled by the facts of the case to address the "broad and important constitutional questions" before it, Justice Sopinka in his opinion for the majority did refer to an earlier pre-Charter decision when the Court acknowledged the four criteria cited by Wigmore for when a motion for confidential privilege should be granted.

It is likely that the Wigmore test will play an important role when and if the Court is presented with the right case requiring a consideration of the constitutional questions not addressed in Moysa. However, from Justice Sopinka's opinion, news media appellants can expect to have to establish with evidence that a direct link exists "between testimonial compulsion and a `drying-up' of news sources."

MEDIA AND THE COURTS

No area of media law has attracted more attention by the courts in both countries than the one involving media coverage of the courts. This area directly involves the conflict of constitutional guarantees: first, freedom of the press with its companion needs to gather information and cover government, including the courts and, second, the defendant's constitutional right to a fair trial.

In the United States, the conflict is between the First and Sixth Amendments. In Canada, it is the conflict between freedom of the press and other media of communication in Section 2(b) and the right to a fair and public hearing in Section 11(d) of the Charter of Rights and Freedoms.

In Canada, prior to the enactment of the Charter in 1982, the rights of individuals and the media to attend and report on court proceedings were much more limited than was the case south of the border. Since then, however, the courts in Canada have issued important decisions that have expanded these rights considerably, but still not to the extent that the courts have in the United States. For example, trial court judges in Canada still have considerable authority to restrain the publication of certain information arising from hearings (publication of evidence tendered in a preliminary hearing is usually banned until after a full trial can be held before an unbiased jury), and journalists have no general right of access to court documents unless specifically provided by statute or court rule.

During the first year of the new Charter, the Ontario Court of Appeal ruled that an absolute ban on the press and public from attending court proceedings was a violation of Section 2(b). While recognizing that the guarantee of freedom of the press is not absolute, the Court acknowledged that "There can be no doubt that the openness of the courts to the public is one of the hallmarks of a democratic society. Public accessibility to the courts was and is a felt necessity; it is a restraint on arbitrary action by those who govern and by the powerful."

It concluded, however, that while absolute bans excluding the press and public from court proceedings did not constitute a reasonable limit, such closures requiring judicial discretion would be allowed under Section 1 of the Charter.

The Supreme Court of Canada offered further instruction in the application of Section 1 in matters relating to the courts in one ruling that struck down an Alberta law prohibiting publication of materials from court proceedings, ruling that such limits were not justified under Section 1.

In another decision, the Supreme Court ruled that an injunction restraining picketing and other activities calculated to interfere with the operations of the court was justified under Section 1, even though the lower court record included an affidavit from a member of the Law Society of British Columbia explaining that the "picket line was orderly and peaceful" and that "Persons appearing to have business inside the Courthouse entered and left the building at will and at no time appeared to be impeded in any way by the picketers."

Further, in Canadian Newspapers Co. v Canada (A.G.), the Supreme Court held that a mandatory ban on publishing the identity of a sexual assault victim was allowed under Section 1, since it was required to achieve Parliament's objective of facilitating complaints by victims of sexual assaults. In a recent decision, the Canadian Supreme Court set aside a ban on CBC from broadcasting a fictional account of sexual and physical abuse of children during a trial in Ontario with similar facts and circumstances.

While ruling that such a ban did not meet the "reasonable limits" test of s. 1, the majority justices offered an interesting observation about differences between the Canadian and American constitutional approaches to issues like this: "Publication bans, however, should not always be seen as a clash between freedom of expression for the media and the right to a fair trial for the accused.

The clash model is more suited to the American constitutional context and should be rejected in Canada." This review of developments in three areas of media law in Canada shows that, while the courts on both sides of the border have expressed a strong commitment to the principle of a free press, Canadian courts have been less likely to provide strict protections for the media to publish without government restraint or interference.

This is most obvious in matters related to coverage of the courts, where judicial restraints on the news media have been more allowable in Canada, although the Court has moved in recent years to balance the importance of press freedom and the constitutional right to a fair trial. Also, Canadian courts have permitted government bans on the publication of truthful information, lawfully obtained, while American courts have held that such bans constitute an unconstitutional prior restraint.

And while media in the United States are allowed greater latitude to criticize public officials, Canadian courts have been reluctant to adopt the American approach to public libel and false light privacy. In other areas, however, involving newsgathering, the duty to testify, and access to information, the courts in both countries have attempted to balance the individual rights of the news media against the broader community interests of society.

DIFFERENCES IN JOURNALISTIC PRACTICE

In order to make some generalized comparisons of journalists and journalistic practice in the United States, in English-speaking Canada, and in French-speaking Canada, it is necessary to indulge in some oversimplifications about groups which, in themselves, tend to be rather complex and diverse. Lysiane Gagnon, in her discussion of "Journalism and Ideologies in Quebec," offers a useful starting point in her review of the classic work by Siebert, Peterson, and Schramm on The Four Theories of the Press, which provides a framework for generalizing about differences between these three groups of journalists and for beginning to identify the French, English, and American influences on the practice of journalism in North America.

While the so-called "social responsibility" theory of the press grew out of the 1947 report of the Hutchins Commission on Freedom of the Press in the United States, American journalists have tended not to accept its basic premise, which calls for government intervention when and if the media fail to act responsibly.

For the most part, they continue to subscribe to the more libertarian view and its imperative that the press be free from government control and influence. However, the most recent national survey of journalists in the United States reveals a shift in the perceived functions of journalism favoring some of the original recommendations of the Hutchins Commission.

As Weaver and Wilhoit explain, "most journalists in 1992 appeared to have a 'belief system' that reflected the Commission's goal of investigating 'the truth about the fact[s]' and providing 'a context which gives them meaning.'" Concerning the appropriate role for government, journalists in English Canada, who share British traditions allowing for more government secrecy and control of information and the reporting of information, are more tolerant than their

American counterparts of government intervention and control.

And by further comparison, journalists on French-language media in Quebec subscribe even more to the tenets of the social-responsibility theory and are willing to accept an even greater role for government involvement in media matters to assure the public's right to information. According to Fulford, English-Canadian journalists have inherited most of their techniques from Britain and the United States, except for the extensive foreign correspondence of British journalism and the investigative reporting in the United States.

Further, and perhaps more important, is his observation that English-Canadian newspapers tend to mix elements of British and American heritage and share the ideal which involves truth, completeness, and justice. Explaining that English-Canadian journalists seek "to report the truth," Fulford quotes publisher Stuart Keate who wrote that "Any publisher, editor or reporter worth his salt recognizes that he has only one basic duty to perform: to dig for the truth; to write it in language people can understand; and to resist all impediments to its publication."

While changes in English-Canadian journalism during this century have paralleled similar changes in the United States, journalism in Quebec has been more influenced by French models that include government distribution agencies, newspapers with more readily identifiable political leanings, and greater acceptance of government intervention in media affairs.

The latter is linked to the basic tenet of the social-responsibility theory of the press which, according to Gagnon, has become more accepted by journalists in the province of Quebec than anywhere else in North America. One of the recent presidents of Quebec's federation of professional journalists, Real Barnabe, supported this observation by writing: "Now that they have acquired the conditions under which they may practice their profession with dignity, never have they [Quebec journalists] been so preoccupied by their responsibilities."

Gagnon further explains that the notion of freedom of the press, which was widely accepted by Quebec journalists in the 1940s and 1950s, has given way to a more complex concept of the public's "right to know," and that this has enjoyed considerable success in Quebec, certainly more than it has in English Canada and, with even more reason, the United States.

Part of the explanation for this has to do with the French traditions and perspectives which place a greater value on collectivism over individualism. As Siebert, Peterson, and Schramm explain in their classic work, the social responsibility theory is "in closer harmony with a collectivist theory of society than with the individualistic theory from which the libertarian system sprang."

Other ways in which the French tradition has contributed to differences between French and English journalism and journalists in Canada include: the emphasis on analysis over simple reporting of facts; the tendency to treat matters conceptually rather than in terms of people and events; the need to rationalize; and a greater personalization of articles and editorials. This is not to say that Quebec journalists are less committed to the facts and to being factual.

A recent study by Pritchard and Sauvageau, for example, found that Quebec journalists are more likely than other Canadian journalists to think that it is important to accurately report comments from news sources. Similarly, an earlier study by Langlois and Sauvageau, which also documented this commitment to the facts, found there to be considerable variation among newspaper journalists in Quebec.

Concerning the greater personalization of articles and editorials, mentioned above, Siegel found in his study of the coverage of the FLQ crisis in 1970 that the French-language papers tended to project an image of self-importance in a variety of ways including "frequent reference to media and journalists; personalized coverage which, at times, included the raising of rhetorical questions which they then proceeded to answer; and editorials written in the first person."

Another conclusion he reached point to still another

important difference between journalism in English and French Canada. Following a comparison of coverage of several major issues or events, as well as a comparison of French and English broadcasting, Siegel found a homogeneity of outlook in the French press system.

"Of particular interest is the leadership role in French-Canadian society in which French-language journalists see them-selves. The articulation of a clearly defined value system is evident in French-language journalism, a practice that goes back a long time."

He found no such uniformity of outlook on the part of the English press, which he termed "fragmented." His conclusion is reinforced by David Thomas, an English-speaking journalist from Quebec: "Unity of thought was, and remains, infinitely more obvious in Quebec's French-language media—a phenomenon implicitly recognized by politicians and journalists who repeatedly point to the harsher treatment accorded the government by the English media."

Dominque Clift, a Montreal author and free-lance journalist who worked for major Canadian newspapers in both French and English Canada, characterized this uniformity of French-language journalists in a different way: the way in which they viewed themselves and their role in Quebec society.

In his article, "Solidarity on a Pedestal: French Journalism in Quebec," he charged that "French journalists see for themselves a much more exalted role in society than do their English-speaking counterparts," adding that: "It is in the actual practice of journalism that French and English writers differ in the most pronounced manner.

It has to do with the way in which journalists look upon themselves, their profession, their public, as well as on their employers." But Florian Sauvageau, in his more systematic study of journalists on French-language dailies in Quebec, could find no such homogeneity in Quebec's journalistic circles.

Instead, he found changes in Quebec media to parallel those in the modern corporate media of North America. Those include: the tendency to view newspapers as, first and foremost, businesses and journalists as "news workers"; journalists talking not so much in terms of "news" but of the "product"; and business and marketing functions gradually replacing the news function.

Journalists are far from all being those radicals trying to control the news, as depicted a few years ago with some help from the pronouncements of the most militant of them. There are some, of course, who still turn for inspiration to the theses of the news as a driving force, and journalism as a tool for development, seeing themselves as agents of change and keeping up with the rhetoric of the 1960s and 1970s.

However, a good number are content simply to report the remarks of the dignitaries they meet, or to get the news out as quickly as possible. The result, he said, is that the work of journalists is becoming more and more routine and fairly unfulfilling, and that this is partly due to the rigid application of certain clauses in collective agreements between journalists and management.

In summary, this brief review of research and commentary on journalists and journalism in the United States, English Canada, and Quebec provides some insight into how the practice of journalism in these different settings has been influenced in a variety of ways by English, French, and American traditions.

Our concern, however, is in how these different traditions or perspectives may have resulted in journalistic practices that vary in their tendencies to promote individualism or to serve the community or broader societal interests.

ANECDOTAL EVIDENCE

Despite the growing body of literature from systematic studies of journalists in Canada and the United States, most of the "evidence" about how journalists and journalistic practices differ between the two countries tends to be anecdotal rather than the result of formal research. There are some exceptions, of course.

For example, we already reported how the most recent

national survey of journalists in the United States shows a shift toward some of the values articulated by the Hutchins Commission, which advanced the "social-responsibility" theory of the press.

Also, French-language journalists in Canada tend to be more willing than their English-Canadian and especially their American counterparts to perceive the press as a public service that can be regulated by the government. As evidence, Langois and Sauvageau found that nearly two-thirds of the French-speaking journalists in their study agreed that the state should intervene in the field of information.

Even before the Kent Commission issued its report and recommendations in 1981, Sauvageau argued that the government might intervene to assure the citizen's right to information, similar to the way it has done in education and health care.

More often, though, evidence is used to explain how the traditions and perspectives of journalists in Canada and the United States vary considerably in terms of tolerance for intervention by government and the courts in ways that limit the media and the practice of journalism.

This chapter began with a good example of this variety by comparing reactions to the decision in the United States to publish the Unibomber's manifesto with reaction to CBC cooperation with the RCMP in meeting broadcast demands of a group of renegades in British Columbia.

Another example is reaction to certain recommendations of the Kent Commission on Newspapers. Following the simultaneous sale of newspapers in Winnipeg and Ottawa by two major Canadian newspaper groups, the federal government established the Kent Commission in 1980 and authorized it to study the new newspaper industry and make recommendations to the government.

One of the more controversial recommendations called for the establishment of a Press Rights Panel within the Canadian Human Rights Commission. Response came mainly from representatives and publishers of newspapers owned by large newspaper groups in Canada.

The reaction was tempered and mild compared to what one would expect in the United States if similar recommendations were to come out of a government committee that spent more than $3 million to investigate the daily newspaper industry. Reactions in the United States to any threat of government intervention or control in media affairs tend to be immediate and predictable.

Media owners and spokespersons for associations of journalists, particularly in the print media, are quick to call "infringement" and issue charges of improper violations of cherished First Amendment guarantees of freedom of the press. Still another example has to do with media coverage of criminal trials.

During the months of exhaustive coverage and commentary related to the O.J. Simpson trial in the United States, a trial court judge in Ontario issued a restraining order on the media in the Paul Bernardo murder trial that included, as well, a ban on publication of most information from his wife's trial several months earlier.

Canadian journalists complained but complied with the court order, while American journalists in neighboring border cities did not, continuing what one U.S. newspaper editor had earlier referred to as a "border battle with Canadian law."

These examples help illustrate the differences between Canada and the United States in terms of their legal systems, judicial traditions, and accepted journalistic practice and show a stronger commitment in Canada to the values of community over the individual rights of journalists and the news media.

Important differences in the traditions of law and in the practice of journalism in Canada and the United States result in different approaches to how the rights of the news media are appropriately balanced against the needs of the community and the broader interests of society. To begin with, while the two legal systems share a similar tradition in English Common Law, their judicial and political approaches are different in important ways.

As Lipset and Pool explain, while both nations seek to protect the rights of the individual while promoting and protecting the general welfare of the community, they do "strike different balances, with Canada tipping toward the interests of the community, and the United States toward the individual."

This review of the development of media law in the two countries shows that the courts on both sides of the border have expressed a strong commitment to the principle of a free press. However, Canadian courts have been less likely than those in the United States to provide strict protections for the media to publish without government restraint or interference.

This is most obvious in matters related to coverage of the courts, where judicial restraints are more allowable in Canada. Also, Canadian courts have permitted government bans on the publication of truthful information, lawfully obtained, while American courts have held that such bans on the press or punishment for publishing such information is unconstitutional.

Also, media in the United States are allowed greater latitude to criticize public officials than are media in Canada, where the courts have been reluctant to adopt the American approach to civil libel. In other areas, however, involving newsgathering, the duty to testify, and access to information, the courts in both countries have attempted to balance the rights of the news media against the broader interests of society.

Apart from differences in the law are differences in the practice of journalism in Canada and the United States. Journalists in Canada are more inclined toward a "social responsibility" view of the role of the media in society. While this particular perspective was proposed by the prestigious Hutchins Commission on Freedom of the Press in the United States, American journalists have tended not accept its basic premise, which calls for government intervention when and if the media fail to act responsibly.

For the most part, they continue to subscribe to the more libertarian view and its imperative that the media be free from government influence and control. Canadian journalists, however, whether sharing British traditions that allow for more government secrecy and control of information or French traditions that are more accepting of government intervention in media affairs, tend to be more tolerant of government intervention in ways that directly affect the media while serving the broader needs and interests of society.

The most recent national survey of American journalists suggests that there may be some shift toward some of the goals of the Hutchins Commission, which originally proposed the social responsibility model.

SOME FUTURE CONSIDERATIONS

There is, and has been, considerable discussion about the Constitution in Canada since the Charter of Rights and Freedoms was adopted in 1982. However, little if any of the controversy centres around concerns over government control of the media or court limitations of Charter guarantees of press freedom.

This is not to say that journalists and media owners in Canada do not have concerns about these issues or that they would not prefer greater freedom and less government control. It is just that these are not major concerns, at least not compared to the larger constitutional issues being discussed. This is not the case in the United States, where journalists and media owners have long been eager and vocal critics of any attempts by government or the courts to limit press freedoms and violate their First Amendment guarantees.

However, the growing criticism and concerns about court interpretations of the speech-press clause in the United States are coming from nonmedia sources who are concerned about too much freedom at the expense of other interests, particularly the rights and interests of disadvantaged groups like women and minorities.

In particular, concerns being raised by feminists, critical scholars and, especially, critical legal theorists are that the court's continuing emphasis on protecting press freedoms serves only to advance the status quo and favors the special interests of corporate-owned media conglomerates. These are variations of the same kinds of criticism and concerns expressed by Jerome Barron, who argued nearly thirty years ago that "Our constitutional theory is in the grip of a romantic conception of free expression, a belief that the `marketplace of ideas' is freely accessible.

But if ever there were a self operating marketplace of ideas, it has long ceased to exist." He went on to argue for a legal right of access to the media to provide citizens with the kind of marketplace originally intended by the Founding Fathers. Barron, an American, raises these same concerns over recent developments in media law in Canada, and a growing number of critical theorists and legal scholars in Canada are expressing concerns of their own about constitutional developments related to court interpretations of the Canadian Charter of Rights and Freedoms.

Michael Mandel, for example, frames his criticisms in terms of what he calls "The legalization of politics in Canada," and argues that the representative institutions like Parliament, the legislatures, and municipal councils "are now being pushed from centre stage and told what they can and cannot do by judges elected by and accountable to nobody."

David Schneiderman, in his edited volume on Freedom of Expression and the Charter, explains that critics are not optimistic about the consequences of the constitutionalization of freedom of expression in Canada and are concerned that the Charter favors the value system of liberal individualism over the collectivist aims of the modern welfare state.

In the United States, concerns are also being raised in journalistic circles about the status of American journalism, about public criticism of the press, and about the appropriate roles and responsibilities of the media in a free democratic society. One of the best recent books on this subject is by Anderson, Dardenne, and Killenberg, who argue for a more ecumenical, constructive, participative, and democratically responsive role for journalism's institutional future.

Other recent authors like Davis Merritt, Jay Rosen, and James Fallows have called for a revision in journalistic practices in order to promote community through civic or public journalism. This approach has challenged the way responsible media report on and relate to the communities they serve. As Dennis and Merrill put it, "The new communitarians are waging a rhetorical war against Enlightenment liberalism—against individualism and libertarianism."

More specifically, Christians argues that journalists should discard the liberal politics of rights, which "rests on unsupportable foundations," and that such rights should be "given up for a politics of the common good." In response, critics of this approach argue that it "confuses journalism with community organization, a social work concept" and are concerned that if journalists became activists and took positions on community issues, they would lose "any claim to impartiality and would sacrifice credibility."

In summary, what emerges from a review of issues like these is the fact that some of the basic foundations of law and journalistic practice are being challenged in very significant ways by credible practitioners and scholars in Canada and the United States alike. This is all part of the important ongoing discussions about how to appropriately balance the freedoms of the press and other media of communication against the larger interests of society, and about how to frame the practice of journalism in the best way possible to serve the democratic process.

The quality of these discussions on both sides of the border can be enhanced by examining the experiences in both countries and, indeed, in other societies, to see how these issues are being played out against the backdrop of different traditions, practices, values, and beliefs.

Each new technology has brought its share of hype from those who would like to see its use for education. In 1922, Thomas Edison said that the motion picture was destined to revolutionize our educational system. In 1945, William Levenson, director of the Cleveland public schools' radio stations, said that the time might come when a portable radio receiver would be as common in the classroom as the blackboard.

In 1961, the Ford Foundation claimed that educational television promises "a whole treasure-trove of new and stimulating experiences". More recently, at the National Education Computing Conference in June 1997, Bill Gates compared the computer and the Internet revolution with the California gold rush of the mid 1800s.

He exhorted educators to use this new technology in the classroom to give students a better chance at success. Researchers have long been aware of such hype and the often unfulfilled promises that educational technology has brought to education. Few are fully aware of the negative effects that these same technologies can bring to education and to our lives. Television has been in schools and in our homes for nearly half a century.

During that time, extensive studies have been conducted on this medium, with some interesting results. For example, second graders from towns without television score higher on reading fluency and creative ability tests. Non-TV-viewing fourth and eighth graders score higher on basic skills tests. Television viewing is a cause of violent or aggressive behaviour.

It also contributes substantially to obesity. Television can make you dumber, less creative, violent, and obese. What do computers have in store for us? Todd Oppenheimer's article "The Computer Delusion" is highly critical of school districts' cutting programs in art, music, and physical education to add computer programs when "there is no good evidence that most uses of computers significantly improve teaching and learning".

ABC's Nightline with Ted Koppel aired a segment on September 30, 1998 titled "Computers in the Classroom: The $50 Billion Gamble," highlighting the fact that there is little, if any, research to prove that there are any learning benefits to using technology in the classroom. One month before that programme, the front page of the New York Times detailed the startling findings of a $1.5 million, three-year study by Carnegie Mellon researchers.

They found that the longer a person spends online, the

more sad, lonely, and depressed he or she becomes. These findings do not surprise critical educators. Every new technology arrives with hype, and years later we find major weaknesses.

Good educational designers should not ignore these findings. They need to find ways to maximize the positive effects of technologies and minimize the weaknesses. Following are three examples of doing just that.

THE NO-SIGNIFICANT-DIFFERENCE EFFECT

One of the most disappointing aspects of using technology in teaching is the so-called no-significant-difference phenomenon. This phenomenon outlines the observation that any technology used in teaching does not make a significant difference in learning.

Statistical comparisons between teaching methodologies, with or without the use of technology, have been made for nearly a century. Researchers have compared how much students learned from a teacher lecturing in a traditional classroom with how much students learned from a traditional correspondence course covering the same material. There was no significant difference.

Comparisons have been made between correspondence courses and radio courses, telnet courses and television courses, and traditional lecture courses and online courses, to name a few. The vast majority of the research resulted in no significant difference. In those few cases where a significant difference was found, the most recent technology in the comparison was not always the winner.

Nearly all of the no-significant-difference studies that have been conducted since 1912 have used a model of a traditional classroom with a teacher lecturing to students. Whether it was a teacher in a traditional classroom, on the radio, on television, on telnet, online, or even via correspondence, they all used the lecture format.

Perhaps the hundreds of findings of "no significant difference" really headline the fact that if you use the lecture format, students will learn the material equally well no matter what media are chosen. That being the case, if you are going to lecture, why not use the cheaper format? Why spend thousands of dollars on technology when less expensive printed materials used in a correspondence course will work just as well?

Another alternative is for course designers to think outside the paradigm of the lecture format. Unext.com is creating Cardean, a "no lecture" university. The company contends that learning only happens when students "do," not when they listen passively to a lecture.

The educational content for the courses is being drawn from several eminent institutions, including Stanford and Columbia. Few schools can afford the millions of dollars being spent on developing problem-based learning courses created by expert designers working with Nobel scientists. However, there are a number of practical ways to begin to develop lecture-free courses.

Project-based activities can give students the freedom to apply learning in practical contexts that are personal and relevant to them. Step-by-step tutorials could allow them to work with applicable software tools to develop digital media for their projects. A good place to start would be to use tutorials that are already online for paint programs, Web page editors, or presentation software programs.

Also, teachers could create links to structured tutorials for surfing the Internet to help students find the best "fair-use" digital materials. Other links could provide students with resources that help them learn how to evaluate sites critically to find good sources of legitimate information. Digital projects could be showcased in an online student gallery or in a student portfolio.

Students could provide feedback as they previewed and learned from each other's work. Course readings or activities could be built around real-world or theoretical problems. Teachers could follow these assignments with threaded discussion forums or live chats.

Students would be expected to read and respond to comments made by those in the class. Once this dialogic process was established, students could use this same model for their own project presentations. Similarly, student groups could be assigned topics of importance to research, develop, and teach to the class. Groups could post Web pages with relevant links for class exploration before conducting formal discussions via live chat or threaded forum discussion.

MINIMIZE THE DEPRESSED AND LONELY EFFECT

Want to be depressed and lonely? Spend more time communicating on the Internet. That is the surprising conclusion of the study conducted at Carnegie Mellon University and financed by a number of technology giants including Intel, Hewlett Packard, AT&T Research, and Apple Computer.

Researchers found that people who spent even a few hours per week online experienced higher levels of depression and loneliness than those who used the computer network less frequently.

These results completely surprised the social scientists because participants used social features such as e-mail and Internet chats more than they used passive information gathering resources to read or watch videos. "We were shocked by the findings, because they are counterintuitive to what we know about how socially the Internet is being used," said Robert Kraut, a social psychology professor at Carnegie Mellon's Human Computer Interaction Institute.

"We are not talking here about the extremes. These were normal adults and their families, and on average, for those who used the Internet most, things got worse". Teenagers, unsurprisingly, tended to spend more time online and showed a greater rate of loneliness and depression. What caused this negative side effect? Here is one possibility: Those who participated in the study reported a decline in interaction with family members and friends that directly corresponded to the amount of time they spent online.

A recent study at Stanford University also found that the more time someone spends online, the less time he or she spends with real human beings. Communicating with someone online apparently is not as psychologically fulfilling as is talking to someone you know. Due to the anonymity of the Internet, unless you really know the people you are chatting with, you cannot be sure that they are being honest about their profession or expertise, let alone any of their personal information.

Several things can be done to minimize the effect of student isolation. One idea is to have students and faculty create biographical pages with visual and auditory elements that briefly encapsulate each individual in an interesting way. Everyone in a class or degree programme should have easy access to this password-protected information.

Password protection prevents search engine spiders from cataloging this information in their databases. Without it, students would soon find their bio-pages listed in the directories of major search engines. Another idea is to group students together when they begin to work on a degree online. Students could be grouped by such factors as interests, personal situations, goals, or the pace at which they plan to work through a programme.

If a group of six students with similar interests starts out together in a programme, real friendships may be fostered on the way to a degree. To help forge a connection with the university, graduate assistants or faculty could be assigned to these groups that meet periodically online.

Another way to develop communication avenues that are valuable to students would be to enable students to establish online clubs based on interests. Dating, chess, foreign language, journalism, or even debate clubs are some possibilities. Access to online student lounges could also be valuable.

MINIMIZE THE NUMBER OF DROPOUTS

The Institute for Higher Education Policy conducted a review of the current research on the effectiveness of distance education. Reviewers found that "in a number of studies, there was evidence that a higher percentage of students participating in a distance learning course tended to drop out before the course was completed compared to students in a conventional classroom".

They concluded that the research did "not adequately explain why the drop out rates of distance learners is higher." They also stated that this "subject mortality" was bad because of "negative consequences associated with dropping out" and also because the research was likely "excluding these drop outs—thereby tilting the student outcome findings toward those who are `successful.'.

If the students who had dropped out had remained in the course, the mean score of the achievement test or student survey could be significantly different." The Corporate University Xchange (CUX) is a corporate education research and consulting firm that helps organizations with training. The company says that one of the biggest challenges of online learning programs is to "retain" e-learners.

Their pilot study of e-learners from Fortune 1000 companies revealed that the number one reason that people drop out of online courses was "lack of time." Solutions for this problem were to create courses that give students: (a) the ability to start a course at any time, (b) flexible deadlines, and (c) 24-hour technical support.

Zielinski (2000, 54) describes a number of concerns about the "design and implementation of many self-paced, asynchronous learning courses," including "higher-than-average drop-out rates or disengaged learners who don't receive the level of interaction, personalized feedback, skills practice, managerial oversight or technical support needed for quality learning experiences." It is hard to address these concerns if learning organizations are not tracking students—specifically those who drop out—to find out about their online experiences.

For example, some may be what Zielinski calls "pragmatic learners," who do not finish all the modules of an online course simply because, with "grazing" learning styles, they take only the content they need, leaving superfluous material behind. Without more detailed data like these, it is nearly impossible to address the dropout situation.

Degree programs should be collecting and developing online-accessible databases of this type of information, as well as more personalized information from students including their interests and learning styles. Instructors and developers should have access to this database.

Finalists for the "1998 Outstanding Online Course Award," sponsored by the Paul Allen Virtual Education Foundation, gave presentations at the "Creating Effective Online Instruction" conference in May 1999. Developers of two of the courses stated that the next wave of development for online courses is to make them more personalized for individual students.

Both planned to develop more personalized Web courses with software such as ColdFusion, which allows developers to create database-driven Web sites. When a student accesses one of these course sites, an individualized course Web page can address her by name, and because it has already parsed through her database of interests and learning styles, it can include a quote or story vignette specifically tailored for her. As she works through assignments and online assessments, the database continues to grow.

If she is found to have a weakness in an area, a Web resource can be offered, giving her a chance to review the same material from a more visual perspective if that matches her learning style strength. One way to begin integrating learning styles into online curriculum is to use the sensory styles. Three sensory styles are traditionally associated with academic learning: visual, auditory, and haptic (or kinesthetic).

An excellent way to address the individual differences of sensory learning styles would be to develop courses using the "Universal Design for Learning" framework. In this framework, curricular materials are developed in "many media so that learners can select one or more ways to approach the subject matter. Text, images with no text, images with text, voice, animation, video, or a sequence of sounds can effectively convey a series of events".

Within this framework, students are able to select media

in the format in which they learn best. A realistic way to begin this process is by creating multiple sensory options for the most difficult concept that will be covered.

VISUAL LEARNERS

Seeing understands for visual learners. Ross and Schulz state that "online course animations, hypertext, or clickable diagrams and video clips can clarify concepts that a static textbook image simply cannot." They further recommend that instructors maintain online archives of slide presentations to assist these visual learners. Additionally, development of charts, graphs, and any other visual rendition of the information to be covered is preferable for these types of learners.

AUDITORY LEARNERS

Auditory learners tend to benefit most from lectures. Ross and Schulz (1999) recommend that instructors establish audio resources and archive digital audio files of fifteen-minute class summaries on the Web. They can add shorter sound clips of instructor-developed materials to clarify course segments.

They can encourage auditory learners to purchase dictation software that converts their voice to text, These programs can often read the text of online materials and e-mail messages out loud. Some phone companies now offer audio-based e-mail services with which you can send or receive messages over the telephone.

Call up, and a computer dictation device will read your e-mail messages to you over the phone. You can then reply to these messages just as you would leave a message on an answering machine. Your response is saved as a digital audio file, attached to an e-mail message, and sent, all without the use of a computer.

HAPTIC OR KINESTHETIC LEARNERS

Learners who prefer to do something more active to learn course materials are referred to as "haptic" or "kinesthetic" learners. "Practicing problems, doing lab experiments, creating solutions, doing physical activities, engaging in manipulative exercises, and brainstorming ideas are all ways to involve this learner in the classroom".

These learners could print out step-by-step directions for more active course-based experiences that are posted online. Ross and Shultz add that "java-programmed jigsaw puzzles can provide a powerful learning and review tool for students."

Nearly two decades ago, Richard Clark said, "Five decades of research indicate that there are no learning benefits to be gained from applying different media in instruction, regardless of their obviously attractive features or advertised superiority." Clark changes this to "70 years" in his foreword to Russell's The No Significant Difference Phenomenon. Apparently, little has changed in the last twenty years.

Will another twenty years pass us by with the same results? One hope is that designers and teachers will try to use other pedagogies of learning that do not embrace the lecture format. Perhaps new leaders of technology will find ways to tap into individual differences to help create meaningful courses that really make a difference.

Additionally, it would be beneficial if students could create real friends and lifelong connections with their peers after experiencing an online degree programme with them. If this hope is realized, two decades from now we may read about online courses encountering the revolutionary "significant difference phenomenon," with students experiencing the "happy and connected" effect.

We might even read articles on the latest methods to stop students from "dropping in" to the class years after they graduate because it was such a life-changing experience.

Chapter 6

Formative Years of the Reporters Committee for Freedom of the Press

When the Nixon pardon was issued on September 8, 1974, the Committee was only four years old and had been engaged primarily in efforts to protect reporters from subpoenas issued by law enforcement officers. Three years later, when the U.S. Supreme Court issued its final ruling on the papers, rejecting Nixon's appeal and upholding the position of the Reporters Committee, the Committee had established itself as a force in what was emerging as a new field in the practice of law, that of First Amendment law.

From the vantage point of more than 30 years, its role in helping establish this new legal specialty is arguably the Reporters Committee's most lasting legacy to the media. But at the time, with reporters in jail for refusing to surrender notes or films, and courts and public officials closing proceedings or records the laws said were public, it was the trench battles that occupied the new organization.

In a nation tearing itself apart, reporters and reporting were vital to a democratic process under extreme pressure. Cautious news executives were uncertain of how to respond, only a handful of lawyers dealt with First Amendment issues on a regular basis, and the media had a genuine enemy in the White House.

The early history of the Reporters Committee is in effect the history of a volatile time in the relations between the news media and government, and the successes and failures of the Committee would prove to be important for succeeding generations of news workers. Early efforts of the Committee reflect the serious distrust between the Nixon Administration and the media, played out at a time of national unrest and an unfolding scandal in the form of Watergate.

As the Committee gained support within its industry, its efforts also opened rifts between working reporters and the powerful publishing interests that funded its operations. Ultimately, the disagreements climaxed in 1983 with a split over strategy at the time of the Grenada incursion, which pitted the more cautious publishers against the "in-your-face" tactics of the Committee and its zealous executive director, Jack C. Landau.

This study of the formative years of the Reporters Committee is a study of reporter-publisher-government relations and how they changed from the angry days of Richard M. Nixon to the relative harmony of the Ronald Reagan White House. For at least a dozen years, the Reporters Committee reflected the anger and paranoia of working journalists in Washington and across the nation, at times reaching a fever pitch in the face of extensive governmental pressures.

This study is a first look inside the Committee itself, the challenges it faced, its decision-making, its financial problems and the donors who rescued it from failure, and finally the internal divisions that sent it in another direction for the remainder of the century.

The author had full access to RCFP records and used interviews with founders, staff members, and leading First Amendment attorneys to fill out the historic record. The early years of the Reporters Committee saw the creation of research and education tools used daily by today's reporters and editors, as they face challenges of open-records laws, closed meetings, and threats of subpoenas.

A corps of First Amendment lawyers was also emerging at the time in parallel with the activism of the Reporters Committee. Publications-legal, academic and professional-began serving this specialized area of the law. Perhaps most of all, the Committee gave working reporters a policy voice separate from that of their employers, and put that voice on a public stage.

The Committee was formed out of the concern generated among reporters by the 1970 demand of federal prosecutors that Earl Caldwell, a New York Times reporter based in San Francisco, turn over notes of interviews he had with members of the Black Panthers. Caldwell refused, citing the need for reporters to maintain confidential sources, and his employers appeared to be wavering in his defence.

Some 35-40 reporters attended a meeting at Georgetown University to examine the Caldwell case; the meeting was called by Times colleague J. Anthony Lukas and quickly turned into a round of testimonials citing other governmental intrusions on the press.

After the meeting, Lukas, Jack Nelson of the Los Angeles Times, and Fred Graham of the New York Times coined the committee's name, sent out a news release, and established an informal steering committee of eleven colleagues.3 It was determined from the beginning that the committee would be governed by working reporters; even sympathetic editors and publishers would not decide policy.

"Reporters needed their own advocacy group," recalled James Doyle, then with the Washington Star, "and we could not be sure publishers would do the job." The group agreed to serve as a clearing house for information on the subpoena threat.

Sam Dash, then head of Georgetown's Institute of Criminal Law and Procedure, offered his office to help sort out inquiries, and it functioned in that manner in the first year, although few inquiries were received because the Committee was not well-known.

Founders saw beyond the Caldwell case to what they felt was a pervasive anti-media bias on the part of the Nixon Administration, including Attorney General John Mitchell. "We had a sense long before the public as a whole that Nixon did not believe in the First Amendment or anything else we believed in," said the late Eileen Shanahan, then with the New York Times.

Mitchell had "a thuggish cast at Justice," said Graham. Well before Watergatē, evidence was revealing that the "New Nixon" maintained much of his anti-media venom from past confrontations. Writing shortly after he left his post in the Nixon White House, William Safire described what he saw as Nixon's attitude toward the press:

When Nixon said, 'The press is the enemy,' he was not saying, as some of us had hoped, 'Be careful, its interest in gathering information is not our interest of developing policy' or 'There is an ideological bias as well as an institutional opposition in the attitude of the press' or even 'They're a pain in the neck, and don't waste your time with 'em.'

He was saying exactly what he meant: The press is the enemy' to be hated and beaten, and in that vein of vengeance that ran through his relationship with another power centre, in his indulgence of his most combative and abrasive instincts against what he saw to be an unelected and unrepresentative elite, lay Nixon's greatest personal and political weakness and the cause of his downfall.8 (italics original)

Accounts of the Nixon years, some written while he was still in office and others decades later, agree that Nixon's hatred of the press was real and deep, and it spread to other elements of the administration. The so-called "Eastern establishment media" had been attacked by Vice President Spiro Agnew in 1969, and federal prosecutors subpoenaed files of Time, Newsweek, and Life later that year as part of the Weathermen investigation.

The Caldwell case followed in 1970, and the Pentagon Papers case broke in June 1971. It was a time of paranoia on both sides, and civil libertarians were alarmed. In 1971 the American Civil Liberties Union issued a study by Fred Powledge, a former reporter, citing cases of Administration moves against the press, and concluding that there was already "a chilling effect" resulting in decisions not to publish sensitive material. Powledge concluded:

The decision not to do the story appears to be multiplying

all over the nation, and before long there will just not be very much interpretation of complex events and social movements. What will be left will be the relatively safe 'hard news' of speeches and statements, that can be easily manipulated.

It is in these ways that the First Amendment is being lost, a little each day. It could and should be argued that the threat would not be nearly so great if the press itself had fought harder for its own freedom.

But it must not matter that the press has chosen to approach this delicate matter with kid gloves on; the First Amendment does not belong to the press, but to the people, and they must not allow it to be given away or traded for a little respectability, or a little immunity from a politician's criticism.

Other civil liberties groups were becoming active. Fred Graham authored a comprehensive background paper for the Twentieth Century Fund Task Force on the Government and the Press, and also served as one of twelve members of the task force, which published its study in 1972.

The task force, about half with news backgrounds and the remainder representing the legal community, provided a remarkably strong defence of press rights, including an absolute ban on prior restraint-this in the wake of the Pentagon Papers case, which was decided while the committee deliberated (this recommendation did gather three dissents from attorneys on the committee).

Turning to the issue that had launched the Reporters Committee, the task force report recommended press protection against subpoenas seeking confidential notes, films, and sources. It backed a strong "reporter shield" law, adding, "If the privilege is to be qualified, the qualifications should be as narrow and as specific as possible.

This could be done by specifying that if newsmen possess information about particular violent crimes, such as murder or kidnapping, they may be compelled to testify." The task force would extend the privilege to "all journalists," specifically to the underground, collegiate, and minority press.

Addressing grand juries, the task force recommended,

"The privilege should shield journalists from having to appear for questioning before grand juries or other secret investigative agencies to the following extent: that when a subpoenaed newsman can make a showing that his newsgathering capacity would be seriously damaged merely by his entry into the secrecy of the interrogation room, then the official who subpoenaed him should be required to demonstrate a compelling need for his testimony before the journalist could be required to appear."

The need for such a policy became apparent when the Caldwell case blew into a national issue for reporters. Caldwell, an African American, won the confidence of some Black Panthers and wrote about the movement. Subpoenaed by a federal grand jury, he refused to testify, citing a promise of confidentiality to his sources.

Joined with two similar cases, those of Paul Branzburg and Paul Pappas, the cases were on their way to the Supreme Court. But the Times appeared to be ambivalent in defending Caldwell; initially he was advised to testify, Times lawyers fearing a loss of some earlier gains for the press. Reporters saw the Caldwell case as emblematic of a growing trend on the part of prosecutors, from the federal to local level, toward the use of reporters as sources.

The use of subpoenas to require reporters to reveal sources was, according to William J. Small, "one powerful tool which the government has used rarely in the past but dramatically and with chilling effect beginning in the late 1960s," particularly in the period following the 1968 Democratic National Convention.

"Over the last decade," media scholar Benno C. Schmidt Jr. wrote in 1973, "journalism and the law have both struggled to accommodate traditional procedures and principles to the development of widespread disenchantment and disobedience in American society." Schmidt noted that the challenge of electronic media has forced print journalists to turn more to investigative reporting and analysis, which rely heavily on confidential sources.

Finally, he added, "changes in official attitudes seem to

have led to the increased use of subpoenas against members of the press. A journalist who has accumulated evidence of official corruption or probed the activities of militant radicals must seem a tempting investigative aid to these pressured officials. Concerned journalists see in the increased use of subpoena a technique to harass the press and to emasculate its efforts at uncovering facts that officialdom would prefer to remain unpublicized."

The practice of a reporter refusing to reveal a source dates at least to 1857, when a New York Times reporter refused to name sources in a story about congressmen taking bribes. J. W. Simonton was held by the sergeant of arms of the House for 19 days before being discharged.

Several rulings over the next century had failed to set an absolute rule regarding confidential sources, and it was clear in 1970 that a major showdown in the Supreme Court was in the offing.

In the uneasy climate of the times, prosecutors often lacked good sources among militant racial groups, the anti-war movement, or the drug culture. Reporters who were able to penetrate these organizations were seen as a source of notes, pictures, and other investigative gems. This was a new challenge for reporters, appearing without warning and in force; it caught them by surprise, and they were uncertain where to turn for counsel.

Commenting in 1987, Caldwell stated the need for such an advocate: Seventeen years ago there was nothing there. It's just like the New York Times one day put a note on the board and said, 'We all feel bad for Earl Caldwell and tho difficult position he finds himself in, The Reporters Committee made it more than individuals being alone out there.

The Reporters Committee really is something that said, we're going to come together and provide (protection for the individual). If you're not a Mike Wallace, which most aren't, but if you're just another reporter out here trying to do your job, we're going to make sure that you're not going to be alone.

The rapid increase in the number of subpoenas was

staggering. Subsequent research by the Committee indicates that from 1960 to 1968, about a dozen subpoenas had been served on reporters; from 1970 to 1976, about 500 subpoenas were served. The Reporters Committee was emerging as the principal advocate of the "no compromise" position on reporter confidentiality.

Graham was a key spokesman, along with Landau, who had just returned to his Supreme Court desk for Newhouse after a fling with John MitchelPs Justice Department. Landau had joined Mitchell as press spokesman when the Nixon Administration took office.

He hoped to be a force for moderation and described himself as a "liberal Democrat" in a regime that was decidedly neither Democrat nor liberal. Although he found himself outflanked by the conservative wing led by Richard Kleindeist, Landau did play a major role in drafting what would prove to be a long-lasting departmental policy on subpoenas.

Working with future Chief Justice William Rehnquist, Landau drafted guidelines under which the Attorney General would be required to personally approve a media subpoena. Failure to get approval would result in the prosecutor's inability to use the material in court.

Three decades later, the rule stands as department operating policy, although it has been amended (and weakened, in Landau's view) by subsequent attorneys general. Landau left Mitchell in April 1970 and shortly afterward joined the Reporters Committee. His parting was described as "amicable," and Landau described Mitchell as one focused on the re-election of Nixon and "not wanting a thoroughly hostile press over this issue (subpoenas)."

MitchelPs idea, Landau felt, was that if subpoenas were reduced at the federal level, state and local authorities would follow suit. That did not prove to be the case, although federal subpoenas were dramatically reduced under the Mitchell guidelines.

Freed from the constraints of the Justice Department and with understanding and supportive editors at Newhouse, Landau plunged into the Reporters Committee with a vengeance. Although some assumed he was "paying penance" for working with the enemy, the mission that became a crusade was typical of Landau's aggressive approach to journalism, a style he brought to the Committee.

"The Reporters Committee was founded to be the way reporters are, "he recalled, "reporters want to move in and slug it out." Landau saw himself as a "First Amendment guerilla" and quickly became the major player in the organization.

When he joined the Committee in 1970, it was essentially a letterhead. Lukas, who had called the original meeting, had engineered a grant to commission an academic study of the confidentiality issue, and the committee had filed an amicus curiae brief on behalf of Earl Caldwell. The academic study, by University of Michigan law professor Vincent Blasi, was of mixed value for the emerging committee.

Blasi surveyed reporters across a broad spectrum, rather than concentrating on those areas that would be sensitive to subpoenas. As a result, he found relatively little direct threat from subpoenas, although most reporters did have some concerns about confidentiality and wanted at least a qualified shield.

Blasi recommended a broad but qualified shield law, falling short of the proposals by the Reporters Committee. The Blasi report gave the Committee some useful data, but did not build a strong case for an absolute shield. Word of the Committee's existence was spreading, particularly in the media centres of Washington and New York, but the Committee had no office, no staff, and no budget.

Because both were lawyers, Landau and Graham initially fielded most of the calls from reporters who had heard about the Committee but had no idea how to use it. By 1972, with interest growing in their work, Committee founders realized a need for a more formal structure. At a meeting on November 29, 1972, an executive committee was formed, including Doyle, Nelson, Landau, Shanahan, and Robert Maynard of the Washington Post.

Graham was in the process of moving to CBS News and

declined to serve, although he remained active. Doyle soon changed jobs and was replaced by Lyle Denniston of the Washington Star. An outside steering committee was set at about twenty-five members, from throughout the nation.

The Committee had a post office box but no telephone and was operating on funds from members' pockets and donations amounting to a few thousand dollars. A financial report on November 1 indicated a 1972 income of $4,334.41 and expenses of $1,253.21

As Graham moved into his new position at CBS, the committee's calls increasingly came to Landau, now the only person on the executive committee with a background in law. Soon he became the group's point man. Landau's view of the Committee's role was broader than some of the others. "They didn't have a concept of exactly what it ought to do, other than the (confidentiality) study.

I did. I knew that they needed legal advice, I knew that we had to start some type of information publication to let people all around the country know what was going on, so they wouldn't feel alone. I also felt that from time to time we might show up in court or file a law suit." Landau said he was using the ACLU as a model for what the Committee might become.

He was working nights and weekends, and in 1973 the first issue of the Press Censorship Newsletter was published, as an April/May issue. The sixteen-page report-essentially an outline of Landau's growing files-was distributed with the Columbia Journalism Review and for most of the working press was the first notice of the Reporters Committee.

The 1972 Supreme Court ruling in the case of Caldwell, Branzburg, and Pappas was a narrow 5-4 decision denying that reporters have a First Amendment right to protect sources but allowing states to adopt such protection. Justice Byron White, writing for the majority in Branzburg v. Hayes, found that the public interest in investigating and prosecuting crime should prevail against the press's argument for a free flow of information.

But the Court left open the door for future interpretation

and acknowledged that Congress and state legislatures were free to legislate a protective shield for reporters. Shield legislation was not entirely new-Maryland had a shield law since 1898, and by 1973 similar laws were on the books in at least nineteen states.

Federal shield laws were first introduced in 1929, but that and subsequent efforts all failed passage. Some fifty shield laws of one stripe or another were introduced in the 92d Congress, primarily in 1973.24 The Reporters Committee joined a conglomeration of media groups to seek federal shield legislation in 1973 and fought the battle for nearly a decade, all to no avail.

There was a record interest in press issues during this period, and in the early 1970s the reporter shield debate was only the most prominent of several battlefields as press and government-often the Nixon Administration-took adversarial positions. From 1972 to 1975 the Washington Post index shows an annual average of more than one hundred stories dealing with "Freedom of Information."

Branzburg v. Hayes launched a full-fledged effort to pass both a federal statute and separate state laws, and the Reporters Committee was the major advocate. Landau and Graham wrote an extensive justification of an absolute shield for Columbia Journalism Review, and Landau debated the issue at a special Nieman Fellows convocation in May.

Committee support for an absolute shield was up against political, legal, and some journalistic support for a "qualified shield" that would require reporters to testify in cases involving violent crime or in libel actions. There appeared to be public support for some sort of a shield. Gallup Polls in 1972 and 1973 showed majority approval of this question: "Suppose a newspaper reporter obtains information for a news article he is writing from a person who asks that his name be withheld.

Do you think that the reporter should or should not be required to reveal the name of this man if he is taken to court to testify about the information in his news article?" In 1972, 57 per cent supported confidentiality, to 34 per cent opposed, with 9 per cent undecided. A year later the figures were 62-27-11, a significant increase as the Watergate investigations began to unfold.

The pollster, The Gallup Opinion Index, noted that the 1973 findings came in the wake of investigations into the conduct of Vice President Spiro Agnew, the Watergate hearings and the jailing of two newsmen, Peter Bridge of the Newark Evening News and William Farr of the Los Angeles Times.

"One argument frequently given by persons in the survey who think newsmen should not be required to reveal confidential sources is that decisions to jail newspaper reporters could eventually deplete the confidential sources on which newsmen often rely to meet the public's right to know," the pollster reported.

Public support for reporter protection continued to grow throughout the decade. Gallup polled again (for the last time) in 1978 and found 68 per cent in favour of a shield, with 23 per cent opposed and 9 per cent undecided. And despite the fact that it was a Republican administration that had squared off against the press on this issue, the polls in 1972, 1973, and 1978 showed Republicans supported protection of sources by heavy margins. In 1972, 52 per cent of Republicans polled supported the reporters' position, with only 38 per cent willing to reveal a source; this compared to a 59 per cent and 31 per cent, respectively, for Democrats.

Support for a reporters' shield increased slightly for both parties in 1973, and in 1978, after all the Watergate-related scandals, Republican support for a shield had increased to 70 per cent, with only 22 per cent opposed. This was even stronger than Democratic support of 66 per cent, with 24 per cent willing to reveal sources.

Considerable public attention was paid to the shield debate. A 1975 debate at the National Press Club, convened by the American Enterprise Institute, saw strong resistance to shield laws from future Supreme Court Justice Antonin Scalia, then an assistant attorney general. Scalia, rebutting Jack Nelson and Charles Seib, the Washington Post ombudsman, grilled the reporters on definition of a reporter and the role of the underground press.

He termed a qualified shield law unworkable and an absolute shield something the courts "could not live with." Scalia was the point man for Justice on this issue, testifying in Congress in 1975 against a shield of any sort. Despite public support and the efforts of several prominent members of Congress, shield legislation foundered and did not survive the 1970s.

The role of the Reporters Committee was pivotal. On the one hand the Committee more than any other group had raised the profile of the issue; on the other, its absolutist view left little room for compromise, even within the profession. Ultimately, Congress was unable to come up with legislation satisfactory to all parties.

In 1975, a compromise bill sponsored by Rep. Robert Kastenmeier appeared to be advancing, but the unlikely combination of the Justice Department (represented by Antonin Scalia) and the Reporters Committee played a big role in failure of the bill. Fred Graham and Jack Nelson, testifying for the RCFP, resisted qualifications in the bill and urged its defeat.

That put the Committee in opposition to the American Newspaper Publishers Association, which testified in support of Kastenmeier's bill. The Committee was part of an ad hoc group, including ANPA, that met irregularly from 1973 to 1977 to work on shield legislation. In 1977, the committee erupted in an angry exchange of memos and comments between Landau for the RCFP and Tim Hanson, general counsel for ANPA.

The Hanson memo branded as "intemperate and unjustified" a Landau objection to Senate 1, the latest attempt to draft a compromise shield law. Additional acrimony ensued between Landau and Jerry Friedheim, the ANPA executive director. The Senate did approve this measure, but with provisions that brought a variety of objections from news groups when the bill went before a House committee.

It failed to gain House approval, and efforts for a federal

shield law soon evaporated. Meanwhile, more states adopted some form of shield legislation. In 1973 alone, shield laws were enacted in Minnesota, Nebraska, North Dakota, Oregon, Pennsylvania, and Rhode Island. By the end of the decade, 26 states had laws granting some measure of protection to reporters under subpoena.

Despite the state laws, the use of subpoenas in both federal and state courts continues to be an issue for journalists. In the most recent phase of a five-year study on the incidence of subpoenas served on the news media, the Reporters Committee reported that 1,326 subpoenas were served on 440 news organizations in 1999.

Forty-six per cent of all news media responding said they received at least one subpoena during 1999. Although shield legislation was the most prominent debate during this period, it was a time of pressures on the news media from many sides.

The Reporters Committee threw itself into the battle, with Landau attempting to raise funds on the one hand and obtain lawyers to carry media cases on the other. With Watergate coming down at the same time, it was a heady time to be a journalist and a heady time for the Committee. Landau was having remarkable success using his connections in Washington legal circles to obtain pro bono attorneys.

At the time only a handful of attorneys really practiced what would come to be known as First Amendment law; most media were represented by corporate firms that knew about tax and labour law but had little experience with the First Amendment.

The host of challenges that came down in the early 1970s gave lawyers a chance to practice this area of the law, and their firms built expertise. One of the agreements among prominent First Amendment lawyers, recalled Cameron DeVore, was to accept requests for pro bono work if it did not conflict with the interests of a client.

E. Barrett Prettyman Jr., a prominent Washington lawyer who became one of the Committee's premier pro bono attorneys, regularly was consulted by Landau and carried several major cases. Landau was "very acquisitive-once he's got you, he's not likely to let you go," Prettyman later observed.

Like several other attorneys who got involved in Committee litigation, Prettyman had been a reporter in his youth (Providence Journal). Prettyman came into play in 1973, when the Boston Globe's Tom Oliphant was sought by the FBI as an alleged participant in the Wounded Knee protest in South Dakota; Oliphant had witnessed an event, and the FBI charged him with crossing state lines to promote a riot.

Landau called Prettyman, who phoned the Justice Department's chief criminal lawyer, Will Wilson, at 2:30 in the morning with a demand that Oliphant be arrested in the District of Columbia rather than in Maryland, because of the differences in the courts he would face.

Prettyman, Landau, and Wilson met at Wilson's office at about 3:30 a.m. and hammered out the deal. Prettyman was tough, Landau recalls; when the negotiating was over, Prettyman turned to Wilson, saying, "Will, if you go back on your word, I'm going to cut your balls off!" The deal stuck, and Oliphant was eventually released.

Prettyman remembers "paranoia on both sides, a mistrust of the press by government and the press wary of Nixon and the others. It was hurtful on both sides, not very clever on the part of the White House." He provided legal advice in many instances, finding "in those days, reporters in trouble had virtually nowhere to turn."

Pressed for time, Landau simply organized his files to create a new magazine, Press Censorship Newsletter fin 1977 it became News Media & the Law. Although lacking in format and readability, PCN was an early attempt to define an entirely new classification of law, specializing in the First Amendment's protection of press freedom.

Most issues had articles grouped under these headings: freedom of information, libel, confidentiality, privacy, prior restraints, secret courts, broadcasting, and labour. The Committee involved itself in most of these areas, staying out of labour issues and generally out of libel matters, the two areas of law that most media attorneys understood.

The committee also declined to intervene in obscenity cases, although pressed by Larry Flynt and others, on the basis that it was not journalism and news people were not involved. The Committee began attracting favorable notice in the profession; a 1973 article in Columbia Journalism Review was titled, "A Reporters' Committee that Works." Author Jules Witcover described the Committee as "a serious and constructive force in the growing fight against executive, judicial and legislative encroachment on the press' First Amendment rights."

Witcover described cases in which quick action by Landau, Graham, and others helped reporters with small newspapers deal with legal challenges. Plenty of examples of help existed. When Jack Nelson and Ron Ostrow of the Los Angeles Times faced a federal court demand for tapes of a confidential interview with Watergate defendant Alfred Baldwin, the Reporters Committee produced a petition signed by some 450 working reporters in defence of the two newsmen.

This form of activism-or guerilla tactic-was foreign to most reporters, steeped in the concept of objectivity and avoidance of any form of political statement. Reporter Robert Bocziewicz of the St. Louis Globe-Democrat faced a contempt proceeding in a state ethics committee; from the hearing room he telephoned Landau, who conferred with Graham and produced a lawyer for Bocziewicz.

The ethics committee retreated. In another 1973 case, the Committee obtained Prettyman as the lawyer for two Louisiana reporters facing a judicial gag order; the judge retreated. The Committee was operating on a shoestring, both in terms of finances and personal commitment. Reporters were unaccustomed to soliciting funds and were busy on their jobs; Landau took the lead, still working without compensation.

Gradually, money was arriving and, despite the Committee's desire to remain independent of publishers, it came from media owners and foundations. Preliminary appeals to the working press for support produced little cash.

Landau began a serious effort at raising funds, targeting major publishers. By year's end, seventeen contributions of $500 or more had been received, totaling $42,500 for the year; Landau had launched what would be an endless search for financial stability.

In that first fund-raising year the Committee also received $5,000 from the New York Times and $5,000 from a triumvirate of media humorists, Art Buchwald, Russell Baker, and Art Hoppe. But individual gifts were unusual-most of the Committee funding then, and now, came from media owners and related foundations.

The injection of cash allowed Landau to open a pigeon-hole office near the Newhouse bureau and hire a part-time secretary and the Committee's first lawyer, a young man named Phil Lehman, the first of many recent law school graduates to do a stint in the office before heading into practice.

This allowed the Committee to step up its interest in advising reporters and pursuing litigation. On that front, 1974 would be a major year, as the Committee stepped boldly into litigation, filing in addition to the Nixon Papers case a major lawsuit against the telephone giant AT&T.

The cases brought out two of Washington's most prominent law firms as pro bono attorneys and launched long and expensive appeals that would wind their way to the Supreme Court. The telephone company had been routinely turning records over to the FBI, without informing subscribers, including reporters, about the transaction.

Columnist Jack Anderson and others protested, claiming this was an invasion of their privacy and also revealed confidential sources. AT&T did agree to notify subscribers of subpoenas, but the FBI and other agencies were allowed to delay notification for ninety days, effectively preventing subscribers from challenging the subpoenas.

This was well short of the reporters' demands, and they announced intent to sue. Prominent Washington attorney Lloyd Cutler carried the case for the Reporters Committee, filing the suit in December 1974 after attempts to negotiate a better deal with the telephone company. Fourteen reporters and news organizations joined the Reporters Committee and Anderson in seeking to stop the practice.

The ATScT case progressed through the federal courts, the telephone company prevailing in district and appellate courts; finally in 1979 the Supreme Court on a 6-3 decision declined to review the case, sealing the AT&T victory. The rulings held that the telephone company owned the records; therefore reporters had no right to protect them from subpoenas.

Pursued simultaneously in 1974, the Nixon Papers case went well beyond the interests of reporters, and Landau forged a broad coalition to fight the issue. After his conversation with Herzstein, he met with Washington Post publisher Katharine Graham, who had heen through the Watergate affair with the Post; she advised that the press should not carry the case alone. "It would look like we were picking his bones," was Landau's recollection of Graham's comments.

Herzstein shared that opinion, and Landau and Fred Graham approached the American Historical Association; Graham had a brother on the AHA board, and the group agreed to join. Next to join was the American Political Science Association, followed by several prominent historians and journalists.

Arnold and Porter agreed to take the case, with Herzstein as lead lawyer. "I never envisioned the depth of Arnold and Porter's commitment; I thought it would be some young lawyers," Landau recalled. "They set up a war room, people working 24 hours a day, and they got the temporary restraining order, which made it so Nixon could not take the papers away."

The Reporters Committee request for a restraining order was combined with a similar request from the Watergate prosecutor, and granted by Judge Charles Richey on October 21. As the lawsuit began its path through the federal courts, Congress passed a law negating Nixon's agreement with the General Services Administration.

The Reporters Committee suit prevailed in the U.S. Court of Appeals, but Nixon then sued to overcome the Congressional act, and the Reporters Committee found itself a defendant in his appeal. The Supreme Court ultimately ruled against the former president in 1977. The long process had put the Reporters Committee on the public screen and cost the Arnold and Porter firm more than $500,000 in pro bono work, Herzstein estimated.

"We lifted the issue above the noise level," Herzstein recalled. The lawsuit had helped save the records from possible destruction.

Attacks on the media seemed to be coming from every comer in the early 1970s, and the Press Censorship Newsletter was becoming more bulky as each edition went to press; Landau was using interns (primarily law students) to keep track of cases throughout the nation.

The original sixteen-page newsletter had grown to forty pages by its third issue in December 1973, and it was a major time commitment to produce. Ironically, considering the widespread readership of the publications on which members of the Committee labored, the Reporters Committee newsletter served in some ways as an alternative publication, in the manner of the 19th-century abolitionist or feminist newspapers.

By compiling and publicizing the numerous cases in which working reporters were under fire, Press Censorship Newsletter helped establish the legitimacy of their cause, alert outsiders to the issue, and-perhaps most importantly-tell reporters under pressure that they were not alone and there was a place to turn for help. These are traditional functions of the alternative press, and they also marked the early years of Press Censorship Newsletter.

A reporter or an editor on a small publication in Kansas or Georgia could know there was a source of help beyond the country-club attorney hired by his publisher, and that he or she was not alone. The August/September 1974 issue of Press Censorship Newsletter had grown to ninety-six pages, a compendium of actions threatening press rights. Clearly, a part-time office and executive committee could not handle the growing workload.

Despite the workload, with Richard Nixon and his administration gone, there was consideration of folding the committee in hopes that the major threat had passed. Fred Graham recalls advocating that position, but he was a minority voice. In fact, the executive committee in September asked the steering committee to pay Landau and launch a major fund-raising effort.

Lyle Denniston, writing for the committee, noted that "without Jack, the Reporters Committee would not be functioning even approximately as well as it does. He personally handles many of our legal defence contacts, involves himself deeply and intimately in the Newsletter's preparation and development, negotiates for us with a widening array of professional and legal organizations, and travels extensively to spread the gospel."

Initially hired at $12,000 on a part-time retainer, Landau was advanced a year later to fulltime employment as executive director, at about $32,000 annually. He continued to write a law column for Newhouse. Fund-raising in 1973 and 1974 was heavily dependent on a few major publishers.

The Boston Globe contributed $13,000; The New York Times Foundation, $10,000; Playboy Enterprises, $7,000; Philip L. Graham Fund, $8,000; CBS, $6,000, and Dow Jones, $6,000. In February 1975 the Committee received a $20,000 grant from the Stern Fund, its first major foundation gift, and one used to expand office capabilities.

With that gift, 1975 contributions totaled $106,558, the first time in six figures. Other major donors that year included the New York Times Foundation, the Philip Graham Fund, HarteHanks Newspapers, Boston Globe, American Newspaper Publishers Association, and the Field Foundation, each more than $5,000.

Landau gives credit for this advance to John I. Taylor of the Globe and to Katharine Graham, who spoke for the Committee at a publishers' meeting. In 1976 contributions amounted to $156,700 and the Committee received its first major gift from Gannett newspapers, $10,000. Through the years, Gannett and its Freedom Forum foundation would become the Committee's largest donors. The Committee also embarked on a sophisticated fundraising effort in 1975 headed by Arthur Taylor, president of CBS; it proved to be an ill-fated and frustrating effort that raised little money beyond an enhanced contribution from CBS itself. Broadcasters had never been prominent in Committee efforts, with the major exception of Walter Cronkite.

The CBS anchor joined the steering committee in 1973 and regularly helped in fund-raising. But he found it difficult to find support among colleagues and the industry. Broadcast organizations, he found, "had a cold attitude toward freedom of the press." He was encouraged, however, when his CBS boss decided to play a fund-raising role.

Taylor entered the field with a news release on May 30, announcing a target of a $2 million trust fund to move the Committee away from its day-to-day need for funds. The campaign was titled "The First Amendment Research and Defence Fund," and Taylor began hiring a professional staff. A veteran fund-raiser, Vincent McGee, was retained, as was an event planner, George Trescher Associates.

The effort set forth with fanfare, and high expectations on Taylor's part. Taylor's concept was that major corporations outside the media would contribute to a First Amendment campaign; a budget was drawn in which 25 per cent of the $2 million would come from these blue-chip companies, along with another $75,000 from advertising agencies, $150,000 from a speakers' bureau, $150,000 from foundations, and $150,000 from individuals.

Taylor hoped that Fortune 500 companies would each give at least $2,500. Little came of the effort, particularly from the big corporations. Luncheons were planned, elaborate material was printed, but the only tangible result was an increase in giving from CBS, to $27,000 in 1976.

Taylor resigned in July 1976, stating that "creation of such an endowment is not feasible until the Reporters Committee can establish a fiduciary entity with reliable long-range administrative and substantive policy-making mechanisms and adequate legal and auditing procedures to meet accepted requirements of public accountability.

When we embarked on this endeavor, it was with the implicit understanding that such procedures would be established. Unfortunately, they have not." Taylor was looking for an organization more suited to a corporate boardroom than to a group of reporters operating on a volunteer basis with a tiny staff, most of whom were law school interns.

The worlds of the boardroom and the newsroom did not converge. Limited corporate support did come, in the form of full-page advertisements in News Media & the Law. The major sponsor was General Motors; others included Arthur D. Little, American Forest Institute, Chrysler, State Farm Insurance, Mobil, and US Air.

No money came from advertising agencies, and individual contributions were small. But the failure of the much ballyhooed Taylor fund made Landau and the executive committee realise that, other than isolated foundation grants, the Committee would be dependent on its own industry for funding.

Special events could raise operating funds-the major successes were a First Amendment Fair at the 1980 convention of the American Society of Newspaper Editors, raising $20,000, and a premiere of Absence of Malice in 1981, which raised $52,230 despite the anti-press tone of the movie itself (the Executive Committee had split 4-2 on sponsoring the show).

The special events took an enormous amount of effort, but also served to draw more support to the Committee and allow journalists to have some fun during a difficult time. The 1980 Fair featured booths with media notables selling things, along with fiddlin" by West Virginia Sen. Robert Byrd, then the majority leader.

"We couldn't get Byrd to stop playing," recalled Landau, "everyone wanted to go home, but we sat around while he played on." The need for an endowment was growing, and the Committee got a big lift in 1977 when John Knight contributed $150,000 to begin a capital fund. Knight had been solicited by Gene Miller of the Miami Herald.

Miller, a steering committee member and two-time Pulitzer Prize winner for Knight, compiled a list of Knight columns supporting the First Amendment and then asked his boss for help. Knight had an assistant research the committee, told Miller his only concern was that "it appeared to be a one-man band," but then sent the check.

The Knight Foundation would contribute an additional $435,500 from 1981 to 1994. The Knight gift was critical; the Committee was literally running out of money. "That was the first real money we had ever seen. Up until then, really, I literally used to hide in the closet when the bill collectors came around," Landau told an interviewer in 1987, "Up 'til then, it (the RCFP) could have disappeared at any time.

That was a lot of money to us, a tremendous amount of money." The Committee did not achieve a measure of financial security until completion of a capital drive under John I. Taylor of the Boston Globe, conducted from 1979 to 1981 with results of $926,605. Taylor, "a First Amendment saint" in Landau's words, worked on the campaign tirelessly, often flying with Landau to meet publishers in some far-flung city.

Landau recalled as typical a two-hour lunch with Taylor, his brother, Davis Taylor, and Arthur "Punch" Sulzberger of the New York Times. After lunch, during which no mention was made of its purpose, the Taylors told an anecdote, "that said Our families have been friendly for several generations and we need a favour/ and that's the way it worked with the people we went to, who were old family publishers."

Publishers were not always comfortable with financing an organization made up of their employees. Landau recalls Marshall Field, the Chicago publisher, listening to a pitch for funds and replying, "Well, Mr. Landau, I'm not really very comfortable funding a group that calls itself the Reporters Committee!" Field did make a modest contribution.

The traditional industry leaders once more came to the

table, and the drive also marked a big increase in help from Gannett and its Freedom Forum. From 1976 to 1993 the company and/or the foundation contributed $743,130 to the Committee for various projects as well as the capital fund. Support continues to the present day; the Freedom Forum pays the lease for the Committee's offices as well as helping in other projects.

Fund-raising was broadened in 1980 to include a state-by-state drive that raised $148,325 under leadership of Gene Roberts, then with the Philadelphia Inquirer. The campaign was repeated three additional years, chaired by Donald Graham, Charles Glover, and C. K. McClatchy.

Funding continued to be print based; only CBS among the broadcasters made a major contribution. CBS contributed $152,500 from 1979 to 1994. Landau estimated the broadcast contribution in 1980 as 3 per cent of operating and 7 per cent of capital. The funding was needed, as the Committee expanded in several new directions during the late 1970s.

Among them were the Student Press Law Centre and the Freedom of Information (FOI) Service Centre, both of which continue as major elements in Committee work. The Student Press Law Centre was a project of the Robert F. Kennedy Memorial Foundation in 1974, and initial funding was shared by the Foundation and the Committee.

The proposal came through Jack Nelson, who had written a book on the student press and was contacted by the Memorial. Initial funding was an estimated $6,400 from the RFK Memorial and $13,000 from the Reporters Committee. The project hired a part-time lawyer to work with high school and college press issues, publish a newsletter, and provide office support. Much of the cost for the first year was carried by the $20,000 Stern Fund grant.

Kennedy Memorial support lapsed in 1982, and the SPLC is now fully supported by the Reporters Committee. The FOI Service Centre came out of meetings between Landau and leaders of the Society of Professional Journalists (SPJ) in 1978 and 1979, at which it was agreed to create a centre to handle state FOI requests. SPJ, with members and chapters in all states, was uniquely situated to handle this work, and the centre was set up in the Reporters Committee office under Peter Lovenheim, a young attorney who was succeeded in 1980 by Tonda Rush.

Grants of $20,000 from the John Ben Snow Foundation and $14,000 from the Kaplan Foundation allowed the centre to establish a computerized cross-index of FOI laws and rules from every state, as well as federal law.

The "How to use the Federal FOI" brochure was started and updated periodically. The original budget of about $40,000 a year was split between SPJ and the Reporters Committee. FOI cases continued to grow as a proportion of Committee work during the next two decades.

A third major expansion was attempted, but failed, during this period. The Committee petitioned the Ford Foundation twice for support of its media law activities; and was twice denied. The Ford contact was Fred Friendly, a former CBS executive and a television pioneer who worked with Edward R.

Murrow. Friendly was now at Columbia University and a consultant to the Ford Foundation. Ford in July 1975 turned down a request to fund legal defence efforts of the Reporters Committee. Friendly informed the Committee that, "We believe that one of our greatest assets in trying to bring people of varying persuasions together is our appearance of neutrality."

Friendly wrote, "On numerous occasions we have had people both from the press and from the judiciary and government comment that a particular result could not have been achieved had it not been for the neutral presence of the Foundation. we think it essential that we make every effort to maintain that appearance and credibility.

" Friendly said Ford had a "broader, more comprehensive view of the whole First Amendment area" than the absolutist position of the Reporters Committee. Shortly thereafter, the Ford Foundation also rejected a Reporters Committee proposal for a media law reporter. At the time, it would have been the first journal in the field and would have greatly expanded the literature available to lawyers working in media law, particularly First Amendment law.

With the formal endorsements of The American Newspaper Publishers Association, American Society of Newspaper Editors, Associated Press Managing Editors, and National Association of Broadcasters, the proposal revealed the importance of expanding the resources available in First Amendment litigation.

The Committee also took its appeal to the Rockefeller Family Fund, again to no avail. Subsequently, Ford issued a major grant to the Bureau of National Affairs for creation of the Media Law Reporter, which largely followed the categories of the Press Censorship Newsletter and continues to this day.

The Media Law Reporter was primarily the creation of attorneys James Goodale and Dick Schmidt, pioneers in what was emerging as a First Amendment Bar. Attorneys for media companies, and other private-practice lawyers working in the field, began sharing their notes early in the 1970s, long before the advent of e-mail lists, recalls Seattle attorney Cameron DeVore.

The major player in this effort was Goodale, who was general counsel for the New York Times in the Pentagon Papers case. DeVore and others credit Goodale with being the organizing arm behind the emergence of a First Amendment Bar. In 1973, Goodale spearheaded the first seminars on media law as part of the Practicing Law Institute.

Attendance, under 100 the first year, now regularly reaches 400 to 500. Schmidt was the moving factor behind the Forum on Communications Law, through the American Bar Association, now the Media Law Defence Centre in New York. Articles began appearing in the prestigious law journals, focusing on First Amendment issues.

Goodale, Schmidts, DeVore, and others were working in parallel with the Reporters Committee, with the Committee providing energy and publicity and the attorneys making the law. Goodale says the Committee, "played a terrific role. raised the level of sensitivity and appreciation, and expressed their own sense of importance (of the First Amendment) to the owners."

In this climate, the First Amendment Bar emerged. Perhaps its godfather, ironically, could be President Richard M. Nixon, for it was during his administration that the issues emerged to create the body of law that became the First Amendment Bar.

The subpoenas, the Pentagon Papers, and other frontline cases created the law and brought forth the lawyers to form this important section of the American bar. "It takes law and lawyers to create a Bar," Goodale reminds an interviewer, making it clear that the First Amendment Bar would have emerged with or without the RCFP.

But in this instance the stridency and advocacy of the Reporters Committee also helped move the cause forward. The Reporters Committee was strident and sometimes off-putting to owners, and its legal ideas were not always in tune with the attorneys it called upon. But the stridency was a factor in helping build the First Amendment Bar.

DeVore cites the Committee for keeping pressure on publishers not to cave on these issues.

"Thank goodness Jack (Landau) was there, pushing and shoving," Goodale says, "They were a sensational advocacy group." Stridency was also creating enemies, both inside and outside the media, as Landau in particular and the Committee in general gained recognition as spokesman for the working press.

The conflict in styles put Landau and Fred Friendly at odds. Friendly had launched, with Ford support, a series of televised seminars or confrontations in which he placed opponents in press-related cases together with a mediator, to see if they could find common ground. Landau and Graham had participated in one of the sessions.

Friendly's theme-let us seek common ground, find acceptable compromise-was antithetical to the zealous First Amendment stand of Landau and most of the Reporters Committee. Landau and Friendly, neither lacking in ego, developed a dislike for each other, and Friendly expressed on several occasions his fear of the Reporters Committee absolutist opinion.

In 1976 he disparaged the aggressive role of the Committee in what became Nebraska Press Association v. Stuart, calling instead for reasonable people to work out differences that had resulted in a gag order in a sensational murder case. Friendly conceded Nebraska was a win for the press, but in an interview he criticized hardline First-Amendment supporters, such as Landau and Graham. "A few years ago I realized that the press had a big chip on its shoulder," Friendly told The New Yorker, "It wanted a confrontation on the free-press issue.

It wanted to fight all the way to the Supreme Court every attempt by any court to limit its total freedom to do as it pleased." Friendly did not agree with this tactic, and he was outspoken. Despite strong support in the profession for the Committee, Friendly was not the only critic.

Landau in particular maintained an absolutist view of the First Amendment and was ready to take on any offense against the press. Moreover, the guerilla campaign had lost some of its sense of impending danger with the removal of Nixon from office. Voices inside and outside the media were calling for moderation.

Michael Kinsley, managing editor of The New Republic, issued a sharp rebuke in 1979: "Despite what you read in the papers, the biggest threat to the First Amendment roaming loose in Washington these days is not Justice Byron White of the United States Supreme Court. It is Jack Landau, the monomaniacal head of the Reporters Committee for Freedom of the Press."

Kinsley was upset at Landau's comments after a Supreme Court decision. He warned that such talk undermined public support for the press. It was inevitable that a group in such constant motion would generate controversy. Sometimes it attracted it like a magnet. In 1976, the Committee was pulled into the furor surrounding CBS reporter Dan Schorr's leaking of an unpublished House of Representatives report on the CIA.

The so-called Pike Papers were published by the Village Voice, and Schorr needed a way to avoid the charge of profiteering from the purloined papers. He approached his colleague Fred Graham and offered to give any profits to the Reporters Committee.

The Committee, as always hard up for funds, took the offer and soon found itself under attack as well. Steering Committee members Lern Tucker and Kenneth Auchincloss resigned to avoid association with Schorr's tactics. In the end, no proceeds were received by the Committee.

More serious, certainly in the long run, was a split between the RCFP and the American Newspaper Publishers Association (ANPA), the major industry lobbying organization, over reporter-shield legislation in Congress. Both groups had been part of an ad hoc committee attempting to negotiate in 1977 with the Justice Department and Senate on proposed legislation.

Landau, testifying before the Senate, held to the usual absolutist view of the Reporters Committee, and was blasted by ANPA counsel Tim Hanson in a letter to Sen. Ted Kennedy (D-Mass). The Committee's view was more strident than major elements of the industry, and Hanson termed the testimony "an intemperate, unjustified attack" on the legislation. Portions of the letter were leaked to the Washington Star.

Despite these criticisms, the Committee, as it neared its tenth birthday, was well-received in the profession. In 1979 it received the first of several national awards, the National Broadcast Editorial Association's Madison Award; previous winners included Eric Severeid and Justice William O.

Douglas. Landau began receiving major recognition, including Freedom of the Press awards from the Society of Professional Journalists and National Association of Broadcast Editorial Writers; also the John Peter Zenger award (University of Arizona), the Elijah Parish Lovejoy Award (Colby College), and Kruglak Gold Medal (University of Southern California).

In 1978 the Committee brought out 400 supporters for a

First Amendment Rally; among the speakers were Katharine Graham and Howard K. Smith. Feelings were running high. Smith compared the use of subpoenas against reporters to the Nazi tactics he witnessed in World War II Germany. Graham warned that, "in the short run we may suffer setbacks, but we and the country will certainly lose more if we pull back, abandon some stories, give up our notes, or otherwise in any way compromise this vital cause."

In 1982 the Foundation for Public Affairs in its annual Public Interest Profiles reported that the Committee "is generally viewed as an authoritative and important advocate for First Amendment rights," and quoted A. M. Rosenthal, executive editor of the New York Times, describing the Committee as "the most effective press organization in the whole field."

As the decade neared its end, the Committee was running at full capacity, and the major innovations for the remainder of the century were in place. They included News Media & the Law, the FOI Service Centre, Student Press Law Centre, Media Alerts (with SPJ, a bulletin on Congressional legislation, sent to news outlets), the First Amendment hotline, and a staff that in 1981 included four attorneys, including Landau as executive director; two administrators; and ten student interns.

The office operated on $310,789 in 1981 and had already accumulated $740,855 in its capital fund thanks to the efforts of John I. Taylor. The fiscally cautious executive committee had set a policy against stock ownership, so the endowment was invested in federal Treasury bonds. The organization now wore the clear stamp of Landau's sometimes manic personality.

Clemens Work, a lawyer-journalist hired in 1980, described the climate as swinging from routine to chaotic. "Jack was brilliant in many ways, but he also liked creative chaos," recalled Work, who went on to U.S. News and World Reports and an academic career. Landau's confrontational style permeated every aspect of the Committee's work, including the magazine, Work found. But press concerns were now shifting from the emotional and confrontational press-shield issues of the Nixon years to conflicts over Freedom of Information and access to court hearings, issues involving more process and procedure and less political activism.

The matter of closed courtrooms had been advancing as a serious press issue since before the Nebraska case in 1975; Nebraska, the case aggressively pushed by the Reporters Committee, barred judges from ordering the press not to publish material obtained in open court. But in 1979, in a case involving a Gannett newspaper, the Rochester Times-Union, the Supreme Court allowed a judge to close pretrial criminal proceedings anytime the judge believes there is "a reasonable probability" that press reports may prejudice a criminal defendant's ability to obtain an impartial jury.

The 5-4 ruling indicated a split court, and later in the year the court agreed to hear a case brought by two Richmond, Virginia, newspapers, in which a judge closed a murder trial to the press and public, without a hearing. The occasion brought a special issue of News Media & the Law, documenting a wave of some 109 court closures and related actions since the Gannett case, and including a "How to fight back" primer for reporters 68.

The spotlight, once focused on reporters' sources, had now moved to the courtroom and conflicts between the First and Fourth amendments. Additional battles were taking place in the always-fertile area of open records, with Freedom of Information issues at the state and federal levels.

In 1977 the Committee tried to expand its victory in the Nixon Papers case by extending it to Cabinet officers, specifically former secretary of State Henry Kissinger, who had compiled transcripts of telephone conversations but refused to open them to the public.

Joined again by the American Historical Association and the American Political Science Association, the Committee relied on its victory in the Nixon case but to no avail. After prevailing at the district and appellate court levels, the plaintiffs lost in the Supreme Court in 1981.

In 1978 the Reporters Committee and CBS correspondent

Robert Schakne challenged the FBI to release its compiled criminal conviction records of four men allegedly involved in organized crime. The FBI claimed that the request violated the privacy of the men, although the information was a public record in the individual jurisdictions in which they were convicted.

The case was not finally decided until 1989, when the Supreme Court ruled unanimously that the records could be withheld to protect the privacy of individuals. The FBI case was the last one in which the Committee was a lead plaintiff; subsequent cases were limited to amicus curiaebriefs or other interventions.

The FOI controversy also was moving on a parallel track in Congress, as the Judicial Conference attempted to narrow the scope of federal FOI laws and Sen. Orrin Hatch (R-Utah) began efforts to reduce the number of documents subject to FOI requests. The Committee strongly opposed both efforts and testified on the bills.

Landau also launched a guerilla attack on Hatch during his 1981 hearings. With his interns, he sent news releases and called every radio and TV station and weekly newspaper in Utah, alerting them to Hatch's role in trying to subvert the FOI. Although few would ever use the FOI, the small news operations showered editorials on Hatch, who was not amused.

"Nobody had ever asked station KLLB in Desert Springs, Utah, to get involved in the First Amendment," Landau recalled. "These guys were fabulous, I mean they got on the radio, virtually nonstop editorials. Hatch called me up and said I was the most unethical reporter he had ever met!"

The Utah ploy was vintage Landau, and it was the sort of action that was needed during the 1970s to get above the noise of a nation in constant turmoil. "Basically, the idea was to fight back, and if you couldn't do it nicely, you did it through warfare.

I'm the guerilla, and if you can't get it one way you can get it another. And that's what we did." A 1981 full-page appeal for funding support, in News Media &1 the Law, was headlined, "The Reporters Committee Fights Back," detailing major cases in which help had been given to reporters or major issues had been raised in court.

In 1982, while the Committee was undertaking a major court effort to overturn a judge's order sealing records in a libel action against the Washington Post, Landau put together a compendium of recent cases that revealed how far-flung and broad-based the Committee's work had become. Among the 56 actions he listed were the following, in which the Committee:

- Helped a McGraw-Hill oil-marketing newsletter overturn a subpoena for confidential sources in a case filed by several states.
- Supported a federal prisoner who wrote a column for a Connecticut newspaper, when authorities wanted him transferred, allegedly because of his writing.
- Obtained a pro bono lawyer for an author trying to get access to records on American-Israeli relations from several presidential libraries.
- Got a federal appeals court to reject former President Nixon's objection to the establishment of public listening stations for the Nixon Tapes.
- Helped The Iberville (Louisiana) South defend itself against invasion of privacy for publishing a 25-year-old story about men convicted of cattle rustling.

Obtained pro bono lawyers for a reporter for a small North Carolina weekly who was arrested for photographing an arrest scene; a National Catholic Reporter reporter who was illegally detained, searched, and handcuffed while covering an anti-war protest; and a Wyoming reporter subpoenaed after interviewing a death-row inmate.

The compendium of issues revealed both the strength and, ultimately, a weakness of the Committee's approach, for it apparently never met a challenge it could resist. It was spreading its resources, personnel, and credibility over an increasingly wide field.

The Committee was also pursuing a wide range of

interests in legislation, often to blunt proposals in Congress. In 1980 the Executive Committee voted to oppose a new CIA charter that included language allowing prosecution of a reporter for identifying an agent, an issue that would emerge 23 years later when columnist Robert Novak acted on confidential information and identified a CIA agent. The charter would also have allowed the CIA to use reporters as paid agents; the Executive Committee strongly resisted. The committee prevailed on both issues.

Although there was no shortage of battles to fight, the mood of the nation and of the media itself was changing, and the First Amendment guerilla style was less in demand. An increasing corps of lawyers was now prepared to file cases, where in 1970 there was only a handful to supplement the Reporters Committee.

When the Committee began, media lawyers almost universally reflected the financial interests of publishers, specializing in libel, tax matters, and labour negotiations. "The Reporters Committee broadened the horizons of media law," says Don R. Pember, whose press-law textbook, Mass Media Law, is widely used in college and university journalism programs.

Pember believes the lawsuits and active involvement in press-shield legislation helped raise interest in those areas of press law. Landau's ability to persuade high-profile attorneys to donate services to defend First Amendment rights was a major factor in the Committee's ability to project itself onto the media-law field.

Staff attorney Clemens Work was astounded at Landau's ability to find outstanding pro bono attorneys, and he was surprised at the extent of the work they put into cases. "We helped shape First Amendment law," he believes, through a matching of Landau, the pro bono lawyers, the magazine, and other publications.

A "First Amendment Bar" of sorts was emerging, through the efforts of James Goodale, Dick Schmidt, Cameron DeVore, Floyd Abrams, and other prominent attorneys.

And media law issues were now seen not only from the

standpoint of publishers and corporate executives; there was a corps of lawyers ready to defend the First Amendment rights of working reporters, some of whom could not count on their own employers to defend them.

But much was changing. The Supreme Court was changing-media friends Marshall, Brennan, and Stewart were gone or planning retirement, President Jimmy Carter had no opportunity to appoint justices who might be friendly toward the press, and a conservative Republican was in the White House.

When Ronald Reagan entered the White House in 1981, a media branded by Reaganites as "liberal" were determined to give the Gipper a break. Watergate was over, reporters were no longer prime-time heroes, and the expansion of soft-news programs on television was changing the public's perception of the news media and of reporters. Nowhere was this more apparent than in the 1983 invasion of Grenada, in which the Reagan Administration completely shut the press out, turning away press boats and essentially dictating that the news be made, compiled, and edited by the American military.

Landau and his interns did a comprehensive search of coverage of past wars, concluding that Grenada was the first "war" in which reporters were excluded and arriving at the conclusion that a lawsuit could be brought on one or more grounds: a First Amendment right of access to combat; equal protection of the law because military reporters were allowed but civilian reporters were barred; damages for false imprisonment of several reporters held aboard Navy ships against their will; or an order prohibiting the government from intentionally giving out false and misleading information.

Landau took the issues to several leading attorneys and law scholars, including E. Barrett Prettyman Jr. and Floyd Abrams, and turned up conflicting advice as to whether a suit should be filed and the best approach to take in such a suit.

Washington attorney Ben Heineman, one of those

researching the issue, drafted a brief for the Committee, challenging the exclusion on constitutional grounds.

"It struck me at the time that reporters couldn't be shut out," Heineman later recalled, "It was more a matter of time, place and manner (of access) than a prohibition." But no lawsuit was ever filed, by the Committee or by anyone else, primarily because of objections from publishers. Landau was finding that publishers had little interest in a lawsuit. "It (the lawsuit) was not terribly popular with the major media players, partially because there was this patriotic thing and partially because of the big tax bill (then in Congress)."

In addition, a turf war of sorts was raging. On November 8, the Committee shelved the idea of a lawsuit in favour of talks between the newspaper industry, represented by the American Newspaper Publishers Association, and the White House. Landau began working with Jerry Friedheim of ANPA and Creed Black, publisher of the Lexington Herald Leader, to put together a team of leading publishers to meet with Reagan's top advisors.

Landau was also attempting to put together a Reporters Committee delegation to the Pentagon, to meet with Secretary of Defence Caspar Weinberger, while publishers were at the White House. He ran this idea by the lawyers for some of the large newspapers and discovered that publishers were "infuriated" by a role for reporters in the negotiations.

After a week of phone calls and negotiations, the efforts broke up abruptly. Things went downhill from that point. According to a memo from Landau to the executive committee, he received a call from Black in which he (Landau) was accused of interfering in ANPA affairs and charging that "the Reporters Committee is fighting the industry," warning that "we give you money and we can teach you a lesson."

Landau fired off a lengthy editorial and background report in the Jan./Feb. 1984 issue of News Media & the Law. The editorial was a damning condemnation of the White House's Grenada actions, but it also asked: "Why then-when this case is stronger than Gannett or Nixon-are many of the media lawyers telling their news organizations that the risk should not be taken? Is this issue less one of morality than access to pretrial hearings? Will this issue be of less importance to the nation than accurate information about the Nixon Administration from its own archives? Is this issue of less interest politically than raiding newsrooms?"

He concluded by calling for a lawsuit if other methods failed. No suit -was filed. Taking on the President, the U.S. military, and public opinion in a highly publicized legal challenge over Grenada would have been a First Amendment guerilla attack of the first order. But it was a battle for which the industry clearly did not have the stomach.

Little came of press efforts to improve the situation; a joint military-media committee headed by retired Maj. Gen. Winant Sidle came up with a formula that was tested in Panama and then used in the Persian Gulf War. Many reporters criticized the formula because they found that it limited access and censorship was endemic.

Two decades later, Landau believes the media lost an opportunity to get better coverage conditions, and paid a price in subsequent military actions in Panama and the first Gulf War. The type of military-media cooperation in the Iraq invasion in 2003 is more akin to what should have happened in those conflicts, he believes.

The residue from Landau's clash with ANPA went beyond the immediate issue, and Landau believes it was a major factor in his forced resignation a year later.85 Publishers had always been leery of funding an organization controlled by reporters, and on high-visibility issues such as Grenada they wanted to call the shots for the industry.

Jane Kirtley, Landau's successor as executive director of the Committee, told an interviewer that a "prominent publisher" told her, "It wasn't so much that we were troubled by Jack expressing an opinion, a point of view; the problem was that in some quarters he was perceived to speak for the media."

But Grenada was also a symptom of a change in the relationship between press and the national government, a relationship that had been gradually improving since the dark days of the Nixon White House. What Landau was not seeing, but others were seeing, was that the era of the media guerilla had come to an end. Publishers were tired of conflict, and reporters had other pressing needs.

To a great extent, the Committee had already begun to serve those needs, particularly with its frequently used FOI Service Centre, and with publications on how to vise the FOI and how to deal with other legal or quasi-legal issues, including closed courtrooms.

However, the Committee staff was still geared up to do battle on the legal front; there was little clerical support for the office and publications staff, and the work depended heavily on interns who changed every semester.

The question of how often to go to court, and which cases to defend, had always been critical for the Committee, and from the beginning there was internal debate over individual cases. Graham tended to take a more cautious view, Landau to be more aggressive in pursuing legal remedies. Even some of the Committee's supporters felt it was overextended. Arthur B. Hanson, a Washington lawyer who had taken pro bono work for the Committee, told an interviewer in 1982, "My feeling has always been that the committee has over-litigated-has cried wolf in a number of cases that had no legitimate value to the press."

In April 1985 the end of the guerilla era was formalized, with a brief announcement that Landau had begun a six-month sabbatical and Jane Kirtley, an attorney hired several months previously from the law firm that represented Gannett, would be acting director. Landau had hired Kirtley to be legal defence coordinator.

The change came after a protracted period of physical and emotional stress on Landau's part, during which relations between him and his staff deteriorated. "I was just plain exhausted," Landau said two years later, "I wasn't handling the staff very well.

Another thing was Grenada. I was also letting the fund-raising slide." Years later, Landau described his physical condition as a nervous breakdown, the combination of personal and professional strain that included a divorce as well as his high-pressure job.

The decision to force a resignation was debated by the executive committee, with several of the founders involved in the decision, including Jack Nelson and Fred Graham. Nelson took the leadership, as the senior member of the committee, citing a loss of communication between Landau and the executive committee, and staff morale.

The change was not without rancor, and Landau left with an agreement for two years' severance pay. "We had to make a change," said Nelson, explaining that it was difficult because, "Jack was the Reporters Committee for a time. We need to give him great credit for his work."

The task of negotiating a departure fell to Nelson, his Los Angeles Times colleague Sarah Fritz, and Hayes Gorey of Time.

Fritz cites personal issues as the major reason for the rift. Committee staff complained to Executive Committee members that Landau was "stuck," unable to pursue Committee work, and the office was barely functioning.

This supports Landau's description of a nervous breakdown caused by overwork and tension. Fritz recalls serious concern on the Executive Committee that the organization might not be able to function without Landau: "He really was the committee for a long time. There was a big question of whether we could survive without him."

Landau was caught in changing times, Graham believes. "Jack was one of us, the original group." Graham believes the early Reporters Committee had a legitimate role as a 'bomb-thrower' but times were different in 1985. "Government ignorance or hubris caused problems, but not malevolence," was his view of the Reagan era. Also important was the rift between Landau and the newspaper industry at the time of the Grenada affair.

Kirtley told an interviewer in 1987 that, in taking an absolutist position on access to the war zone, Landau was "somewhat strident. and I think there were a number of news organizations that felt that by taking this very hard line they were going to end up with a worse situation than was already the case."

The Committee changed focus in the ensuing 15 years, partly to reflect changing times and partly as a reflection of the different personalities of Landau and Kirtley. Landau was a reporter with a law degree, Kirtley a lawyer with a journalism degree; their style reflected this difference.

Kirtley reduced the number of cases where the Committee was a major player, feeling that in the early 1980s the Committee "took very extreme positions that were not always legally supported." The Committee, she felt, should become an organization that "will become authoritative on issues, including some that others may not -want to weigh in on."

Threats were increasingly coming from the private sector rather than government, she noted, including a rising incidence of privacy-press conflicts, an area in which she wanted the Committee to take the leadership." Landau's concept of the Committee involved litigation, which he felt was necessary to keep press issues alive and publicized, and maintain a spirit of aggressive defence of the First Amendment.

"Once you lose the fire, you begin to constrict your vision," he said later, "You don't want to lose your political or financial base." But the Executive Committee, Fritz recalls, wanted a lower key presence and less litigation. "Jack loved the politics of the First Amendment crowd," but Kirtley was instructed to pay more attention to organization and pursuing Committee goals without the high visibility.

"We wanted to stay out of the First Amendment politicking, but continue to be a force," Fritz recalled.Kirtley changed the emphasis of the Committee, picking up the role of publications and education; additional brochures were published regularly, guiding reporters in such areas as photo-journalism and privacy, access to electronic records, and others.

In a 1987 interview in Washington's City Paper, Eleanor Randolph, who covered media for the Washington Post, was quoted as saying: "Several years ago I found that the Committee worked so hard to be advocates that you really couldn't get the kind of solid information you needed about some of the really important things that were going on. since Jane Kirtley has taken over.

I have noticed that the information has become more useful for a reporter." Kirtley's administration got off to a contentious start in November, with a nasty split on the steering committee over a proposal to host a special showing of the HBO film, "Murrow." Broadcasters on the committee, particularly Walter Cronkite, were incensed at some of the portrayals in the film.

Howard K. Smith labeled it, "a libel on Frank Stanton," and Smith, Cronkite, Tom Brokaw, Ed Fouhy, and Dan Rather all voted against sponsoring the film. Only Peter Jennings among the broadcasters voted with the majority in a 16-10 split in favour of sponsoring the showing.

Staff and Committee members agree that the organization functioned more smoothly under Kirtley, who left in 1999 to become a professor of media ethics at the University of Minnesota. A polished spokesperson, she made a strong television appearance and wrote a regular column for American Journalism Review.

With the advent of the Worldwide Web, the Committee moved to a web-based publication and offers guidance to reporters through the web. The Reporters Committee offices now are quiet and orderly, a marked contrast to the cramped, noisy, and often chaotic days of guerilla tactics.

Litigation that in the past might have been pursued by Committee pro bono lawyers is now more likely to be pursued by the growing "First Amendment Bar", some of whom obtained their start as interns for the Reporters Committee. The only founder still on the steering committee is Fred Graham, although Jack Nelson maintains an active interest. The Committee in 2000 had an operating expense of S403.145, and its endowment fund held common stocks valued at $1,476,754.

One of the largest holdings was its old antagonist, AT&T.

It remains the only organization of its kind, governed by working reporters and serving the working press on First Amendment issues. Its publications, vastly expanded in the Kirtley years, are well regarded and used in newsrooms throughout the nation. Legal fellows, recent law graduates, have replaced much of the early reliance on law-school interns, lending more of a professional air to the Committee's efforts.

The executive director since 2000, Lucy Dalglish, has both a news and legal background. As the Committee matured and was more cautious in selecting its targets, its legal work became more credible in the view of attorneys such as Goodale and DeVore.

For working reporters, the environment three decades later is less dominated by government than were the guerilla days of the Reporters Committee. Today's reporters work in a new technological environment with competitors that did not exist in 1970, and they are far more likely to work for one of a handful of increasingly powerful media conglomerates.

The camaraderie of an earlier day existed side-by-side with news competition, but today concentration rather than competition is the norm. Owners of the media giants need no pro bono lawyers, and pro bono lawyers don't offer help to Gannett or Knight-Ridder. Yet the media giants, through their foundations, are the largest donors to the Committee.

Some of the economic and journalistic reasons for the Committee have gone the way of media mergers, bottom-line corporate managers, and editors with management degrees. More than the passage of Richard Nixon and John Mitchell, this has changed the landscape in which the Reporters Committee functions three decades after its beginnings.

Public support for journalists has also declined. Three decades after the epic struggles between the news media and the Nixon Administration, much of the public support for press freedom appears to have evaporated.

Some of this, according to the Freedom Forum, the primary chronicler of press freedom issues, can be traced to September 11, 2001, but even before that tragedy there was an erosion of public support for the First Amendment. In its 2002 survey of First Amendment support, the Freedom Forum found 49 per cent of those surveyed feel that the First Amendment "goes too far in the rights it guarantees." That is up from the 39 per cent of 2001 (pre 9/11) and 22 per cent in 2000.

The least popular First Amendment right is the press, with 42 per cent feeling that the press has "too much freedom," about the same as in 2001. And more than 40 per cent said the press should not be allowed to freely criticize the American military about its strategy and performance.

In spite of these feelings, 48 per cent of those surveyed also want more information about governmental actions, and 94 per cent support the right to be informed by a free press. The Reporters Committee in 2004 has regained some of its former prominence by involvement in a series of issues resulting from the attacks of September 11, 2001.

Provisions of the Patriot Act and the government's secrecy regarding prisoners held at Guantanamo Bay and at other federal facilities have brought the Committee into a more active public role than was the case prior to 9-11. The Committee played a major role in exposing a secret court docket in Miami's federal district court, and it was later called into service when reporters began receiving subpoenas in several federal cases.

Dalglish, who had maintained a low public profile in her first years as RCFP executive director, began to be a familiar face as First Amendment cases increased in the wake of 9-11 and Bush Administration efforts to close down information in the name of national security. Despite this increased visibility and controversy, the Committee in 2004 is still largely known within the profession, where its comprehensive Web pages are an invaluable resource for reporters, and its publications are a staple in newsrooms around the country.

That the Committee is more professional, better organized, better financed, and less contentious seems beyond doubt as it enters its fourth decade. But it seems also beyond doubt that the lasting legacy of the Committee was created in the guerilla years, from the anger of the Nixon-era confrontations and subsequent struggles with closed courtrooms and locked files.

"I'd never seen such anger," Eileen Shanahan recalled of the early executive committee meetings. Herself never one to walk away from a fight, Shanahan found herself cautioning, "indoor voices, please," as the arguments proceeded. Today's Committee has more of an "indoor voice," but the anger of the 1970s, directed against specific abuses and specific abusers, left its mark.

"Without us, who knows what would have happened?" asks Fred Graham. "We have become a voice that's respected, a place to call for help, the recognized source of comment on reporter's issues." Landau, typically seeing the issue in confrontational language, cites two "revolutions" from the guerilla days: "The first revolution was getting the press to fight back.

In effect a revolution in the psychology of the press, who had never believed in litigating. and the second was we broke down the categories (of press law) and started collecting the cases, providing the momentum to get people to think about this. now there is something called press law and it is (separate) from other law."

The guerillas of the 1970s waged their war without fax, e-mail, the Web, and a host of other electronic marvels, along the way proving that notoriously independent reporters could not only join forces to help colleagues but forge and govern a team that was right for the challenges of that time.

Chapter 7

Staying Close to Distant Sources

Several scholars have complained about the lack of theory concerning journalism and technology. The most substantial set of technologies that requires the development of theory is the one that journalists use for sourcing of publishable news information, outweighing news dissemination, storage, and presentation technologies, the results of which may be displayed, distributed, or stored subsequently by other technologies.

As the nature of knowledge acquired by reporters may be shaped by the manner in which they acquire it, these devices may be perceived as "epistemological technologies," the study of which could help answer key questions about the nature of journalism, such as the extent to which journalists perform activity in time or space, tend to rely on firsthand witnessing or mediate the second-hand experience of others, use technologies allowing for interrogation of sources or acceptance of source versions as is, and employ their technologies proactively or for passive reception of source-initiated materials.

This study seeks to lay the foundation for a theory of epistemological technologies, based on their actual use for sourcing in different media. To obtain a comprehensive picture, the study incorporated nonmediated contacts as well (i.e., face-to-face interviews and news-scene presence).

Data were gleaned in a series of face-to-face reconstruction interviews, during which reporters described how they obtained a sample of almost 850 news items published by nine leading national Israeli news organizations in three different media: print press, radio, and online news Web sites.

The fourth medium, television, was omitted because it embodies certain apparent production and visual biases4 and could overextend the scope of an already broad study. The three designated media were studied concurrently using the same research tool.

Data deal specifically with recollected sources of information subsequently used in published (or broadcast) stories, comprising the entire sourcing process. Although serving the core journalistic functions that yield the public news diet is probably the most significant role of communication channels, the study does not cover the whole reporting process by any means, primarily because it lacks three essential components.

First, it may overlook non-item-oriented information, such as reading newspapers or visiting news Web sites, that does not necessarily end up in specific published items, its prominent place in daily journalistic routines notwithstanding.

Second, even item-oriented information may leave no traceable residues if items are subsequently dismissed during the selection phase or if information possessed an auxiliary journalistic function and consequently reflected an indirect, abstract, or supplementary character, such as background information, self-updates (about a particular issue), or searches for a suitable source or a specific datum.

Third, the method is not immune to memory inadequacies and possible interviewee bias. To mitigate the first and second shortcomings, a complementary study was conducted using traditional interviews with reporters that focused on Web uses other than sourcing. To minimize memory problems, reconstruction interviews were conducted as close as possible to the date of publication.

Generally speaking, there is no justified rationale for considering Israeli news media to be significantly different from other Western, free, modern, commercial, and competitive media. Obviously, Israel has several unique structural, political, and cultural characteristics, but any attempt at determining the precise manner in which these macro attributes-and especially their composite-are translated into micro patterns of technology use would be highly speculative.

Therefore, the extent to which the Israeli case is representative may only be determined after this study is repeated in other locations and news cultures. The study follows an inductive pattern, beginning with introduction of the findings and then proceeding to generalization and the proposed theoretical framework.

TECHNOLOGY AND JOURNALISM RESEARCH

Numerous scholars have recognized the role of communication technologies in shaping newswork, as well as the information that reporters may or may not acquire by using them. The most prominent channel types, mentioned in the literature as tools of sourcing, are new technologies such as the Internet and e-mail.

The other two are non-mediated channels, such as news-scene attendance and face-to-face interviews and more traditional technologies such as landline telephony.The importance of communication channels in journalism lies in their possible impact on news information, enhancing or limiting its scope, quality, diversity, depth, and accuracy, as well as their role in shaping the epistemological qualities of news information.

For example, the face-to-face interview is considered a channel that enables nonverbal information to be obtained, and the telephone interview is one that allows reporters to negotiate source versions and implement interview techniques. E-mail, in turn, is described as a dubious channel that strengthens a source's control over messages and invites untraceable involvement of PR practitioners.

The connection between episteme (knowledge) and techne (art) is an ancient concept, dating back to Greek philosophy and addressed by modern thinkers such as Innis and McLuhan.

In this study, however, the concept of epistemological technologies is employed neither as an embodiment of scientific or practical knowledge nor as a tool for shaping the knowledge of media consumers, but rather as the means that media producers use to obtain information.

Not all scholars agree that new technologies necessarily change news practices: "Reformists," probably the largest school of thought, claim that technologies created a significant shift in the work of reporters; "Traditionalists," apparently the smallest group, identified long-range trends in news production methods that may limit the effects of the new technologies significantly; while "Selectivists" assert that journalistic work has changed dramatically for television reporters, whose speed of reaction and ability to gather information have been accelerated by new technologies.

Three shortcomings of the existing body of empirical research may thwart theory-building that would address both journalism and epistemological channels:

- Fragmentation. Most studies focused on a small subset of technologies and sometimes even on one technology only. This fragmented scope limits their generalizability, inviting overestimation or underestimation of the technologies studied. Multi-technology studies were not only scarce but also limited to the public relations field.18 At least one study exhibited a multi-technological and multi-source perspective, but was restricted to print press reporters, who are not necessarily the most advanced among technology users. Moreover, the study was conducted before the new generation of mobile and broadband technologies became popular and possibly revolutionized newswork.
- Non-journalistic Theories. Most studies applied nonjournalistic theories - such as diffusion of innovations or uses and gratifications - that are virtually blind to the specific context of the journalistic field.
- The Novelty Bias. Naturally, new technologies attract

extra research attention, especially when perceived as a remedy for the weaknesses of journalism. Nevertheless, exclusive focus on new technologies as "one of the biggest hopes (and hypes)" of journalism, with some studies appearing "upbeat and at times even Utopian in their conclusions," renders all but brand new conduits symbolically extinct.

The current study tries to overcome these shortcomings, supplying a comprehensive picture of old and new channels, both mediated and non-mediated, determining their actual contribution to published news and integrating the results within a broader journalism theory.

Following McManus, the present study distinguishes between two principal stages of the newsmaking process:

- News discovery, during which the reporter becomes acquainted with the existence of a potential new story, and
- News gathering, in which the reporter obtains the building blocks of the news item, as news discovery data is often incomplete and insufficiently substantiated.

Both phases were studied only regarding items that were subsequently published or aired, however. In keeping with its exploratory nature, the study addresses research questions and expectations rather than formal hypotheses.

RQl: What are the relative contributions of the respective communication channels to news published in the three media studied?

With some caution, based on several of the studies mentioned previously, one might expect to find that while most news information is technology-mediated, telephony is still widely used and textual channels serve primarily as news discovery conduits.

RQ2: How often do reporters use the Web as a news source? Do online reporters do so more than their counterparts in other media?

According to several prominent studies, journalists use the Web extensively. Furthermore, online reporters are expected to rely on the Web more often than their counterparts in other media, as they also use it as a vehicle for display and consequently acquire considerable Web savvy.

Traditional methods might prove problematic in examining the journalistic role of technology, as surveys and interviews capture per- ceived functions of the various channels that may differ substantially from their actual use; moreover, observation alone cannot detect the full spectrum of channels operated by different reporters in different settings to obtain information from different sources.

Consequently, the present study uses face-to-face reconstruction interviews, a method that has proven its ability to identify the respective contributions of different entities to the production of news.

The procedure consisted of three steps (prior to the interviews):

- Random Selection of Beats: Ten parallel print press, online, and radio news beats were chosen randomly from nine leading Israeli national news organizations.
- Identification of All Published Items within Beats: The sampling period extended over four weeks (beginning November 15, 2006), reflecting the attempt to achieve a fair balance between variety of stories and use of material still fresh in reporters' memories. News Web sites were visited four times a day.
- Random Sampling of News Items: Ten items per reporter were selected randomly (average monthly output per reporter: fifty-three items) to address the necessities of source confidentiality. The sample is thus large enough to allay any concern that stories could be matched to their descriptions but not so large as to tax reporters' focus and patience.

Further measures to maintain source confidentiality included asking reporters to describe how they obtained each of their sampled items without revealing any identifying details about them, as well as the seating arrangements: the reporter (with a pile of sampled stories) and the interviewer (with a pile of coding sheets) sat on opposite sides of a table with a screen between them.

Reconstruction interviews were conducted during the month following the sampling period, each approximately ninety minutes in duration. Although nearly all interviewees cooperated, the goal of deciphering 300 items per medium was not entirely achieved because of structural constraints applying to the organizations studied, such as insufficient number of business items for one of the radio stations and the need to avoid double-length interviews of Haaretz reporters who work for both print and online media.

To preclude the distorting effect that the missing items may exert on comparability, each medium was weighted to 300 items, maintaining the internal proportions of the sampled newsbeats.

For the most part, data were displayed and analysed as percentages, thus presenting an overall picture of the channel mix with each channel displayed in the context of other channels and other media. Because of its exploratory nature, the study uses effect size measures (D-statistic) rather than significance tests. Effect values of 0.20 through 0.49 are customarily considered small, 0.50 through 0.79 medium, and 0.80 and above large.

Obviously, no method is without its shortcomings. The current method's drawback is that data deal very specifically with recollected sources for information subsequently used in published (or broadcast) stories. To compensate for this shortcoming and study the uses of technology beyond the specific item, a supplementary personal interview was introduced.

As these interviews were conducted after the rather long reconstruction interviews, however, only 49-61 reporters out of a total of 80 agreed to respond to them (depending on the specific question). The data display unambiguous differences between common and rare uses of the Web and as such will be used only in the Discussion as a general indicator of Web use for purposes other than news sourcing. The findings supply an initial overview of the ways in which reporters in three different media operate a comprehensive set of epistemological channels to obtain their news.

RELATIVE CONTRIBUTION

The data show that channel use across media is highly homogeneous except for a few aberrations, concentrated in the discovery phase, that may be explained chiefly on organizational grounds.

The greater use of landline telephones among online reporters is not really substantial, as their total use of telephony is very similar to that of their counterparts and the greater use of pager messages among radio reporters is counterbalanced by their limited use of e-mail.

Furthermore, greater use of pagers may reflect the correspondence between the short and instant nature of both pager messages and radio items, as well as the mobility and urgency of radio newswork, at least in the Israeli case.

Similarities across media intensify if the data are clustered according to the three major channel types embodying the epistemological qualities of the interactions they enable:

- Non-mediated channels, involving the reporters' physical presence at news scenes and face to-face interviews, constitute the smallest group: ranging (across media) from 7% to 10% of the contacts in the discovery phase and 15% to 18% in the gathering phase. The remainder consists of technology mediated coverage.
- Oral channels, led by telephony-mediated contacts (landline + cellular), contribute the main course to the news menu: ranging from 46% to 50% in the discovery phase and 54% to 65% in the gathering phase. This cluster's share is actually even greater, as it also includes the non-mediated channels.
- Textual channels comprise a rather formidable cluster, particularly in the news discovery phase, in which it accounts for 39%-43% of the contacts, decreasing to only 18%-29% in the gathering phase.

INTERNET USE

RQ2 focused on the actual contribution of the World Wide Web, the most celebrated technology in journalism literature, across different media. The Web's contribution to published content as a news source was no more than 3%in both phases. Even online reporters do not use their publishing platform as a sourcing tool to any greater extent than their old-media colleagues do.

The Internet's contribution rises substantially if we include e-mail: ranging from 8% to 21% in the discovery phase and 4% to 15% in the gathering phase. This increment is puzzling, however, as reporters play a proactive role when using the Web and generally adopt a passive or reactive one in e-mail use.

DISCUSSION

Four aspects of reporter behaviour are particularly challenging. The discussion begins with the more general aspects, namely the surprisingly modest use of non-mediated coverage and the lack of any substantial differences among the three media. The remaining two aspects are oriented towards specific technologies: the Web's marginal role as a news source and the enduring dominance of telephony.

The image of extensive non-mediated coverage is fostered not only by scholars (who contend that such coverage prevails in conjunction with telephone interviews), but also by the traditional ethos that extols "shoeleather reporting" as the supreme news gathering method, as well as by journalists themselves, who do not go out of their way to expose the truth behind a deteriorating work pattern that still establishes their occupational legitimacy and authority.

Many have even developed a set of practices to conceal their remote coverage. Although some American reporters declared that face-to-face interviews are their second choice as a newsmaking channel, the current findings indicate that, in practice, non-mediated coverage is far rarer than might be expected, or, as the legendary Jimmy Breslin observed, "in many newsrooms, the shoe-leather reporters are regarded as throwbacks or has-beens."

The overall similarity of channel use across media challenges the widespread belief that at least online reporters embody "new regimes of content creation" with a distinct media logic. Apparently, tendencies toward journalistic "isomorphism" overshadow medium differences, at least insofar as methods used to source information are concerned, reflecting similarities in organization around newsbeats and news sources, perceived newsworthiness, and the inclination towards homogeneous news products.

Two of these relatively homogenous patterns challenge common wisdom regarding specific technologies: the use of telephones and the Web for news sourcing.

THE WEB AS A NEWS SOURCE

The limited use of the Web observed in this study appears to challenge findings suggesting that the Web had become a "dominant" and "indispensable" newsgathering tool that had changed the face - if not the soul - of journalism. Interestingly, the Web's contribution as a source for published news is not only marginal but also stagnant, having displayed no growth over time - at least with regard to the Israeli print press, studied in 2001 using the same method and research tools as the present study.

However, in contrast to its limited use for sourcing, the Web is widely used for more general newswork functions. Personal interviews with reporters show that they use the Web for two hours and fifty minutes a day for journalistic purposes, plus one hour and twelve minutes for personal matters - about four times more than the average Israeli citizen and about an hour less per day than American computer reporters, who are probably among the most intensive Web users.

During those long hours, reporters were using the Web for the functions. The rich assortment of Web functions used by reporters may be categorized into three basic types:

- Productive: These include core journalistic functions directly involved in sourcing publishable news materials, such as discovering and gathering news information, followed by two types of auxiliary functions that exert less direct impact on news products and more on news processes and news environments.

- Referential: Including self-updates, monitoring other publications, fact checking, locating potential news sources, and finding background material.
- Communicative Functions: Communicating with different stakeholders-superiors, news sources, counterparts, and competitors, mostly via e-mail.

Functions performed routinely (i.e., on a daily basis by at least half the reporters) are mostly referential. The only exception is the highly frequent use of e-mail for receipt of press releases. This still does not guarantee an impact on publications, however, as many if not most press releases are discarded during the selection process.

The highly infrequent use of e-mail for interviews may surprise scholars who described e-mail as "the killer [Internet] application" for journalists. On the other hand, it will relieve those who condemn e-mail interviews as a "method of last resort for conducting anything approaching a candid interview" because it avoids real interaction and invites hoaxes and "canned" PR responses.

Journalists' paradoxical use of the Web - seldom for sourcing and often for more general newswork assignments - suggests that although journalists enjoy "cutting edge gizmos," they are choosier about using them for core journalistic assignments such as sourcing.

Hence, until another study refutes the current findings by taking the exhausting route of investigating - source by source - a sample of published items outside Israel, using the current method and research tools, one cannot rule out that limited use of the Web for sourcing, together with extensive use for more general newswork assignments, extends beyond the case at hand and may even be a relatively universal phenomenon.

It is definitely not an Israeli peculiarity, as shown by initial findings of another study employing the same method and research tool to study Chilean national press reporters in the summer of 2007. Those reporters used the Web for only

5% of discovery contacts and 7% of gathering contacts. There is some indication that figures for the United States, Portugal, and Greece do not differ dramatically.

At least part of the difference between the current study and those claiming vast use of the Web may thus be rooted in method (reconstructions of specific published items versus general estimations of technology use in surveys and interviews) and research focus (specific uses for sourcing of published items versus more auxiliary uses for reporting).

This line of reasoning is supported by current findings reflecting heavy daily use of the Web, mostly for functions other than sourcing. Some American scholars agree that the Web has not become a major news source despite its numerous advantages. According to one observation, American newsroom adoption of computer-assisted reporting yielded mixed results.

Another opinion maintains that the journalistic advantages of the Internet "are counterbalanced by a number of inherent weaknesses," some of which have already been mentioned in the relevant literature: poor quality of information; limited reliability, believability, and accuracy; as well as time constraints, lack of training and navigation and design faults.

The following drawbacks should be considered as well:

- The Proactive Role: While most other textual channels, including e-mail, assign reporters a passive or reactive role, the Web calls for their proactive performance in such tasks as database analysis or investigation - demands that go against the grain of mainstream news reporting, which is reactive in nature.
- Impersonal Data: While other channels enable and improve communication with human agents, the Web usually bypasses them in favour of largely impersonal data. Hence those who perceived the Web as a promising news source were not wrong about the technology, only about its users. Journalists, it turns out, are not in the general information business

but rather supply information originating among human agents.

- The Extra Burden of Corroboration: Constant suspicions concerning the trustworthiness of Web materials could have been resolved by crosschecking with additional sources. As their time frame shrinks, however, reporters may wonder why they ought to use a news source that requires additional sources a priori instead of simply contacting these sources themselves.
- Unqualified Material: Apparently, the Web's marginal contribution to published news (and that of other mass media) contradicts the nature of news producers as heavy news consumers above all, who start each day by reading one another's publications. Media consumption does not necessarily contribute directly to specific news items that are subsequently published, however, but rather informs reporters about current events in general and the output of competitors and counterparts. Furthermore, the Web offers "too much information or [.] too little information" and is loaded with previously published items that are useless to reporters who refrain from plagiarism unless they find their own angle or follow-up, employing an independent sourcing process.

Some of these weaknesses are the strengths of a much older technology, whose contribution to the public news menu tends to be overlooked.

THE ENDURING DOMINANCE OF THE TELEPHONE

The enduring dominance of telephony challenges the assertion that newsmaking was conquered by new technologies, especially when combined with insistence that the golden age of the telephone in journalism ended during the 1950s. Some scholars have mentioned the ongoing prominence of telephony together with face-to-face interviews but did not specify the respective contributions of each.

The continuing dominance of the telephone in the new technology-saturated news environment, after a hundred years of service and despite more sophisticated alternatives, can no longer be explained in simple terms such as the immediacy and efficiency of the given technology.

At first glance, it may appear that numerous factors motivate reporter and source alike to avoid oral communication. Why should reporters trap themselves between oral input and textual output, adding the burden of translating vocal utterances into written stories?

Why would they work with loosely structured, ephemeral raw material that leaves no paper trail and is replete with redundancies, inconsistencies, and multiple, interwoven threads of thought?

And why would news sources, in turn, use channels that impede realization of a speaker's full potential and downgrade control over verbalization, precision of expression, lexical richness, and grammatical sophistication, thereby forgoing the advantage of imperceptible emendation and rendering themselves vulnerable to audible self-correction that sounds like "denial and patchwork"?

Several considerations may explain the persistence of the present situation:

- *Naturalness:* Oral channels are a "primary form of communication for humans." They are "addressed by a real, living person [.] at a specific time in a real setting" and are more "natural to thought and speech" than writing, more spontaneous and more dynamic and vivid, as vocal expression is itself a live event in space and time, anchored in the "life-worlds" of real people.
- *Informativeness:* Oral communication always includes "much more than mere words." Even telephone conversations retain many attributes of face-to-face interactions, including "use of language [.] the way words are pronounced, elements of intonation or prosody, syntax and semantics [.] variations of loudness and pitch beyond that involved in

intonation, tempo, resonance, pauses and nonfluencies, as well as nonlanguage sounds such as laughing and sighing."

- *Unavailability of Suitable Texts:* Journalists generally search for news within a narrow time slot once a new event or story begins to unfold and before others cover them - at least in the same news market. During this short period, texts may be unavailable, unsuitable, already published, or authored by PR professionals.
- *Participatory Role:* Oral channels are actually the only conduit through which reporters may play a participatory role in shaping the raw materials of news.

This role corresponds with four aspects of newswork:

- As a "negotiated phenomenon" (i.e., an output of bargaining between reporters and sources), news tends to flow through channels such as the telephone, that enable negotiations between the parties.
- As news constitutes a co-production by reporters and their sources, the former perceive their authorship as including mandatory participation in the formation of raw news material and not only post hoc reduction of source-initiated texts.
- Oral channels increase reporters' control over their raw material, whereas written versions accord their writers the advantage, giving them more leeway to hide, slant or frame information as they see fit.

Oral channels enable interview techniques that may not only improve source accountability but also reinforce the status and legitimacy of reporters as trustees of the public who pose questions on its behalf.

- *Competitive Advantage:* While many written materials are distributed to or may be approached by numerous journalists, oral channels give reporters a chance at exclusivity. Most of the time, such exclusivity does not apply to the items as a whole, that are shared by their counterparts and competitors, but rather to certain details thereof.

- *Smaller (Perceived) Risk:* When leaks are involved, both sources and reporters are especially careful to avoid textual channels, as they may leave clear traces in case of investigation. Although they cannot promise full protection, oral channels are perceived as safer than others except in cases of serial leaks, such as the Pentagon Papers, in which randomly chosen pay phones were the instrument of choice.

Epistemological channels, a collection of communication technologies and non-mediated conduits of news coverage, are probably the keystone of technology and journalism theorization, thanks to their crucial role in shaping the scope and quality of information that subsequently becomes the public news diet.

The current study suggests an initial theoretical outline for the role of these channels in news sourcing, based on a careful analysis of their contribution to a random sample of about 850 stories from three different media.

Just as a hierarchy of credibility prevails in the realm of sourcing, according precedence to certain informants over others, a technological hierarchy governs the world of communication channels that echo the logic of sourcing, determining which conduits are to be given priority.

The subordination of these channels to a higher order of sourcing considerations is observed both in the combined tendency of the reporters studied to rely on human agents (in 87% of their contacts in the discovery phase and 92% in the gathering phase) and to communicate with them orally (57% and 75%, respectively).

Heavy reliance on technology-mediated coverage suggests that reporters accord much lower priority to the demands of space than to those of time. Hence the basic role of communication technologies is to release reporters from spatial constraints, thereby enabling them to meet temporal demands.

According to the findings, reporters sourcing their published news prefer various remote data excavation technologies to first-hand witnessing, and prefer reliance on human agents to technological sources such as the Web and oral communication to textual. Hence the principal role of epistemological technologies is to enable remote coverage while keeping close to human informants.

The methods journalists employ to obtain published news indicate that news is a social product, fabricated chiefly through interpersonal reporter-source contact. As such, news is more a matter of trust between humans than of independent witnessing, fact finding, or fact checking.

This process is none too compliant with "foundationalist epistemology" that expects validation of facts by empirical findings or rational substantiation, but rather conforms with social epistemology that makes do with facts established by communal agreement within "specific epistemic communities."

Furthermore, news is a textual product of oral processes. This "oral culture" allows reporters to omit, edit, select excerpts, and "tidy up" quotes in a manner that often bears the seeds of tension between parties. To a certain extent, this may explain the vast quantities of journalistic errors, misunderstandings, misquotes, and source statements taken out of context.

As one Wall Street Journal reporter put it, "It's your notes against their word." This study focuses on the most substantial role of communication channels as conduits for generating the public news diet. Despite the meticulous methods employed, however, it is not free of weaknesses and blind spots, as it addresses involvement of different channels only in items that were subsequently published or aired, relying on the recollection of reporters themselves.

Hence, the current study sets a broad agenda for further studies, especially those considering other types of reporters who probably employ different patterns of channel use, particularly TV reporters, investigative reporters, citizen journalists, multimedia and multi-skilled reporters, and so on.

Subsequent studies should focus on other news cultures especially that of the United States, testing the hypothesis of limited use of the Web as a news source and extensive use for other newswork functions. Newsroom observations may contribute another missing link by mapping the inevitable gaps between reported and actual uses of communication channels.

These may also focus on the oral culture that associates reporters and sources, the patterns in which oral raw materials are transformed into final news texts and the extent to which this transformation is susceptible to errors, misunderstandings, and disputes between the parties.

Chapter 8

Public and Traditional Journalism

What does the public need to know? What role should news play in local community life? What are the central characteristics of good journalism? Debates and discussions about these fundamental questions primarily have been limited to journalists and those who study journalism. But what about consumers of journalism? This study set out to discover what everyday citizens think about journalistic practice and the role of journalists in reporting local news. For decades, a few journalists and many scholars have wondered how journalistic practice may affect the public.

For a decade and a half, a smaller group has wondered whether journalistic practice has contributed to Americans' dwindling interest in news and declining participation in civic life. Davis "Buzz" Merritt, then editor of the Knight-Ridder-owned Wichita Eagle, spearheaded one of the first journalistic projects to reengage the public in local news and civic life. Concurrently, New York University journalism scholar Jay Rosen, then director of the Project on Public Life and the Press, began asking pointed questions about the role of journalists and journalism in public life.

Eventually these efforts led to a new journalistic movement and scholarly area called civic or public journalism that connected journalistic practice, the public, and the fabric of civic life in new ways.

What does the public think of journalism practice in general and civic journalism in particular? What does the public expect of local news? By gaining greater insight into the public's expectations of local news, it may be possible to identify key issues that could, in the long run, increase the public's interest in news and civic life.

THE PUBLIC JOURNALISM LITERATURE

A review of forty-seven public journalism studies conducted from 1995 through 2001 revealed that public journalism has primarily been studied in three areas: content, journalists, and effects of public journalism on the audience. Content and Public Journalism.

Studies have found that public journalism content has distinct characteristics. For example, McGregor, Comrie, and Fontaine studied coverage of a New Zealand election campaign, comparing papers that endorsed public journalism and papers that did not, and found the public journalism papers covered the race more constructively.

By comparing the Seattle Times Front Porch Forum Project coverage with the coverage by the Times in earlier years as well as content in the Seattle Post-Intelligencer, Blazier and Lemert found that among eleven public journalism traits, providing mobilizing information was the most distinguishing factor between the public journalism project and earlier coverage by the paper and coverage by the competition.

Moscowitz also found mobilizing information in a study comparing coverage of homelessness in the Knight-Ridder-owned, civic journalism-oriented Charlotte Observer with the Gannett-owned, traditional journalism-oriented Indianapolis Star. The Charlotte Observer was also less likely to use official sources and more likely to include solutions to problems in its coverage seeking out citizen sources rather than relying solely on official sources has been identified as a characteristic of public journalism.

By comparing two papers, one civic, the other not, Kennamer and South found the civic-affiliated paper had a much greater number of unaffiliated sources than the other. Kurpius also studied sources and found that local television news stories, employing public journalism techniques, used a larger percentage of African American sources than represented in the general population. Furthermore African American, Latino, and female journalists were more likely to use minority and female sources in their stories. Rather than focus on the text of a story, Coleman compared the visual elements in public journalism and traditional journalism content.

Although for the most part, visual elements did not distinguish public journalism and traditional journalism, Coleman did find that public journalism stories were significantly more likely than traditional journalism stories to include visual elements that facilitated contact of the media by the public.

Because interactivity lends itself to citizen involvement and public journalism principles, Choi compared public journalism and traditional journalism newspapers in an online environment, expecting that online public journalism newspapers would exhibit more public journalism characteristics.

Content analyses of online stories from the Rochester Democrat, Charlotte Observer, Orlando Sentinel, online versions of public journalism-oriented newspapers, and the Buffalo News, Winston-Salem Journal, Florida Times Union, online versions of traditional journalism-oriented newspapers, found little difference in the content of online newspapers that represented public journalism and traditional journalism newspapers.

JOURNALISTS AND PUBLIC JOURNALISM

Because a decision to practice public journalism usually rests with a senior editor or producer, Kurpius examined the relationship between management and content. In two separate examinations of local television news, Kurpius found that visionary managers were the key for the civic-model of successful issues coverage at local television stations, but he also discovered that market forces may hinder civic reporting efforts in local media in the long run.

Factors that may influence journalists' attitudes toward public journalism were studied by scholars in New Mexico.

After journalists at the Albuquerque Journal and Albuquerque Tribune and journalism students at the University of New Mexico completed self-administered questionnaires as part of a convenience sample, the results showed "a progression of socialization that begins with students supporting civic journalism."

Journalism students without newsroom experience appeared to be more supportive of civic journalism than practicing journalists and journalism students with newsroom experience. The authors suggested that civic journalism appeared to be inconsistent with autonomy, an attribute greatly valued by practicing journalists and journalism students with newsroom experience.

Indiana University scholars asked journalists directly about civic journalism in their most recent national survey. Although their previous national surveys of journalists, which were conducted in 1982 and 1992, had documented the backgrounds, attitudes, and values of journalists, the latest national study represented the first time that specific questions about public or civic journalism practices were asked.

According to "The American Journalist in the 21st Century," 72% of journalists approved of giving ordinary people a chance to express their views on public affairs and 58% endorsed providing possible solutions to society's problems. Only 32% approved of convening meetings to discuss public issues.

EFFECTS OF PUBLIC JOURNALISM ON THE AUDIENCE

The sixteen audience-centreed studies identified in the Massey and Haas review examined the effects of civic journalism on the public rather than the public's expectations of journalism." For example, one study reviewed by Massey and Haas found evidence that public journalism produced positive results.

In a study of broadcast and print media that included Wisconsin Public Television and Radio, WISC-TV, the

Wisconsin State Journal, and the Wood Communications Group and their collaborative effort to provide a more civic-oriented approach toward election coverage, Denton and Thorson found respondents in Madison said the project made them more knowledgeable about the election, encouraged them to vote, and gave them useful tools to assess campaign information.

Although the literature found civic journalism practices improved public attitudes and increased knowledge of election issues, overall, the Massey and Haas review of public journalism studies found mixed audience effects. Public journalism was found to both increase and suppress voter turnout, to both increase participation in civic projects and have no impact on civic participation, and to produce both strong and weak agenda-setting effects.

After reviewing forty-seven empirical studies, Massey and Haas criticized the public journalism literature for its lack of methodological rigor and for narrowly focusing on "jewel box" civic journalism projects that were conducted at the Wichita Eagle, Charlotte Observer, and Wisconsin State Journal.

Only one of the authors' six recommendations for future research involved the public and that was to conduct laboratory experiments that "could prove more useful for more convincingly identifying whatever causal factors may be behind any public-journalism influence on news audiences."

Surprisingly, none of the recommendations that resulted from this comprehensive review of public journalism studies focused on the public as an independent, active, and integral component of the communication process with opinions and expectations about a new type of journalism that ventures to re-engage the audience in the civic arena.

RESEARCH QUESTIONS

Although civic journalism has been discussed, practiced, debated, and studied for over a decade and a half, the public's perspective on civic journalism has not been studied empirically. Understanding the public's view of local news and civic journalism is important for the practice and business of journalism as well as society as a whole.

Without an assessment of what the public expects of local news, it will be virtually impossible to identify journalism practices that may help reverse declining attention to news, restore dwindling public trust in news as a whole and journalists in particular, and bring back the vanishing participant in civic affairs.

Unlike much of the research on public journalism, which has focused on the effects of specific public journalism projects on voting rates and other measures of civic participation, this study explores the public's views about journalism as well as the public's expectations of local news and the underlying dimensions of those expectations.

Specifically, the following research questions will be answered:

- *RQ1:* What do survey respondents regard as the important attributes and roles of journalism and how does that compare with the norms of traditional and public journalism?
- *RQ2:* How do survey respondents compare with journalists on the importance of practices and norms associated with traditional and civic journalism?
- *RQ3:* What segments of survey respondents as defined by race or ethnicity, age, income, education, and gender are more likely to endorse civic journalism and traditional journalism norms?
- *RQ4:* What are the underlying dimensions of survey respondents' expectations of local news?

As part of a research project for a local newspaper and local NPR affiliated public radio station that was starting up a local news division to complement the national news broadcast from NPR, the authors worked with the radio station managers to design a research study that would ascertain public opinion about local news. A Pew Centre for Civic Journalism grant provided funding for the audience study. The radio station manager believed that understanding the public's expectations of local news was a prerequisite to building a radio news division that would report local news of importance and meet the public's needs.

The spring 2001 survey, conducted in a southwestern metropolitan area by a professional telephone survey unit, used random digit dialing to select the sample. Interviews were completed with 600 adults, representing a response rate of 62.2%. Calculation of the response rate was based upon the number of completed interviews (n=600) relative to the number of completed interviews plus refusals (n=286), incomplete interviews (n=37), and persons contacted but not interviewed due to illness, language barriers, or other impairments (n=36).

Answers to the four research questions were based on survey respondents' ratings of roles of local news media and characteristics of news coverage. Respondents were asked: What do you think is the most important role of local news media? Rate each on whether you think it's "extremely important," "somewhat important," or "not very important."

The roles were (1) report the widest range of news; (2) concentrate on certain topics; (3) provide a forum for community views; (4) be a watchdog of powerful people and the government; (5) highlight interesting people and groups in the community; and (6) offer solutions to community problems.

Respondents were also asked the following: What is the most important characteristic of news coverage you want? Rate each on whether you think it's "extremely important," "somewhat important," or "not very important." The characteristics were (1) accuracy; (2) rapid reporting; (3) understand the local community; (4) unbiased reporting; (5) care about your community; (6) be inclusive of different points of view; and (7) provide explanation of issues and trends.

To determine how survey respondents compare with journalists, the survey respondents' opinions about practices and norms associated with traditional and civic journalism were matched with journalists' opinions from "The American Journalist in the 21st Century" national survey.

Specifically, the opinions of survey respondents and

journalists were compared in four areas: offering solutions, providing a community forum, being a watchdog, and rapid reporting. Although both studies used random sampling and "extremely" on the measurement scale, there were several methodological differences.

The question wording in the national survey of journalists differed on the four opinions that were compared. For offering solutions, the national survey asked journalists how important it was "to point people toward possible solutions to society's problems."

For providing a community forum, the national survey asked journalists how important it was "to convene meetings of citizens and community leaders to discuss public issues." For being a watchdog, the national survey asked how important it was to "investigate claims and statements made by the government."

For rapid reporting, the national survey asked journalists how important it was to "get information to the public quickly." In addition to the difference in wording, the present study relied on a three-point scale to measure opinions about journalistic norms while the national survey of journalists relied on a four-point scale of "extremely," "quite," "somewhat," and "not really important."

The difference in question wording and the number of points on the measurement may have affected the number of respondents that chose "extremely" as an option. The final methodological difference was that the present study was conducted in spring 2001 in one southwestern metropolitan area while the national survey of 1,149 journalists was conducted summer and fall of 2002.

The survey questionnaire also included questions about socio-economic backgrounds and media use. Standard survey questions were asked to ascertain number of years lived in the area, marital status, level of education, income, age, and race or ethnicity. Respondents were also asked if they had children living at home and their gender was recorded.

To establish media use, respondents were asked if they read the primary daily newspaper 4-6 times a week, 1-3 times a week, less frequently, or never. Similarly, respondents were asked if they read the primary Sunday newspaper 3-4 times a month, 1-2 times a month, less frequently, or never. Respondents were also asked how often they heard news on the radio, which TV stations they watched for local news, and how often they obtained local news from the Internet.

Bivariate analyses with appropriate statistics were used to determine if opinions about public and traditional journalism practices and norms differed by race or ethnicity, age, income, education, or gender. A factor analysis was used to identify underlying dimensions of survey respondents' attitudes about the roles and characteristics of public and traditional journalism.

RESULTS

SOCIO-ECONOMIC BACKGROUND AND MEDIA USE

Survey participants had established roots in this southwestern metropolitan area. The median number of years lived in the area was twelve; 55% were married and 42% had children at home. Although education was high, different educational levels were represented: 21% had a high school degree or less, 27% had some college, 28% were college graduates, and 24% completed at least some graduate school.

Different income groups were also represented: 34% had a household income of less than $40,000; 31% had incomes between $40,000 and $69,000, and 35% had incomes of $70,000 or higher. Slightly more than one-third of the respondents were ages 18 to 39; 31% were ages 40 to 69; 35% were 70 years or older.

Respondents were fairly diverse: 68% were white, 19%; were Latino, 7% were African American, and 5% were Asian American or other. The remaining 1% did not specify race or ethnicity. When asked how many times a week they read the primary local newspaper, 30% said never or less frequently than 1-3 times a week, 25% said 1-3 times a week, and 44% said 4-6 times a week.

Survey participants were more devoted to the Sunday newspaper with 64% reporting they read it 3-4 times a month. In addition to the newspaper, survey participants relied on other local news sources: 80% watched one of the five local TV news outlets, 59% often heard news on the radio, and 18% often turned to the Internet.

THE PUBLIC'S VIEWS ON JOURNALISTIC NORMS

The overwhelming majorities said that accuracy (94%) and unbiased reporting (84%) are extremely important, but two major tenets of traditional journalism did not receive strong endorsements.

The traditional journalistic norm of being a watchdog of powerful people and the government was supported by only 49% of survey respondents and rapid reporting was endorsed by only 35%.

THE PUBLIC'S VIEWS ON THE ROLE OF LOCAL NEWS

Slightly more than half (51%) said offering solutions to community problems was extremely important, and 49% said providing a forum for community views was extremely important.

To answer RQ2, these views were compared with journalists' views about civic journalism practices.

COMPARING THE PUBLIC AND JOURNALISTS

Although the survey of the public was conducted in a southwestern metropolitan area and the survey of journalists was conducted nationally, results from the two surveys were compared because both studies used random sampling techniques, included similar questions about characteristics of traditional and public journalism, and incorporated "extremely important" on the measurement scale.

A difference in proportions test on independent random samples was used to determine if survey respondents were significantly different from journalists in their endorsement of two civic journalism norms and two traditional journalistic norms. Even though the majority of survey respondents strongly endorsed the fundamental characteristics of journalism, accuracy and unbiased reporting, there was a statistically significant gap between survey respondents and journalists on two roles that are an integral part of traditional journalism: watchdog and rapid reporting.

Only 49% of survey respondents said being a watchdog of powerful people and the government is extremely important, but 70% of journalists said that traditional journalism role is extremely important. Survey respondents were also significantly less likely than journalists to say that rapid reporting was extremely important (35% vs. 59%).

The roles and characteristics of traditional and civic journalism displayed were analysed by five socio-economic characteristics (race or ethnicity, age, income, education, and gender) to better understand survey respondents' opinions about traditional and civic journalism roles and characteristics.

Although there was no statistically significant difference between survey respondents and journalists in their endorsement of the civic journalism role of providing solutions to problems, there were significant differences when this civic journalism role was analysed by sub-segments of survey respondents.

SOLUTIONS

African Americans and Hispanics were significantly more likely than whites and Asian Americans to say that the civic journalism role of offering solutions to community problems was extremely important.

Almost three quarters (72%) of African Americans and 64% of Hispanics said offering solutions was extremely important, but only 45% of whites and 47% of Asian Americans said this civic journalism role was extremely important.

Segments of survey respondents that made less money and had less education were more likely than wealthier and more educated segments to say offering solutions to community problems was extremely important. Almost three-fifths (59%) of adults who had incomes of less than $50,000 compared to 44% of adults with incomes of $50,000 or more said offering solutions was extremely important.

This inverse relationship was also apparent when offering solutions to community problems was analysed by education. Adults with a high school education or less (68%) were more likely than adults with some college (54%) and adults with a college degree or higher (42%) to say offering solutions was extremely important.

Females were also more likely than males to attach greater value to the public journalism role of offering solutions with 56% of females compared to 44% of males saying it was extremely important for local news to offer solutions to community problems.

WATCHDOG AND RAPID REPORTING

The traditional journalism characteristics of watchdog and rapid reporting were also analysed by the five socio-economic variables and three were significantly related.

The oldest age group (55+) was more likely than the youngest age groups to value the watchdog role of traditional journalism, with 62% of adults 55 or older compared to 47% of adults 35 to 54 and 45% of adults 18 to 34 saying being a watchdog of powerful people and the government was extremely important. An inverse relationship emerged when the traditional journalistic characteristic of rapid reporting was analysed by education. Among adults with a high school degree or less, 47% said rapid reporting was extremely important; 30% of adults with a college degree or higher said rapid reporting was extremely important.

Females attached greater value to rapid reporting than males. Among females, 40% said rapid reporting was extremely important but only 30% of males said this traditional journalistic practice was extremely important.

The Underlying Dimensions of the Public's Expectations of Local News

To better understand the underlying dimensions of

survey respondents' expectations of local news reporting, researchers factor analysed the six roles of local news and seven characteristics of journalism. The good neighbour dimension that emerged included attributes of public journalism: caring about your community, highlighting interesting people and groups in the community, understanding the local community, and offering solutions to community problems.

The watchdog dimension was represented by four roles of local news including being a watchdog of powerful people and the government, concentrating on certain topics, providing a forum for community views, and providing explanations of issues and trends.

The unbiased and accurate reporting dimension was defined by those two traditional characteristics of news; the fast dimension was represented by the traditional news characteristic, rapid reporting. Providing a wide range of news and being inclusive of different points of view did not load high on any one dimension. In fact, the inclusive factor loading was similar for the good neighbour, watchdog, and unbiased and accurate dimensions.

DISCUSSION

Although more than fifty empirical studies have been conducted on public or civic journalism, none of the studies has tried to gauge public opinion about this new approach to journalism practice.

This study provided insight into a journalistic practice that developed over the past decade and a half in response to the vanishing newspaper reader and disappearing participant in civic affairs. Furthermore, this study provided insight into the public's views on traditional journalistic characteristics.

At a time when newspaper readership, participation in civic life, and the credibility of journalism are at all-time lows, this study helped answer broader questions about journalism: Is traditional journalism meeting the public's expectations? Is the civic journalism movement on the right track?

The results of this survey suggest that, in many cases, the public and the press, including traditional journalism and the civic journalism movement, are on separate tracks headed in different directions and unless something is done to better meet the public's expectations, civic participation, newspaper readership, and the credibility of the press may continue to decline.

While it is reassuring to know that the survey respondents overwhelmingly endorse accuracy and unbiased reporting, it is important to recognize that these same expectations can cause the public to turn away from the news.

When Jayson Blair fabricates the news at the New York Times or star foreign correspondent Jack Kelley is accused of inventing parts of stories reported by USA Today, the public's trust in the news media is shaken and the reasons for reading the news are threatened.

It is also important to note that long-held norms of traditional journalism, being a watchdog and rapid reporting, are not strongly valued by a majority of the survey respondents. Only 49% said being a watchdog of powerful people and the government was extremely important, and 35% said rapid reporting was extremely important.

But when the survey respondents were analysed by age, the press as watchdog was popular in the oldest age group. Over three-fifths of adults 55 years or older said the news media's traditional role of being a watchdog was extremely important.

Offering solutions to community problems, a characteristic of civic journalism, was strongly endorsed by only half of the survey participants as a whole, but when different segments were analysed, this public journalism practice was found to be more popular than first thought. The popularity of offering solutions is most evident among those who have traditionally been disenfranchised from the power sources of government and business: African Americans, Hispanics, adults with less income and education, and women.

Perhaps these groups are looking to news media as a

source for help. Do the public's expectations of local news fit the traditional journalism model, the civic journalism movement, or some other ideal? The factor analysis of thirteen roles and characteristics of journalism revealed four dimensions with being a good neighbour-not watchdog, unbiased and accurate, or fast-representing the dominant expectation.

Being a good neighbour included caring about your community, highlighting interesting people and groups in the community, understanding the local community, and offering solutions to community problems. The expectation that the press should be a good neighbour may be related to declining trust in the news media and declining attention to news.

If the public expects the press to be a good neighbour but the press fails in that role because it sees its professional responsibility as a watchdog, there is clearly a disconnect between the public's expectations and the press' expectations which civic journalism practices may not be able to fix.

Buzz Merritt and Maxwell McCombs argue for an expanded watchdog role of the press that is consonant with the good neighbour perspective: News media need to be creative watchdogs and agenda setters scanning the horizon for the gaps in current public life.

Part of this larger watchdog role is functioning as social radar, not just a chronicler of what government and other institutions are doing right now, whether good or bad. This means discovering the concerns of citizens and defining what the public needs to know in very expansive terms.

But for this expanded watchdog role to resonate with the public, the news media must educate the public and even persuade the public that in the role of watchdog, they are looking out for the public in the same way that a good neighbour would. According to Andrew Kohut, director of the Pew Research Centre for the People and the Press, a decade and a half ago, which was about the time of the first civic journalism projects?

The public thought the press was "too sensational, too pushy, too rude, too uncaring about people and the public."

But most people saw journalists as moral, professional and caring about the interests of the country. Today, the public considers the news media even less professional, less accurate, less moral, less helpful to democracy, more sensational, more likely to cover up mistakes and more biased.

These are not exactly attributes of a good neighbour. Because this study represents only one metropolitan area in the Southwest, additional studies should be conducted in other parts of the country.

Because different communities have different characteristics and needs, it is possible that they have different expectations of their local news. It is also possible that even with different community characteristics and needs, the public's expectations of local news are similar, regardless of community size or geographic location.

Only by replicating this study in other communities can the public's expectations of local news be determined. According to a 3 May 2005 New York Times article, the 1.9% drop in daily circulation and 2.5% decline in Sunday circulation reported by the Audit Bureau of Circulations represented the "largest circulation losses for the industry in more than a decade, and indicate an acceleration of the decline."

The magnitude of the circulation decline for 814 daily newspapers suggests that it is imperative that future studies determine how the public's expectations of local news relate to readership of newspapers and use of other news media. Future studies should also determine how participation in civic life is related to the public's expectations of local news. Finally, it is important for future studies to focus on the public's expectations of news with special attention paid to the concept of the press as a good neighbour.

By gaining greater insight into the public's expectations of local news, it may be possible to initiate a dialogue between the public and the press. This dialogue may lead to a closing of the gap between the expectations of the public and the press that could, in the long run, reverse declining attention to news and waning participation in civic life.

Perhaps more than any other profession, journalism grapples with an apparent contradiction between autonomy and public service. Sociologists define professional autonomy as wide latitude of judgment in executing occupational duties.' Autonomy provides discretion in the application of techniques and separation from influences that threaten a professional's ability to apply expertise in service to the public.

Thus, practitioners adhere to norms of public service even as the lay public itself is excluded from formal decision making. This conception of autonomy becomes problematic when applied to the press, according to advocates of civic (or public) journalism. This reform movement is based on the premise that news media should go beyond the mere reporting of information to act as a catalyst and as a forum for the revitalization of democracy.

But according to civic journalism opponents, these goals threaten the institutional independence of the press and thereby jeopardize journalistic autonomy. Under the traditional view of journalism, autonomy allows the press to cover public affairs with some protection against partisan bias and other corrupting influences.

If civic journalism is to succeed in the long run as a reform movement, it must meet head on the tension between the profession's autonomous identity and its role in democracy.

Civic journalism has focused on the implementation and consequences of professional values, but it has been less concerned about understanding the origins of these values as a function of professional socialization. The purpose of this study is to model the process by which professional socialization predisposes college students to reject or embrace civic journalism.

We will first assess the extent of support for various dimensions of civic journalism within two groups: journalism students and professional journalists living in the same community. Our general expectation is that students will be relatively supportive of civic journalism while professionals will express reservations in light of their commitment to autonomy.

We will then consider college experiences that might help to explain when and why this gap emerges.' Our intent is not to argue for the merits of civic journalism, but to provide insight into why support for it might erode as a consequence of professional socialization. For those who do support civic journalism, this line of inquiry could suggest implications for curriculum reform geared toward enhancing-or preventing the erosion of-civic journalism support.

This approach will also allow us to make an empirical contribution to the ongoing debate as to whether civic and traditional journalism principles coexist in harmony, or whether the two perspectives necessarily conflict as values take shape during professional socialization.

Why Autonomy Is Important to Journalists. While autonomy for all professions is ostensibly a mechanism of public service, it also accommodates the psychological needs of the practitioners. Autonomy contributes to group identification-the perception of belonging to a particular human group. Cheney and Tompkins observed that identification helps to sustain "an individual's or a group's 'sameness' or 'substance' against a backdrop of change and 'out side' elements."

Prior research shows autonomy strongly correlated with both professional identification of journalists and job satisfaction. Management trends in news media have increased the need for autonomy in recent decades. Comparison of the findings of Johnstone, Slawski, and Bowman in 1976 with those of Weaver and Wilhoit for 1986 and 1996 reveals that perceived autonomy declined.

As Johnstone, Slawski, and Bowman surmised, the bureaucratization of media organizations diminishes the sense of autonomy among rank-and-file reporters. In the first two surveys, 60 per cent of respondents reported they were almost entirely free to select the material on which they worked; this dropped to 51 per cent in the third study.

Potential threats to autonomy include increased corporate

chain ownership, the crumbling of the metaphorical wall between business and editorial, competition from Internet sources of news and entertainment, and the blurring of editorial and business functions in news organizations. With an erosion of perceived autonomy, and without the organizational protection and academic credentials of other professions, journalists are likely to feel vulnerable in the face of structural changes.

This probably accounts for some of the defensiveness, if not outright hostility, many prominent journalists express toward civic journalism, a reform movement that is itself an explicit challenge to traditional notions of autonomy.

CIVIC JOURNALISM AS A MULTI-DIMENSIONAL CONCEPT

In efforts to document the amount of support among reporters and editors, researchers have sought to isolate specific values associated with civic journalism. Bare developed a "personal public journalism" scale that formed a continuum from general goals to specific practices.

Support decreased along the scale in the movement from abstract goals to practices that violate professional detachment. One purpose of this study is to identify where students and professionals might depart in their evaluations of specific goals and practices. We will consider first the possible reactions to a questionnaire item that explicitly mentions "civic journalism" as a reform movement.

"CIVIC JOURNALISM" AS A POLITICIZED TERM

Several proponents of civic journalism have lamented that the term itself has become politicized in that it evokes disdain in professional circles instead of contemplation. Consequently, we expect that the professional respondents, and perhaps some students, will react negatively to a question that merely mentions "civic journalism."

Analysis of responses to this item could help us to evaluate responses to the other questionnaire items: if respondents express support for specific goals and practices, yet object to "civic journalism" itself, this would suggest that they are responding to something not captured by the other attitudinal items.

Given the lack of prior research on differences between professionals and students in support for civic journalism, we propose a research question rather than a formal hypothesis: RQ1: In comparison with professionals, will students express stronger support for "civic journalism" as a general description of the reform movement?

CIVIC JOURNALISM GOALS

The press traditionally understands its role as a disseminator of accurate information that allows individuals to participate as competent citizens. This requires neutrality in the coverage of political actors, institutions, and issues. By contrast, civic journalists argue that news media should not be neutral about the quality of civic participation in their communities.

We asked respondents to assess their support for two goals associated with civic journalism: going beyond the mere transmission of information to increase political participation, and focusing on news that helps a community to solve problems. While these goals are potentially problematic in light of the norm of detachment, they are described at a fairly abstract level, with the threat to autonomy more implicit than explicit.

Thus, we again propose a research question instead of a hypothesis: RQ2: In comparison with professionals, will students express stronger support for civic journalism goals? Civic journalism Practices. We do anticipate differences between professionals and students in the evaluation of practices that might jeopardize autonomy.

For example, we asked respondents to assess their support for news media sponsoring meetings to address local problems. According to professional critics, such events cripple the ability of journalists to remain critical of the favored policies. We also asked respondents to evaluate the use of polls to help journalists decide what should be covered.

Critics have dismissed this technique as another manifestation of how marketing has intruded into the newsroom. Handing news judgment over to the public directly violates the profession's traditional understanding of autonomy. H1: In comparison with professionals, students will express stronger support for practices associated with civic journalism.

ANTECEDENTS OF SUPPORT FOR CIVIC JOURNALISM

A review of prior literature suggests that college experiences and attitudes adopted during professional socialization will influence students' acceptance of civic journalism.

Potential predictors of civic journalism support include the amount of college instruction, anticipatory socialization as a psychological construct, working for a campus paper, and support for traditional roles of the press.

FORMAL INSTRUCTION

Participation in a college journalism curriculum should influence the likelihood of students adopting values similar to those of professionals. Weaver and Wilhoit reported that alumni of journalism programs expressed a connection between their formal education and their current news values. Students are likely to adopt a commitment to professional autonomy-and consequently a reticence about civic journalism-to the extent that instruction emphasizes the conventional understanding of professional detachment and neutrality. Prior participation in a civic journalism project should also predict support, but we did not include this variable because of the minimal presence of civic journalism in the journalism programme where we recruited respondents. The programme had provided only one civic journalism class (in 1998), with an enrollment of eleven students.

ANTICIPATORY SOCIALIZATION

Individuals typically view themselves as members of a

profession long before they join a specific organization. "Anticipatory professional socialization" represents the extent to which an individual has thought seriously about a particular career. An important dimension of this process is "identification," or the perception of belonging to a particular group.

This need for professional membership and acceptance might predispose students to reject civic journalism. A central argument of civic journalism is that news media should display their inner workings, thereby becoming more accountable to the public.

But if students begin to value an insider's perspective on newsroom culture, this group identification could evoke an aversion to the civic journalism critique.

WORKING FOR A COLLEGE NEWSPAPER

While these two factors should facilitate the adoption of traditional values, neither duplicates the degree of autonomy experienced by professionals. Working for an independent college newspaper, however, might represent an indelible socializing experience that produces a resistance to civic journalism.

Campus newspapers vary in their degree of independence from journalism departments and university administrations, but a tradition of American universities is that student newspapers should maintain substantial institutional independence.

The experience of working for a campus newspaper-including the sense of empowerment gained from reporting and editing with little or no instructor supervision— should instill an appreciation for autonomy that cannot be duplicated in the classroom.

Theorists of human development have observed that a young person's identification with an occupation or profession facilitates a realization of self identity, and thus many students might become attracted to journalism precisely because it allows them to express independence and personal identity through their writing and news judgment.

H2: Students with campus newspaper experience will be less supportive of civic journalism compared to other students.

SUPPORT FOR TRADITIONAL ROLES

Civic journalism opponents argue that its goals and practices are not compatible with the traditional mission of the press as an institution that relies on autonomy to provide accurate and balanced information. In the case of journalism training, the question is whether the formation of a professional identity will allow for not only multiple role conceptions among students, but for acceptance of roles that are potentially incompatible.

Prior surveys of professionals provide evidence that journalists do identify with more than one role. Weaver and Wilhoit identified three highly correlated but distinct attitudes about professional purpose: interpretation, dissemination, and adversary orientations."

The interpretive function resonates with a recommendation of the Commission on Freedom of the Press-that journalists should investigate the truth about facts while providing a context that gives them meaning. The disseminator function highlights the need for the press to transmit information that is useful to a large audience, while the adversary function reflects the importance of acting as a "watchdog" of government.

In a survey of newspaper staff members, Arant and Meyer concluded that the majority of journalists do not support practices that violate professional autonomy, but those who did also supported traditional roles of news media. In the context of this study, we anticipate that students would support the traditional roles.

But with relatively little concern about journalistic autonomy, measures of traditional values might correlate strongly with civic journalism support among the students, given that the overarching commitment to public service is reflected in all of these role conceptions. We propose the following research question: RQ3: Will support for the dissemination, interpretive, and adversary roles predict students' support for civic journalism? The student respondents attended the University of New Mexico (Albuquerque), and the professional journalists were recruited from two daily newspapers published in the same city. While the restriction of respondents to one community in the Southwest limits the external validity of findings, the design eliminates regional factors as alternative explanations for possible differences between students and professionals.

SAMPLING

We used a purposive sample of students in courses taught within the university's Communication & Journalism Department. The intent was to include a large percentage of students who identified to some degree with journalism as a profession.

During April of 1999, we administered questionnaires to classes that contained students in four undergraduate major tracks: print journalism, broadcast journalism, public relations, and advertising. We would expect that some students would be sharply focused on journalism, with some fully involved in internships and writing for the campus paper.

Other students, however, would have little or no interest in journalism as a career, but they would have at least some knowledge of news media as an academic topic. This diversity of student background creates the possibility for variance within the variables used to predict civic journalism support.

The sampling frame for the professional journalists was defined as all reporters and editors on the staffs of the Albuquerque Journal and the Albuquerque Tribune. The family-owned Journal represents the largest newspaper in New Mexico with a circulation of approximately 121,000. The Tribune is delivered in the afternoon to about 16,000 subscribers, the vast majority of whom live in Albuquerque. It is owned by Scripps Howard.

We were given permission to distribute questionnaires during the same time period in which we sought responses from the students. The staff list for the Journal included 144 reporters and editors while the list for the Tribune totaled.

INTERVIEWING

Questionnaire items for students and professional journalists were identical in every respect practical. We used paper-and pencil, self-administered questionnaires for both groups. The availability of students in classroom settings allowed us to directly distribute and administer their questionnaires (N=317 respondents), but this degree of supervision was not practical for the professionals' questionnaires.

In both newsrooms, we requested that an administrative assistant place a questionnaire, cover letter, and return envelope in the mail slots of all reporters and editors. Two weeks after the questionnaires were distributed, we distributed a reminder letter to coax potential respondents who had failed to complete a questionnaire.

This procedure produced a response rate of 59% for the Journal and 57% for the Tribune. These can be considered relatively high response rates given that the interviews were voluntary and unsupervised. The final sample consists of N=117 professional journalists.

DESCRIPTION OF SAMPLES

Descriptive statistics reveal a range of interest within the student sample regarding journalism as a career goal. When asked if they plan to pursue a career in journalism, 55% disagreed or strongly disagreed, 16% indicated they were not sure, and 29% agreed or strongly agreed.

For the sample of professional journalists, we sought to gather data reflecting variance in newsroom status among reporters and editors. When asked how many years they had worked in journalism, 42% indicated 1 to 10 years, 26% indicated 11-20 years, and 32% reported more than 20 years.

CIVIC JOURNALISM MEASURES

One question asked explicitly about civic journalism: "Several newspapers in recent years have initiated projects known as 'civic journalism.'

Indicate the extent to which you agree with the goals of

civic journalism." Respondents were asked to answer using a 1-5 scale for each question, with 1 meaning "strongly disagree" and 5 indicating "strongly agree." No answer (NA) was coded as 3.

Two items described goals: "Local media should focus on news that directly helps a community solve its problems." "Local media should go beyond simply reporting news in efforts to increase public participation."

Two items described practices: "Local media should sponsor community meetings to help citizens solve problems." "Reader or viewer interest polls should be used to help journalists decide what should be covered."

Predictors of Support for Civic Journalism. Variables used to predict students' support for civic journalism include journalism experiences in college and support for traditional media roles.

College Journalism Instruction. A summed two-item scale (r=.40) assessed the extent of formal instruction:

"Are you a major in the UNM Department of Communication & Journalism?"

"How many news writing courses have you taken at the college level? Include any courses taken this semester."

Career Anticipation. A summed 6-item scale (alpha=.85) measured the extent to which students had anticipated a career in journalism. Responses to the first two questions were coded as yes=2; no, NA=1.

"Do you plan to write news for the Daily Lobo?"

"Do you plan to undertake a news writing or editing internship?"

For the remaining questions, respondents used a 1-5 scale with 1 meaning "strongly disagree" and 5 "strongly agree."

"I plan to pursue a career in journalism."

"I hope to work in a newsroom."

"My interest in a news-related career is growing stronger.

"I have always wanted to be a journalist."

College Newsroom Experience. A summed two-item scale (r=.38) assessed the extent of involvement with the university newspaper.

"Have you been a news writer for the Daily Lobo?"

"Have you worked as an editor for the Daily Lobo?"

Dissemination Role. A single item measured support for the role of news media in disseminating information. Respondents used a 1-5 scale, with 1 meaning "not important" and 5 indicating "extremely important."

"How important is it for the media to concentrate on news that is of interest to the widest possible public?"

Interpretive Role. A single item scale measured support for the interpretive role of news media in covering public affairs.

"How important is it for the media to provide analysis and interpretation of complex problems?"

Adversary Role: A summed two-item scale (r=.18) measured support for the role of the media in acting as an adversary of government.

"How important is it for the media to be an adversary of public officials by being constantly skeptical of their decisions?"

"How important is it for the media to investigate claims and statements made by government?"

The five civic journalism measures were first entered together in a one-way repeated-measures multivariate analysis of variance (MANOVA), with journalism experience (student without newsroom experience, student with newsroom experience, professional) as the independent variable. Using all four algorithms, the analysis showed a significant effect for the dependent variables considered together.

When the civic journalism measures were subjected to separate one-way ANOVAs, significant effects were obtained for the following items: local media should go beyond reporting news to increase participation, local media should sponsor meetings, and polls should be used to help journalists decide on news coverage.

With respect to the premise that news media should attempt to increase participation, there was not a significant difference between students with newsroom experience and professionals-both expressed significantly less support for this goal compared to the students without newsroom experience. The same pattern occurred with the practice of local media sponsoring meetings.

These results suggest that students with newsroom experience were becoming more like professionals and less like their fellow students in their evaluations of civic journalism. Finally, the professionals expressed significantly less support, in comparison to both groups of students, for the use of polls to help journalists decide on coverage. Collectively, the three cases show a clear pattern of decreasing support for civic journalism as the respondents gain experience via newsroom participation.

The first research question asks whether college students, in comparison to professionals, express stronger support for the attitudinal item that explicitly mentions "civic journalism" as a reform movement.

No significant difference was found. RQ2 addresses whether college students express stronger support for civic journalism goals. The means for students and professionals are nearly identical with respect to the premise that local media should focus on news that helps a community to solve problems.

But in the comparison between students without newsroom experience and professionals, a statistically significant difference exists for the item that concerns media going beyond reporting to increase public participation. While the first goal describes an agenda-setting function that facilitates a community response to a problem, it apparently does not evoke suspicion among the professionals to the extent of the second goal.

To "go beyond" the reporting of news might have suggested a kind of advocacy journalism to the professional respondents. Hi states that the students will express stronger support for practices associated with civic journalism. Both measures generated significant differences between the student and professional respondents, in support of Hl.

The second practice in particular (use of polls) would challenge autonomy if respondents interpreted it as diminishing the importance of professional expertise. In the interpretation of these results, it is useful to consider that civic journalism has existed for only about ten years, and consequently the older professional respondents would not have been exposed to it while in college.

Meanwhile, neither of the Albuquerque papers had conducted projects identified as civic journalism. As for the students' exposure, their journalism programme had not adopted civic journalism as a regular component of the curriculum.

Thus, we urge caution in making inferences that would generalize these results. For example, Arant and Meyer found that the amount of civic journalism support was related to whether a newspaper had previously conducted a project.

H2 proposes that students with campus newspaper experience will be less supportive of civic journalism compared to other students. Lending support to H2, students with newsroom experience were less supportive of the goal in which media go beyond reporting to increase participation. This is also the case for the practice of news media sponsoring meetings.

We consider next the importance of campus newspaper experience in relation to other experiences that might explain the erosion of civic journalism support. We decided to examine this deterioration of support with respect to a civic journalism practice in light of our theoretical argument that specific techniques, rather than abstract goals, would more likely generate opposition as professional socialization proceeds.

The largest variance in student responses occurred with the item that advocates media sponsorship of meetings. This variable was used as the dependent variable in a multiple regression model in which the three indicators of educational experiences are entered as an initial block of independent variables. The second block includes the measures of support for traditional media roles.

In the first equation, only newspaper experience accounted for a significant amount of variance. The beta is negative, demonstrating that writing and editing for a campus newspaper diminish potential support for civic journalism.

The second equation addresses RQ3: Will support for traditional media roles predict support for civic journalism? The attitudinal measure for the interpretive role did account for significant incremental variance, but support for the dissemination and adversary roles did not.

All of the betas were positive, however. While these results do not provide overwhelming support in favour of RQ3, they certainly do not suggest a scenario in which the adoption of civic journalism values is accompanied by a rejection of the traditional roles for news media. This study represents the first empirical effort to model the origins of civic journalism values as a function of professional socialization during the college years.

The results confirmed that students tended to be more supportive of civic journalism in comparison to professionals who work in the same community. Gaps between the student and professional respondents emerged when questionnaire items described specific practices that violate the norm of detachment, such as news media promotion of town hall meetings. A subsequent analysis of factors that might explain these results suggests a scenario of professional socialization that begins with students predisposed to support civic journalism. Acquisition of these values during the college years, meanwhile, is not associated with an erosion of commitment to traditional roles.

However, in leaving the classroom for the newsroom, the unmaking of civic journalists might occur as reporters and editors develop a stronger sense of autonomy. One experience in particular— working for the campus paper-appears to instill a sense of autonomy that diminishes acceptance of civic journalism.

A BROADER VIEW OF AUTONOMY

College instruction would ideally promote an open-minded orientation to journalistic roles and an appreciation for both the limitations of routine reporting and the potential for innovation. But those who would reform the curriculum to promote civic journalism must acknowledge the inherent need for increased autonomy during the beginning stages of professional socialization.

The desire for autonomy is an inevitable outcome of the process by which students identify with the profession. Journalistic autonomy, consequently, should be appreciated not as a fixed disposition but as a developmental process.

From the perspective of civic journalism advocates, the results of this study highlight the need for college instruction to encourage a broader conception of journalistic autonomy. However, would-be reformers should acknowledge the importance of autonomy for students and for professionals rather than issuing a wholesale attack on editorial detachment.

The irony of professional autonomy is that it is the best hope for implementing reform even as editorial detachment appears to preclude civic journalism. Civic journalism can challenge students and professionals to reconceptualize autonomy as the independence to transcend conventional practices that would otherwise limit the contribution of the press to democratic life.

LIMITATIONS AND FUTURE RESEARCH

The results of this chapter are based on a single study in one community, thus restricting any inferential claims based on an assumption of external validity. But the findings reflect a certain degree of construct validity given our emphasis on autonomy as a professional value that should dampen support for civic journalism.

Students who work for a campus newspaper should be moving closer to professionals and away from fellow students; the data consistently fit this pattern across various measures of civic journalism support.

Future research would ideally incorporate a panel design of at least two years' duration, with a larger and broader sample of respondents, to track the development of journalistic values as students enter the initial stage of their professional careers. Studies should also incorporate direct attitudinal measures of autonomy as a professional value to supplement the attitudinal and experiential measures used in this study.

We suggest a framework for field research based on the development of operational measures that represent the twentieth-century ethos of professional journalism (e.g., detachment, free press, watchdog role, people's right to know, criticizing institutions) alongside the civic journalism approach (e.g., social responsibility, community building, self-criticizing press institutions, problem-solving).

This approach might generate insight that can be used for the reform of journalism instruction as educators promote autonomy in service to democracy. Public journalism began as a series of experiments in the late 1980s and early 1990s, and soon developed into what Schudson has called "the most impressive critique of journalistic practice inside journalism in a generation" and "the best organized social movement inside journalism in the history of the American press."

Also known as civic journalism, the movement arose in response to a perceived crisis in the role of the press in constituting a public sphere in which citizens could understand and engage productively with the issues of the day. During the first decade, the movement generated an array of innovative practices in newsrooms and communities, as well as an extensive network of journalism practitioners and educators committed to reshaping professional and institutional norms.

The primary philosophical emphasis of public journalism, as manifest in the writings of its leading theorists and practitioners, is on the relationship between the practice of journalism and the democratic work of citizens in a self-governing republic, and suggests journalists are ideally suited to help constitute vital "publics" to deliberate complex issues and engage in collective problem-solving activities.

Public journalism, thus, has set out to help members of the public come to see themselves as citizens, and hold them accountable for grappling with the full complexity of issues and become participants in civil society rather than mere spectators of it.

Still, after more than a decade of practice of public journalism, empirical knowledge of whether and how public journalism has met these goals remains largely based on in-depth case studies. Early literature focused on cases generally acknowledged as the seed-beds of the public journalism movement.

Subsequent comparative research examined other best cases, focusing on changes in newsroom reporting and editing practices, community recognition of public journalism efforts, and shifts in community problem-solving and public deliberation. While researchers found positive evidence in each area, elements were not disaggregated and case studies were often idiosyncratic, making it difficult to measure impact or establish clear relationships among elements.

In their critical review of forty-seven evaluative studies of public journalism, Massey and Haas found that public journalism practices have had limited effects on the attitudes, beliefs, and behaviours of news audiences. They criticize existing research for focusing on "a handful of showcase public-journalism news organizations and projects."

In doing so, they highlight the methodological shortcomings of many of the efforts to assess public journalism, and recommend that future research capture a wider array of experiments and trace the effects of these efforts on community life. With prior research lacking a broad, systematic assessment of public journalism efforts, we set out to provide a holistic analysis of the movement, shedding light on participating organizations, practices, and effects.

An inventory of the archives of the Pew Centre for Civic Journalism found 651 public journalism projects conducted from 1994 to 20027 Our research analyses the inventory using hierarchical regression analysis to trace the effects of organizational factors, project features, story frames, and efforts to involve community members and assess public opinion on three civil society goals:

- Improving citizens' civic competencies,
- Influencing policymaking processes, and
- Increasing civic volunteerism.

The literature on public journalism is extensive, but extracting clear empirical propositions is challenging. First, much of the best literature is normative, advocating a role of the press in improving public life, and tends to draw case-based observations about changes public journalism creates in news organizations.

Second, the large body of case literature is very uneven, ranging from anecdotal and polemic to qualitative and comparative case observation. While it is difficult to untangle the effects of public journalism on civil society given these inconsistencies, there are important insights to be gained from the extant research.

Public journalism research has primarily concentrated on several flagship public journalism newsrooms and projects. Additionally, there are numerous case studies of other cities and regions. These cases, however, have not been analysed using a systematic empirical-quantitative framework.

Here, we consider the scholarship in three domains of public journalism:

- Organization of newsrooms and their effects on individual journalists' values, norms, and behaviour;
- Links between public journalism efforts and changes in news content, framing, and sourcing; and
- Public journalism's impact on electoral knowledge and behaviour, and on citizen participation in public life.

MEDIA ORGANIZATIONS AND NEWS VALUES

There are two broad types of newsroom studies: (1) of news organizations; and (2) of journalists' beliefs and attitudes. While there are no inherent methodological contradictions between them, each tends to have its own understandings of how public journalism is established in newsrooms.

Organizational studies see the adoption of public

journalism from the top down, with publisher and editor orientations as the important predictors of public journalism practice. An investment by news organizations in public journalism shapes reporting routines and story content, and accounts for the adoption of the practice over longer periods of time.

This approach posits institutionalization as a property of the organization, with organizational decisions molding the actions and routines, if not beliefs, of individuals within them. Evidence suggests that newsrooms institutionalizing public journalism (i.e., commitments to partnerships with other community organizations and lengthy projects) produce stronger public effects.

A second approach looks at the effect of values of journalists on attitudes and behaviour. Here, the adoption of public journalism values is a prerequisite for genuine individual transformation that leads to newsroom change. Proponents of this approach hold that positive attitudes toward public journalism should precede behavioural change."

This values approach, then, sees change in beliefs and attitudes as generating new public reporting behaviour that underlies the transformation of news organizations. From their review of public journalism studies, Massey and Haas found that journalists are most comfortable with the more "traditional" shadings of public journalism, though some support for more "activist" roles exists.

These mixed results indicate traditional and public journalism beliefs seem to coexist in many newsrooms and within individual journalists, suggesting an "occupational pragmatism." Not surprisingly, "mixed-change" characterizes virtually every case of public journalism, positing a kind of "tipping point" within newsrooms and individuals.

If newsrooms have not tipped, public journalism practice should be weak. As this suggests, both the organizational approach and the news values approach ultimately focus on the degree to which newsrooms have adopted and integrated public journalism practices into the newsroom culture, regardless of whether the spur of this transformation is from the top down or the bottom up.

NEWS COVERAGE AND CONTENT

Research on changes in reporting spurred by public journalism is sparse, with little attention to whether certain topics or frames of reporting are particularly suited to public journalism. Although public journalism often implicitly focuses on community, efforts have addressed a plethora of issues confronting localities, including crime, diversity, education, environment, health, poverty, and, of course, elections and government.

Public journalists have utilized a range of issue frames to structure their reporting, from established conflict and human-interest frames to more novel problem-solving and historical frames. However, little is known about the potency of these framing devices for civil society outcomes or whether certain topics lend themselves to successful public journalism as defined by increases in civic competence and volunteerism.

Instead, most coverage studies focus on the type of content and sources used in public journalism stories, with inconsistent evidence. Some indicate little difference in content, while others have found that public journalism efforts have a greater focus on local concerns and help citizens engage in civic activities.

There is also inconsistent evidence on sourcing. Thus, it remains unclear whether certain public journalism tools, such as encouraging citizen involvement or giving citizen voices greater prominence, improves civil society outcomes.

EFFECTS OF PUBLIC JOURNALISM

The evidence for public journalism effects on civic and public life is partial and incomplete. Studies divide broadly into those investigating the effect of public journalism on electoral outcomes and those addressing civic and public problem solving.

First, there is evidence supporting a positive relationship between citizenfocused journalism and knowledge, trust, and civic participation in elections. There is, however, some evidence to the contrary. Thus, on the whole, studies support a moderate effect of civic electoral coverage in the areas of voter awareness of issues and traditional forms of political participation.

Although untangling political cause and effect is difficult, there is a case for public journalism efforts and broader public engagement. Studies have found an increase in political participation. There is also some evidence that public journalism increases public deliberation and civic problem solving. Moreover, Friedland's study of the "We the People" project in Madison, Wisconsin, found project longevity to have substantial cumulative impact on opinion leaders, media cooperation, and institutional effectiveness, with mixed effects on citizen engagement. If there is episodic coverage with little follow-up, however, a project's cumulative problem-solving effects were attenuated.

In sum, the case-based evidence shows effects of increased civic and public problem solving in limited areas. Past theorizing and case studies concerning the practices and effects of public journalism do not present a clear picture of the consequences of this shift in coverage for civil society. Scholars have focused on different levels of analysis-organization, newsroom, story, and citizens-and attended to a wide range of outcome variables.

Results have not been consistent, though this inconsistency may be a function of community and organizational factors that are not the focus of a particular case study. After a decade of broad practice, it is unclear which organizational factors beyond length of adoption and integration of public journalism contribute to the success of public journalism efforts.

Likewise, beyond attention to certain patterns of sourcing and shifts in content, it is not known whether the success of public journalism efforts is connected with attention to certain topics-such as poverty or crime-and particular frames of reference - such as human interest or problem-solving.

On a more basic level, evidence is lacking on whether

particular ways of giving voice to the perspectives of citizens improve civil society in the ways that theorists of public journalism attest. Accordingly, we examine here the effects of a wide range of potentially explanatory variables on assessments of the outcomes of a wide cross-section of public journalism efforts between 1994 and 2002. This study attempts to answer how the influence of organizational factors, project features, story frames, and efforts to involve community members and assess public opinion uniquely contribute to three broad goals of public journalism: (1) improving civic skills among citizens; (2) influencing the policymaking process; and (3) increasing levels of civic volunteerism.

Accordingly, we offer the following research questions to guide our analysis:

- RQ1: What features of news organizations involved in public journalism projects appear to influence whether sponsored efforts increase civic skills of citizens, public input on policymaking, and levels of civic volunteerism?
- RQ2: What features of public journalism projects appear to influence whether sponsored efforts increase civic skills of citizens, public input on policymaking, and levels of civic volunteerism?
- RQ3: What types of story frames used by journalists involved in public journalism projects appear to influence whether sponsored efforts increase civic skills of citizens, public input on policymaking, and levels of civic volunteerism?
- RQ4: What types of efforts to involve community members and assess public opinion appear to influence whether sponsored efforts increase civic skills of citizens, public input on policymaking, and levels of civic volunteerism?

METHODS

Data

This study is based on data collected at the University of

Wisconsin-Madison from the archives of the Pew Centre for Civic Journalism. During its ten years of operation as the principle incubator for the movement, between 1993 and 2003, the Pew Centre collected examples of public journalism projects submitted by U.S. newsrooms seeking funding, competing for awards, and/or seeking informal recognition and advice.

Between January 2000 and May 2001, this archive was systematically examined for all evidence of public journalism experiments, with the archive structured into a set of cases organized by discrete projects and publication dates.

A qualitative coding scheme was developed to capture a descriptive account of project attributes, including, but not limited to: the news organization (circulation, population served, partnerships); the project (topic, publication dates, presentation format); the news frames, sources, and civic linkages used in news construction; and the civic practices, polls, and public deliberative events used to give citizens a voice.

In addition, outcomes such as improved civic and deliberative skills, increased public funding and volunteerism, and improved public policy processes were gauged from these reports.

A quantitative coding guide was developed so that statistical tools could be used to more systematically analyse these data. The final inventory of the archive contained a total of 651 cases of public journalism completed between 1994 and 2002.

Although the study sample is limited to public journalism projects in the Pew Centre's archive and undercounts the full range of public journalism work conducted by U.S. newsrooms during this period, it captures public journalism as practiced by the most dedicated of self-identified public journalism practitioners.

Thus, the sample, while biased in favour of best practices, provides a solid foundation upon which to assess a broad range of public journalism practices and evaluate the movement's reach and impact on community life.

Measures

Items coded from the public journalism projects were used to operationalize six general clusters of variables: (1) outcomes of the public journalism project, (2) features of the news organization, (3) features of the project, (4) features of the stories, particularly story frames, (5) citizen involvement, and (6) public assessment.

In the analyses reported in this chapter, the outcomes of public journalism were used as dependent variables predicted by the other five sets of variables.

OUTCOMES OF PUBLIC JOURNALISM

Initially, six outcomes of public journalism projects were identified: improved citizenship skills, enhanced public deliberative processes, increased private funding and donations, expanded volunteer efforts, and greater public policy and civic organization responsiveness.

These items were dummy coded with "present" coded as 1, "absent" as O. The six items were then examined through exploratory factor analysis and three factors emerged.

First, improved civic competence is an additive index consisting of two measures of public journalism outcomes: improved citizenship skills and improved public deliberative processes second, improved political process was constructed by adding two items: changes in public policy and the formation of new civic organizations.

Finally, heightened volunteerism is a two-item additive index consisting of measures of raised private funds and donations, and increased level of volunteer efforts.

FEATURES OF THE NEWS ORGANIZATION

For news organizations' publication schedule, daily publication was coded as 1 and all other scheduling formats as zero. Level of circulation was measured using a six-point scale with 1 representing circulations under 50,000 and 6 representing circulations over 5 million.

Type of population served was measured on a four-point scale with 1 for smaller populations and 4 a national audience.

Level of involvement in public journalism represents the length of time in years the news organization experimented with these practices.

Partnerships was coded for evidence of other media or civic organizations involved in the project with "none" coded as 0 "either media or civic" as 1, and "both civic and media" as 2.35

FEATURES OF THE PROJECT

Eleven specific categories were identified to code each project according to the primary topic covered, including community, crime, diversity, economy, education, environment, health, poverty, youth, election, and government.

These items were dummy coded with "present" coded as 1, "absent" as 0 Project branding was constructed with three items, each used to develop a unique project identification,- including evidence of a formal presentation format, clearly stated aim of the projects, and guide for reader comprehensiveness. Each item was dummy-coded with 1 being "present," O being "absent."

Mobilizing information consisted of two items: empowerment information (to help citizens engage in civic activities) and civic linkages (contact information for public officials and civic leaders). Each item was dummy-coded with "present" coded as 1, "absent" as 0.

STORY FRAMES

Each project was coded according to six frames used in journalistic reporting: investigative frame, conflict frame, issue-oriented frame, problem-solving frame, human-interest frame, and historical frame. These items were dummy-coded with 1 representing a frame being "present," 0 for "absent."

CITIZEN INVOLVEMENT

To measure a project's effort to include citizens' input, each case was coded for evidence of (a) inviting citizens to provide feedback, and (b) giving them a voice in the publication of their community's conversation. These two variables were dummy-coded with 1 for "present," 0 for "absent."

Each project was also coded for evidence of the news organization's effort to assess the climate of opinion on the project and/or issue including (a) survey and (b) focus group research. Surveys could be the organization's own scientific or informal surveys, or surveys provided by other sources. Each was dummy-coded with 1 for "present," 0 for "absent."

RESULTS

In order to examine the relationships between public journalism efforts and their purported impact on civic competence, the political process, and volunteerism, we performed hierarchical multiple regression analyses in which organizational factors, project features, story frames, and efforts to involve community members and assess public opinion served as independent variables predicting the three criterion variables.

Tables are organized in a manner that highlights the order in which the different blocks of independent variables were entered into the regression and indicates the incremental variance in the criterion variable explained by each successive block. We consider how each additional block affects the standardized betas of the variables being considered simultaneously, and focus on the final standardized coefficients for the full model.

IMPROVED CIVIC COMPETENCE

The regression model predicting improved civic competence performed quite well, as it accounted for a total of 52.9% of variance. The features of the news organization were substantial predictors (20.4% of variance), with news organizations that served small or medium communities and that partnered either with civic organizations or other media the most successful.

Improved citizenship was also anchored in the actual features of the public journalism project (16.4% of incremental variance). The focus on certain social problems such as poverty seems well suited for the purpose of improving citizenship. On the other hand a focus on negative or individualized concerns such as crime and health counter this objective. The news frames utilized in public journalism stories accounted for 10.3% of the variance in the model. Among the frames, it seems clear that the problem-solving frame was most closely linked with reported improvement in citizenship. Conversely, the human-interest frame appeared to produce the opposite effects, reducing the perception of an increase in civic skills among the audience exposed to public journalism efforts.

Above and beyond characteristics of the news organization, features of the project, and selection of story frames, enhanced citizenship seemed to be contingent on involving citizens in the process of public journalism. In our model this block accounted for 4.6% of the final variance, with inviting audience/reader feedback and giving citizens an actual voice serving as key contributors.

In addition, administering surveys in the community was also positively related to improving citizenship in the community. In the final model, public journalism's reported ability to improve citizenship was linked

- To news organizations that serve smaller communities and partner with other community organizations,
- To projects that focus on topics such as poverty as opposed to crime or health,
- To reporting that adopted problem-solving story frames over human interest story frames, and
- To project elements that involved citizens through feedback, sourcing, and surveys.

These findings support many of the conclusions drawn from case study analysis, while clarifying how these different factors intersect to shape citizenship.

IMPROVED POLITICAL PROCESS

The regression model used to gauge political process

improvements—accounted for 22.6% of the variance. In this model, the features of the news organization were not as critical as in the previous model, accounting for only 4.2% of the total variance explained. In the final model, only a single organizational factor-partnerships with other community or media organizations-was a significant predictor of improvements in the political process.

The features of the project were substantial predictors of an improved political process, with 10.8% of the variance explained by this block. Among this group, community and education topics are positively related with the dependent variable, while concentrating on the poverty topic is negatively related.

This suggests limited responsiveness in terms of process responsiveness when projects address the needs of the underprivileged. The framing of news also explained variation in improving the political process, with the investigative frame as the strongest predictor, followed by a problem-solving frame. Conflict, explanatory, and human-interest frames appear to be irrelevant for this purpose, while the use of a historical frame is negatively related.

This seems to indicate that attention to long-standing community issues is less effective at spurring political responsiveness than focused attention on current problems or scandals. Engaging citizens with the project or seeking their opinion does not seem to be particularly consequential for improvements to the political process.

These two blocks only account for.5% of the incremental variance and yield no significant predictors. In the final model, then, partnerships, reporting on community and education (as opposed to poverty), and investigative and problem-solving (but not historical) story frames appear to spur responsiveness in terms of improvements to the political process.

IMPROVED VOLUNTEERISM

The model predicting levels of volunteerism in the community explained 22.7% of the variance. As was the case for improving the political process, organizational features do not play as large a role as they do in improving citizenship, explaining only 3.1% of the variance in reports of improved volunteerism, whereas project features explained a sizable amount (13.5%) of incremental variance.

Again, establishing a partnership with another news or civic organization is positively related to increased volunteerism, making this a consistent predictor across all three models. Project topics such as community, crime, and education are linked with reports of increased volunteerism.

In terms of news framing, concentrating on human-interest seems to increase civic volunteerism, whereas historical frames have the opposite effect, consistent with the negative association in the model explaining political process improvement. This block explains 5.0% of the incremental variance.

Finally it seems that citizens' engagement with the project and seeking citizens' opinions are not necessary to improve volunteerism. The model shows a small incremental contribution of these two blocks (incremental variance explained 1.1%) with only the use of surveys actually being negatively related to volunteerism.

In sum, partnerships; reporting on community, crime, and education; and human-interest (but not historical) story frames appear to spur reported increases in volunteerism. This study is the first to explore a broad range of public journalism projects, incorporating a near census of the field of efforts between 1994 and 2002 and tracing the reported effects on civil society.

Further, it incorporates multiple levels of specificity, examining the effects of organizational features, particular projects, story frames, and citizen involvement in civic and public life. Our findings, thus, provide the first holistic assessment of the impact of public journalism on U.S. civil society and critical insights for future research and practice. Before we discuss these implications, we first offer an interpretation of these findings and discuss some of their limitations.

Although we find organizational features such as publication schedule, circulation level, and population type are associated with certain civil society goals of public journalism, most of these effects appear to be mediated through the structure of public journalism projects and journalistic framing.

One organizational feature is consistently found to shape the general success of these efforts: partnerships with other organizations. In our final models, partnerships predicted improved citizenship, political processes, and volunteerism, indicating me centrality of organizations' connections for efforts to renew civil society.

This seems most true of efforts to improve citizenship, where institutional connections may provide the basis for civic recruitment and broader project scope. Additionally, a project's focus also appears to be linked to certain civil society outcomes.

A focus on education, community, crime, and poverty were found to relate to the achievement (or failure) of civil society goals. The potency of a particular issue varied across these goals. For example, focusing on community and education was related to positive effects on the political process and civic volunteerism, with projects focusing on crime also linked to volunteerism.

The positive association of the these topics on political process and volunteerism outcomes suggests that projects directed at issues affecting larger cross-sections of the population are particularly effective at improving processes and spurring action.

Notably, a negative relationship was detected between a focus on crime and health topics-individualized issues typically directed at those with higher socio-economic status- and the improvement of civic skills, whereas a focus on poverty was found to have a positive effect on the development of civic competencies, as might be expected.

However, a focus on poverty was negatively related to improvements in the political process, suggesting a lack of elite responsiveness to issues affecting the underprivileged.

Future research must work to disentangle these effects and identify the types of issues that produce desirable community outcomes.

Particularly notable are the results regarding the emphasis on certain story frames. Our findings suggest that problem-solving frames have the most pronounced effects on efforts to improve citizenship and the political process, and investigative news frames were also positively correlated with improvements in the political process.

In sharp contrast, however, human-interest and historical news frames appeared to generally reduce the success of public journalism efforts at achieving civil society goals, particularly in relation to citizenship. Our results for human-interest frames show a reduction in the development of civic skills, yet an increase in civic volunteerism, which is surprising given past research on episodic framing and the reduction of a sense of shared responsibility.

46 For historical news frames, we observed negative effects on both political process and volunteerism outcomes, suggesting that projects revolving around long-standing issues are less effective at spurring political or public responses. This pattern of results points to the importance of journalistic choices in framing news stories around certain themes and organizing devices.

Investigative and problem-solving frames would appear to spur involvement and action, whereas historical frames, and to a lesser extent human interest frames, appear to reduce responsiveness to community problems. While not invalidating frames that spur long-term reflection on deep-seated problems, these results do question how stories are organized and presented.

Further, it may be that the cross-sectional nature of these case assessments does not allow an observation of the effects of certain story frames over time. Finally, efforts to involve citizens in public journalism-i.e., inviting feedback from citizens, giving them a voice in coverage and their communities, and surveying their attitudes and behaviours-were linked to the improvement of civic competencies.

In total, these results suggest that journalists who understand the perspectives of citizens are more able to construct projects that improve citizens' civic and deliberative skills. It may also be that asking citizens for their perspective and giving them public forums is fundamentally mobilizing, something we might call a type of "civic Hawthorne effect."

This study, while comprehensive, is not without limitations. Most notably, the cases that function as our units of analysis rely on some self assessment of effects by the editors and journalists involved in the projects. This may create some biases. However, these would seem to be equivalent across all news organizations in the study, thereby rendering differences observed meaningful.

Moreover, every effort was made to validate the outcome variables, which were often self-assessed against real world indicators of change. The reliability of these self-assessments was found to be well above the threshold for acceptability, further suggesting the validity of the data. The implications of this study, even with these limitations, are broad-reaching. They can be used to inform the next generation of public journalism efforts and structure research efforts. Future research should consider the longitudinal effects of public journalism projects on civil society. Using small-N comparative historical methods, researchers might more closely explore the precise configurations of organization, project, and story frame that lead to the most effect on civic and public outcomes.

Finally, there are broad theoretical implications of our study. If historical frames are demobilizing, for example, what alternative frames could address long-term, deep-seated community problems addressed by journalists interested in democracy? If problem-solving and investigative frames are mobilizing, what are the specific features of these types of projects that encourage changes in civil society? If certain topics seem to lend themselves to successful public journalism outcomes, how might coverage of other issues be constructed to spur responsiveness on the part of the public and policymakers?

Clearly, there is much that remains to be learned about the effects of public journalism projects on civil society. Nonetheless, if the findings presented here are any indication, the effects of the projects are considerable and broad reaching, and certainly provide empirical support for the normative project of public journalism.

Chapter 9

Network Theory to the Use of Hyperlinks in Journalism

Recent research into the growth patterns of the Web has uncovered principles that help us understand networks of all types. Unlike many networks which evolve slowly and imperceptibly, the Web has exploded before our eyes. From a few hundred Web pages in the early 1990s to more than a billion a decade later, the intricately linked Web became a perfect natural experiment for the study of network growth. Contrary to an early hypothesis that much network structure occurs randomly, researchers discovered a predictable order in its evolution, one that applies to a wide and diverse range of network structures.

The present study applies the lessons learned from the Web as a whole to a unique subset of the Web, journalism Web sites. Like the larger Web, stories on news Web sites are linked, both internally and externally. If the patterns of this linked network follow newly developed theories, predictions about the use of hyperlinks in Web news may be possible. This study began preserving Web data in 1997 for future examination and attempts to answer two primary questions.

First, do Web news stories follow the growth pattern typical of the Web as a whole second, what types of stories are heavily linked? Contextual potential is offered as a predictor for the use of hyperlinks by Web journalists. A typical news story's mix of new fact, old fact, assertion, and interpretation has changed over the last two centuries. From 1790 to 1980, Schudson found a "decline of 'facts'" and a corresponding increase in interpretation in reporting on the State of the Union address.

Barnhurst and Mutz documented a century-long shift toward long journalism, long on interpretation and context, short on new fact. The role of technology in these changes has also been explored. Nerone and Barnhurst found a shift in newspaper design that resulted in fewer small individual news items.

The effects of television on the content of newspaper stories have also been examined. Iyengar found print coverage of elections to be more contextually bound (or thematic) compared to television coverage that was more episodic. Over time, the decline of fact-driven reporting first seen in print revealed itself in television news, which also shifted to more analysis and speculation.

Journalism scholars disagree on the proper use of contextual material in news stories. Barnhurtz and Mutz say the shift to long journalism is unfortunate for several reasons. Isolated events are ignored; interpretive journalism is often boring; and facts are replaced with opinion, abstraction, and "discouraging problems."

Others disagree. A prominent journalism association recently concluded that, "Journalism's first obligation is to the truth. Democracy depends on citizens having reliable, accurate facts put in a meaningful context." In this view, facts alone aren't enough; a framework for interpretation is required.

Some have concluded that more, not less, context is needed. Schudson appreciates both views. He was among the first to document the decline of facts in journalism amidst a shift toward what he called a culture of criticism. At the same time, he is wary of the media's "fetishism of the present" that reports events absent historical context.

The technology of the Web allows news presentations that might satisfy both those wanting shorter fact-driven accounts and those wanting context, interpretation, and opinion. Take, for example, a CNN.com story that was posted to the Web at 8:58 a.m. on 23 March 2003 and headlined,

"Iraqis Put Up Fight at Umm Qsar." The story covers events of the war with Iraq during the preceding twenty-four hours. The main page runs about 800 words and recounts eight distinct incidents. After a two- or three-paragraph summary of each incident, the reader is offered a link to the "full story."

One incident has a link to two stories; one is the U.S. version of events, the other the Iraqi version. Along the right side of the screen are links to additional material. Within one click there are approximately 8,000 words of contextual material, two slide shows, two interactive maps, and five video reports. Most of these pages have links to still more related material.

The primary 800-word story is event-focused and short on context. The linked material, however, provides historical, geographical (maps), political, and international context. This material also includes opinion and alternative interpretive frames through the publication of readers' views, both pro- and anti-war.

This story is not typical, even for the Web. But its existence is predictable and follows from newly published theories governing networks of all types.

NETWORK THEORY AND THE GROWTH OF THE WEB

Networks, or graphs, have been an object of study for centuries. Swiss mathematician Leonhard Euler introduced the idea when studying a problem concerning bridges and land masses. Any distribution of similar objects (nodes) that are interconnected in some way (links) can be considered a network. They occur in nature, such as neural networks, or can be man made, such as power distribution grids. The first explanation for how commonly occurring network structures form came more than two hundred years after Euler's discoveries in the work of mathematicians Paul Erdos and Alfred Renyi.

They proposed random graph theory, the idea that networks are essentially the end result of links being formed between random pairs of nodes. Each link forms independently of all others and the clustering of links around some nodes is explained by chance.

This explanation went unchallenged as most researchers focused instead on information flow through networks rather than evolution of the network itself. In the 1960s, Rogers studied the flow of ideas through social systems. This work explored both the individual adoption process and the large group diffusion process.

In the latter area, Granovetter argued that ideas are spread most widely not by persons in the middle of a cluster of acquaintances, but by peripheral members who spend time in multiple social circles. Granovetter's work suggested that the independence assumption of random graph theory was violated in the case of social networks.

His conceptualization of the "strength" of a social tie included how much time individuals dedicated to its establishment and maintenance. Because an individual's time is limited, establishment of future ties is dependent, in part, on the existence of current ties. Certainly geography and other factors also limit possible social ties. For this type of network, and many others, an alternative structural explanation is needed.

Barabasi and Albert used the rapid growth of the Web as a testing ground to construct a theory of network development. Each Web page has a number of ties (links) to other Web pages. If random graph theory applied in this context, there would be a small number of pages with few or no links, a small number with a huge number of links, and the majority with an average number of links; in other words, a normal distribution.

For the Web, they found a curve with a degree exponent of 2.1 for incoming links to a page and an exponent of 2.5 for outgoing links from Web pages. There are a small number of pages that have hundreds or even thousands of links; these are called hubs. The majority of Web pages have very few links. To say the average Web page has ten links means little, then, because most will have fewer and some will have a hundred times that.

Distributions following a power law also conform to Pareto's law, the so-called 80/20 rule. Pareto, a nineteenth-century engineer, observed that approximately 20% of the population earns 80% of the income. Only in the late 1990s did researchers begin understanding why naturally occurring networks follow this pattern.

Using computer simulations, Barabasi and Albert discovered two principles that explain all distributions that follow a power law: growth and preferential attachment. Another example from the Web helps illustrate the theory. If we plot Web pages by links pointing to them we will find that some (yahoo.com or ebay.com) are linked to by thousands or even millions of Web pages.

But most Web pages have very few other pages that link to them. So why do the hubs have so many links pointing to them? One reason is that some sites have been around a long time (for the Web this means since the mid1990s). As more pages and more links appear, older sites have a disproportionately greater chance of being linked to than those that are young.

So the very growth of a network favors the original nodes. But if this were the only way hubs grew, then instead of a power curve we would see a relatively straight line with old nodes having the most links, "middle age" nodes having a mean number of links, and young nodes having few links. The reason this is not the case has to do with the second principle of network growth: preferential attachment.

When choosing which pages to link to, most will choose ones that are already heavily linked. If many others find a site useful, then it becomes more likely to be chosen than more obscure pages. In this way the "rich get richer," and, proportionally, the poor get poorer.

Preferential attachment, coupled with growth, invariably leads to a distribution following a power law. Naturally occurring distributions of this type depart from scale free power curves in one respect: they are not truly scale-free. The tails of true power curves stretch to infinity, whereas real networks are finite.

One reason for this is the cost associated with adding links. Network theory assumes a low cost. Where the cost of establishing new ties is high, growth of hubs is stunted. The particular value of Barabasi and Albert's theory is its universality. It can explain networks from many unique contexts including power distribution grids, social networks, the Web, and even the neural networks of organisms.

These two principles are tested here against a subset of the Web, those pages appearing on national news Web sites. If the patterns hold for this data set, we may be able to predict what types of stories will be favored by the linked Web.

HYPOTHESES AND RESEARCH QUESTIONS

Web news editors use links in stories to point readers to additional material. If Web pages about news follow the growth patterns of the Web as a whole we should expect to find evidence of Barabasi and Albert's two principles, growth and preferred attachment. Therefore: H1: The number of links in news stories will increase over time.

As news sites' digital archives grow (stories, maps, photos, graphics, etc.), there are more opportunities for linking. While growth in the use of linking within news stories should rise across the board, preferential attachment predicts that some stories will grow at a faster rate than others.

There are a number of factors that might explain which stories are "preferred." One is context. Recall the findings of Barnhurst and Mutz concerning the use of context and interpretation in newspaper stories. They documented a century-long upward trend. Their study concerned news stories on three topics: jobs, crime, and accidents. Each type of story lengthened, but accident stories were the shortest and job stories the longest.

This makes sense if one considers the possible context a journalist could include in different stories. Many accidents will lack obvious historical, geographic, economic, social, or political context.

And consequences may not be known at press time. Stories concerning jobs, however, are likely to involve economic and political context and may also have historical and geographic aspects.

If the choices Web editors make concerning linked material are driven by contextual possibilities then we can predict that some types of stories will benefit from preferred attachment. This proposition was tested by selecting categories of news that would logically require a great deal, or very little, context. First: H2: Stories about international relations will be more heavily linked than other stories.

Stories involving negotiation or conflict between two or more countries present numerous possibilities for geographical, historical, and political context and in some cases economic and social context. Contrast this with another category used by journalism professionals: spot news. As this label implies, these are stories concerning discrete events such as accidents and crimes.

While adding context to these types of stories occurs, the possibilities may be fewer than for other news stories. Therefore: H3: Spot news stories will be less heavily linked than other stories.

The power law distribution is believed to result from the interaction of growth and preferred attachment. If this is the case, then not only should story types differ in the quantity of links but also in their respective rates of increase. Therefore: H4: The gap in the number of links used between spot news and international relations should widen over time.

Media type may also affect linking practices. When compared to print news, television news has been labeled event-driven or episodic. If this is the case we might expect Web news stories produced by television-affiliated companies to use fewer links than those produced by print-affiliated companies. However, television-based Web sites may be more likely to link to audio or video material because of its availability.

Rather than a hypothesis, the following research question is explored: RQ1: Do print- or broadcast-affiliated Web sites make greater use of hyperlinks in news stories?

Other variables that might play into preferred attachment

for Web news are considered in the conclusion. Ten U.S. national news Web sites were examined for a period of five years, from 1997 to 2001. At the beginning of this period, the 10 were the news organizations with the largest viewing audiences or circulations that had a Web news presence. Five are the Web counterparts of newspapers or magazines.

Answering the research questions required a content analysis of the Web sites. An after-the-fact data collection scheme, such as one that might be conducted for a newspaper content analysis, would not be practical for the ever-changing Web. Instead, a sample of Web news content was created by periodically recording the home pages of the 10 sites.

A systematic sample was recorded using the following scheme. In March of each year the 10 Web sites were visited every four days, with a random start for a total of seven days each year. Main page stories appearing on the screen of a standard-sized monitor were coded. This process yielded 1,493 stories or about 300 a year.

CODING AND RELIABILITY

Over the course of the project a number of variables were measured including topic, links per story, node modality (audio, video, text, etc.), internal versus external links, etc. Two of these are of interest here: topic and links per story. Hyperlinks were initially defined as any clickable text or graphic that leads to additional material related directly to the story.

What constituted "related" was left to the coders but specifically excluded standard site navigation icons and advertising links. Also excluded were next-page links and those beyond the first level. Following a hypertext story beyond the main page is problematic for coders if the story is hierarchically constructed and/or circular.

Limiting the coding to the main page is also consistent with the standard industry practice of using one primary story page and linking from it to prior and related stories as well as, in some cases, multimedia elements. Rarely do Web editors require lengthy scrolls by the user. This coding procedure thus provided some control for story length, although variance in the primary text was observed. Coding occurred at two points. In the first year of the study, testing the reliability of the links variable was logistically cumbersome due to the ever-changing nature of the Web, a fact that has been noted by others.

It was accomplished by having two coders access, on computers in separate rooms, two stories on each of the seven coding days. The 10 Web sites were sampled in alphabetical order; each was represented by one or two stories in the reliability sample. These 14 stories represented 5% of the total sample that year. Reliability on links per story was very high by Krippendorf's alpha. In 1999 the definition of hyperlink was expanded to include material obtained by placing the cursor on, but not clicking, certain Web elements (rollover graphics). By this time Web news stories had become more sophisticated, but software made it easier to preserve digital copies of hypermedia stories. Another test of reliability was conducted, using a simple random sample of 100 cases.

To these 100 cases, 66 more from the first two years of data were selected following the same method. Each story was coded for topic using the headline and sub-head. There were twelve categories including the two of interest here, spot news and international relations. Spot news was any story about a crime or an accident posted within one day of the incident. International relations stories involved conflict or cooperation between two or more countries. When two or more news categories applied, the coder was instructed to select the one considered primary. Coder agreement on story topic was by Krippendorf's alpha.

RESULTS

The links variable is heavily skewed as a result of a high number of stories (29%) having no links at all and cannot be normalized by data transformation. Use of ANOVA is not recommended for data that are skewed because results can be unreliable and statistical power forfeited, especially for smaller sample sizes. Because the sample here is large accurate p values are likely; these analyses are presented here. Nonparametric tests, which do not rely on normality, are also presented. The first hypothesis concerns a test of trend in the use of hyperlinks in Web news stories.

In 1997 the average main-page story on a U.S. national-news Web site had three links to related material. By 2000 that number more than tripled. A Kruskal-Wallis test was performed to confirm significant differences among groups. Additionally, a test of linear trend using two-way ANOVA was conducted. The growth hypothesis was confirmed.

The remaining hypotheses concern preferred attachment and were tested using a sub-sample of the Web news data which included 398 spot news and international relations stories. Those news categories were selected to test the idea that context would drive preferred attachment.

The second hypothesis predicts that stories about international relations will be more heavily linked than other stories. A Mann-Whitney U test confirmed this hypothesis. International relations stories had almost three more links than other stories during the five-year period. This gap was not consistent over time, but grew from only 0.5 (not significant) the first year to 5.5 by the final year.

The third hypothesis predicts the opposite result for spot news stories and is also confirmed by a Mann-Whitney U test. Spot news had three fewer links than other stories during the period of study. The gap was more consistent than the one observed for international relations, growing from about 2.5 in the first year to 4 in the final year.

H4 concerns the relative rates of growth between spot news stories and international relations stories. Specifically, it proposes a linear interaction between the growth and preferred attachment concepts proposed by Barabasi and Albert. If true, the gap between spot news and international relations stories should widen over time.

There is no procedure for testing a two-way linear interaction (with unequal cell sizes) with nonparametric statistics, but ANOVA can provide a conservative p value for reasons described above. The p value is not large but the limitations of ANOVA for nonnormally distributed data may be preventing a significant result. With a Type 1 error held to 5%, the fourth hypothesis is not supported.

The research question requires a comparison of Web news stories produced by print and broadcast companies. A two-tailed Mann-Whitney U test confirms what is apparent in the figure: stories on Web sites affiliated with broadcast outlets are considerably more "linked" than stories on sites associated with print publications.

Broadcast Web stories had more than twice the number of links. Initially, only a small difference was apparent, but the gap widened to 7 links by 2000. A narrowing of the gap was observed for 2001.

ALTERNATIVE EXPLANATIONS

The data suggest an increased use of hyperlinks over time and a statistically significant variance by topic. Alternatively, story length could be driving both trends. If news stories on the Web are getting longer, the opportunities for linking might likewise increase. An extensive literature citing Web news professionals suggests otherwise, but a test for this possibility is worthwhile.

Word counts were not recorded during the live coding done in the 1990s, but by the final year a complete digital record was preserved. This year of cases (n=241) was used to test the relationship between links and topic while controlling for story length. In addition, one site in the sample, CNN.com, maintains a Web archive of stories which was utilized to attach word counts to the existing data for CNN (n=157).

Unlike many of the 10 sites studied, this site has never limited page lengths by breaking the primary text into sequential chunks, so variance in words per main story page is substantial; CNN is an ideal test of the notion that story length and links may co-vary. Using these two sources of data, we can explore the effect of story length on the identified relationships.

During the five-year period, CNN.com stories did not vary significantly from a mean length of 647 words. That word count is consistent with the optimum page length recommended by Web professionals. There is a significant correlation between length and links. Longer stories did have more links.

By dividing links by words, a composite variable was created to test the trend over time. ANOVA revealed a significant linear contrast. Controlling for story length, the number of links increased over time; the growth hypothesis (H1) was confirmed for the sub-sample.

The second and third hypotheses were retested to control for length using the 2001 sub-sample. A links-per-word composite variable was computed for each case and normalized using a log transformation. Spot news did not differ significantly from other topics when controlling for story length.

International relations did differ significantly from other topics. For this sub-sample, the second hypothesis was rejected and the third confirmed. In 2001, stories from broadcast sites were shorter (763 words) than stories from print media sites (909 words) but used more links (11.6 compared to 6.6). Controlling for story length, broadcast stories had more links.

Previous studies on the increased use of context and interpretation in journalism and new theories about how networks grow led to the hypotheses and research question explored here. The growth effect of Hl was tested and confirmed. Two instances of preferential attachment were also discovered. Story topic (H2 and H3) affected the amount of linking in the predicted manner, although H2 was not supported when controlling for story length. Medium also made a statistically significant difference (RQ1).

Stories on Web sites of television companies were more heavily linked than on Web sites of print companies. This supports a recent study by Lin and Jeffres that found greater use of linking on local television Web sites than newspaper sites, although this study used the site rather than the story unit of analysis.

The additional linking on national broadcast sites is not

attributable to a significantly greater use of audio and video clips. That difference accounts for only 0.28 links per story while the overall gap between print and broadcast sites is 4.4 links per story. More likely, the difference stems from national broadcast outlets writing Web stories from scratch, while print sites can rely more on shovelware.

More than 400 stories (28.6%) contain no links at all, but 5 stories have more than 60 links. As a result, stories with the mean of 6 links cannot be convincingly described as "typical." The curve is very similar in shape to one depicting the Web as a whole although somewhat more gentle. Rather than following the 80/20 rule, this one follows an 80/31 distribution. That is, 31% of the stories in the sample accounted for 80% of the links.

Why is the curve more gentle? The purpose of journalism may limit the number of links a news story will offer on its main page. The story with the most links in this sample had 81, a relatively small number compared to the most-linked pages on the Web.

Stories that offered more links than this would fail at one of journalism's primary missions: providing the reader with a clear view of what really matters. Adherence to this mission may cap the effects of growth and preferred attachment and limits the length of the tail on the distribution. This may also explain why the growing gap between spot news and international relations failed to reach statistical significance.

An examination of the most linked stories is useful. The number-one story was from 28 March 1999 and appeared on CNN.com. This was the fifth day of NATO bombing during the Kosovo conflict that had been in the news for two years and was heavily covered in the preceding weeks. This provided editors with ample historical context and recently produced material.

The result: links to 37 internal pages of text, 18 other Web sites, 10 video clips, 8 photos, 6 maps, 1 audio clip, and 1 discussion forum. Although not investigated in this study, it is reasonable to conclude that the time a reader spends on such a presentation would, on average, exceed the time spent on a story that did not provide any linked material. In this way the technical characteristics of the Web could drive coverage the way television's news is driven, in part, by its technology. The next 5 most-linked stories shared the same topic: the stock market. This may be an example of the interaction between growth and preferred attachment.

The business audience was among the first to take advantage of the new medium. If Web editors targeted this audience then stories of this type would have received preferred attachment early on and would have grown at a faster rate than other stories.

During the five years investigated, financial stories were more heavily linked than stories about international relations. The sample for this study has some limitations which affect generalizability. For each of the five years, systematic sampling occurred in March rather than throughout the year.

Only the top stories for each sampling day were recorded; stories further down on a news Web site are likely less "linked." And because story length was not recorded until the final year, a more detailed examination of that variable is warranted.

This chapter addressed the increased use of hyperlinking but did not examine where those links lead. Are the points of view available to readers being broadened by linking, or are the same types of sources being used on the Web as in traditional journalism? When news organizations link to other Web sites, which ones are linked to and which are not? Are there trends already discernable that allow us to predict which kinds of ideas become "hubs" in the electronic network and which become isolated pockets?

Does the linking of news stories to discussion forums, a common practice on the Web sites examined here, affect the pattern of discourse surrounding current events? Two types of preferential attachment were confirmed in this study. Stories produced by broadcast companies were more heavily linked, and story topic also had a statistically significant effect on linking practice.

Another bias of Web editors that may affect link usage

is commercial. If television news favors good pictures to hold an audience, we might expect Web editors to use links strategically to keep readers on their sites. The special characteristics of the Web could be changing the way news stories are crafted.

By linking to contextual material instead of including it in the primary text, a separation may be occurring between "events" and "context." In this scenario individual stories may become at once more event-driven and more contextual (through the use of links). If this is the case, an examination of linking patterns becomes critical if we are to understand the way stories are framed in the Web of context.

CASE STUDY: THE NARRATIVE OF CORE TRADITIONAL VALUES IN REIMAN MAGAZINES

Reiman Publications is one of the largest publishers of magazines, with thirteen magazines devoted to cooking, country crafts, and reminiscence, all presented within a traditional values context and a "home-style" aesthetic. Six are in the top 100 in circulation.

Its most popular, Taste of Home, is the best-selling food magazine in the country; others include Country Woman, Birds & Blooms, and Reminisce. Taste of Home's editor sums up the company's approach: "We are proud to be the comfortable shoe, not the stiletto, of food magazines."

This approach is shared by readers-one described reading the magazines as "like visiting with people across the country for relaxing conversations among friends." Within the context of shelter books, the magazines present a singular model in important ways: they are ad-free and 80% of content is submitted by readers.

This case study describes how these magazines fit into the American cultural landscape and addresses how a conservative aesthetic is built around core values. Within the pages of the Reiman magazines, the role of suburban middle-class white women is tied to traditional values, religion, and a valorization of country taste as "authentic" expression.

Analysis of narrative structures shows that the magazines

tap into deeply shared assumptions about the American past and a discussion of rhetorical devices shows how the editors foster agency on the part of contributors and shape their submissions into a seamless whole. This study shows how an imagined community is constructed, describes the social space readers share, and suggests how the magazines frame and build core values.

It thus allows us to examine the larger cultural role that journalism fulfils as an "essential social narrative," and also to examine the role of journalism in binding readers into a community and in voicing shared values and a shared self-image.

The magazines embody a country aesthetic and a nostalgia for small-town life, a mythic construction that might seem ever more remote from American life and culture yet one that continues to appeal to a broad public. Given the persistent sense of social crisis and the increasing focus on the salience of traditional values in the press and the political sphere, it is critical to understand the appeal of such an approach.

The editors have responded to changing norms not by ignoring changes in women's lives but by placing them within the "feel good" sense of a simpler time that the magazines construct.

What has made these particular titles so attractive to readers, and what do they tell us about the current media landscape? After all, women's magazines have traditionally published anecdotes sent in by readers and have supplied guides for food and decorating. Likewise, shelter magazines have catered to "country" taste. Further, as in other magazines directed toward women, the editorial stance crafts a setting in which its readers feel at home, both emotionally and culturally. What makes the Reiman titles compelling is the presentation of seemingly unedited direct testimony from readers in an ad-free environment.

Due to the reader submissions, the editorial content nurtures and rewards reader investment. This helps create a devoted following-readers who, by contributing, join an imagined community, one in which participants are encouraged to feel that they are having a conversation with one another. Founded in Greendale, Wisconsin, in 1965 by Roy Reiman, this model, unique in the industry, has proven successful; despite the lack of advertising, the company has become a media empire, producing revenues of over $300 million a year and valued at $760 million when bought by Reader's Digest in 2002.

Yet, the company has received little scholarly attention, and even the magazine industry has largely ignored the company. Further, like the magazines, their readers-white, middle-aged, middle-class, suburban Midwestern women-are also understudied."

As a cultural form, magazines have not received the attention they deserve. In addition, as Johnson recently noted, few published studies place magazines within cultural and historical studies or address their role as reflectors and/or shapers of culture. Yet, as Kitch notes, magazines' "national reach, narrative style and physical permanence make them important sites of cultural commentary and community-building."

This study, like Kitch, views the role of journalism as binding readers into a community and voicing a shared self-image and values. Narratives order experience, and by doing so, they "make the world make sense." One focus of media studies is the narrative form news coverage takes and the function of the stories journalists tell. Such studies allow us to examine the larger cultural role that journalism fulfils-that of an "essential social narrative."

As symbolic texts, news narratives, "like myths, do not 'tell it like it is,' but rather, 'tell it like it means." The Reiman editors work to order the flux and chaos of life into a comforting narrative, approaching the task with a preconceived narrative structure that draws on a heritage of rural America as a site of traditional values and community.

Reiman magazines' narratives thus draw on American cultural resources to make sense of social and cultural change. They also tap into the nostalgia trend in today's media and assuage anxiety about the role of popular culture in contemporary life by portraying the nostalgic view that life was better, more relaxed, and more enjoyable in a previous era.

As one commentator wrote: "The world of Reiman Publications is all benevolent rolling terrain, the sunshine always sparkles and there's nary a smokestack in sight." Reiman credits the magazines' popularity to their helping readers connect to their rural past: "Close to half of all people in America have rural roots at least through their grandparents.

We're selling a two-hour escape to those people." This approach is intimately tied into identification as being an American, an identification crafted into every issue; Reiman's stated goal is for American readers to put their "chins up, chests out."

Kitch describes a contemporary "generational-memory trend" tied to the burgeoning number of media devoted to nostalgia in America in the last twenty years. She defines nostalgia as a social experience and identifies the role of magazines in that experience: "Nostalgic media products anticipate an ongoing dialogue between the producers and the audience, as well as shared values and wishes. This sense of mutual understanding is an editorial quality of most magazines, which speak conversationally to their readers about topics of common interest."

While conservative critics charge that many people feel disconnected from one another, dissatisfied with the mass media, and surrounded by a mediated culture over which they have no input or control, Reiman magazines have crafted a traditional, nostalgic model, that of an "old-fashioned exchange of stories and recipes over the backyard fence."

The editors provide a setting in which contributors believe their point of view matters, one where they can peruse others' memories and share their own. Kitch argues that reminiscent media merit attention because they are sites for social identity formation and because, due to their dialogic nature, they offer insight into the social function of magazines.

This study argues that the Reiman tides deserve attention for similar reasons.

Andersen's theory of imagined community is much invoked, but the actual process through which an imagined community is constructed is more rarely examined. The imagined community constructed in the magazines is organized around core values, what Gans calls "motherhood values"-family; community; church; reliance on pastoral, small-town virtues; and the image of the past as an ideal, safe place-that continue to resonate.

These deeply held, majority values are embedded in the narrative structures of Reiman submissions which present the creation of meals and country crafts as a way to knit family and community together. The magazines are vehicles through which a dialogue about those values is shared through reader submission of stories that are shaped and shared with other readers.

The reader interprets the modern world through a template of "traditional" values and behaviour, which are recalibrated to address contemporary stressors, such as the changing roles of women. These values are activated in material ways, in a "country" aesthetic celebrating an aggressively "American taste" centreed on country crafts, birding, and gardening.

The text, the projects, the howtos-all deliberately middlebrow-embody an aesthetic that can be created by the readers themselves, in the process working to make the reader feel both validated and creative. This analysis of the Reiman magazines was conducted through a close reading that led to narrative and rhetorical analysis.

Every issue of each title published between January 2003 and October 2005 (231 issues) was examined. The number of elements (recipes, letters, stories which included recipes) in the various publications ranged from 75 to 85 per issue, totaling about 18,249 items, the majority of which, in the food magazines, were recipes.

For example, in one issue of Taste of Home, 37 of 68 pages were recipes. This was followed by a textual analysis of every article that was not solely a recipe, with particular attention paid to Taste of Home, the most popular title, to capture the food category which comprises four of the thirteen titles, and Country Woman, to analyse one of the non-food magazines.

Although recipes are embedded in all sorts of stories, this analysis focused on the longer articles, as it is in these pages that the narratives of family, religion, and pastoral values are most pronounced. This close reading led to analysis of the narrative construction of values and of rhetorical strategies. This study examines the magazines at the level of production.

However, the meaning in the magazines is a co-production between readers and editors. We can make some claims about how the magazines function as a site for the creation of community. Even though we don't know to what extent the published versions are filtered through the editors' lens, the magazines would not exist unless the readers submitted content, so the content, however altered, is representative of readers' interests and lifestyle.

NARRATIVE STRUCTURES IN REITNAN MAGAZINES

The narratives in the magazines tell stories of individuals in their everyday lives. This presentation assigns value to the personal and the local, forming the image of a homogenous social gathering foregrounded by geographic region. Thus, the private life is privileged over the public life, and that private life is one that any reader can duplicate through recipes; homey design; and non-threatening, familiar, country decorations.

The appeal to the local works to resist standardization and presents the contributor as an individual of a given place and of a given church. Under the pretext of the magazines being not theirs but the readers', the editors foster the sense of agency that the reader feels.

This process eases the strains of modern life that cut off community and creates a product with which the targeted demographic feels comfortable. In this way, the magazines help define contemporary thought-that of visualizing nostalgia for a country lifestyle. These narratives reflect the values of the older, more conservative reader that appears in the magazines: married white woman, with husband and children. The narratives follow a common formula: we learn about the cook's family, what she and her husband do, her activities, her children, her mother's role in getting her cooking, and the story of her marriage.

These common narratives help tie the publications together at the same time they provide a normative model for the ideal life. They also serve as models for ways to order contemporary life and the proper stance to take toward the world: for the female reader, it is best to be a stay-at-home mom who devotes herself to her family.

If that is not possible, the next best thing is to duplicate as much as possible her mother's life and to incorporate the demands of working into the pleasures of creating a comfortable home. In either case, the role of religion is a defining frame for volunteer activities, social values, and social networks.

An interesting aspect of this narrative style is the ability to adapt and "domesticate" societal changes that might threaten this comfortable nostalgic view, including demands on working women, changing roles of women and men in the home, divorce, and alternative lifestyles. Otrum credits the readers for these responses: "Those are the interests that they have expressed to us over the years and we've responded."

Editorial copy does not shy away from demands on women's time that necessitate changing patterns in home life, but they are presented within a frame that makes them "safe." Therefore, there is the sense of modern life made palatable; in spite of changing norms, stresses on family life, and threats to traditional family structures, the old values hold.

These narratives, then, negotiate the tension in the lives of women leading contemporary lives but whose values are traditional. The narratives affirm that although she cannot stay home like her mother, the contemporary mother can still make dinner from scratch; despite the divorce rate in the United

States, traditional marriage is the norm; despite growing levels of immigration, the heartland is still a Christian world.

THE ROLE OF WOMEN

There is a strong focus on the nuclear family, particularly the role of women. Each recipe begins with a narrative about the cook; many note that the writer learned to cook from her mother and is now passing that wisdom down. This theme of carrying on traditions helps create a nostalgic look at the American past, a theme codified in the feature, "My Mom's Best Meals," which combines security, the importance of holidays, and the role of the mother in the family.

Stories often mention that both the submitter and her mother are stay-at-home moms, and tie that status to creating family bonds. For example, Norma Harder writes that her mother was "a stay-at-home mom with four children, and we were often greeted with the aroma of freshly baked bread after school."

Stories look back to when meals were made from scratch, a luxury modern cooks do not have. In this way, modern demands are recognized and incorporated into the contemporary scene. Catherine Dawe writes: "Nowadays, I do use some convenience products and am the queen of speedy weeknight dinners. But I like to cook from scratch when I have time." Genny Monchamp writes that "One thing Mom taught me is a real 'taste of home' can't be bought at a drive-thru window." Thus, despite the demands on the modern family, old values hold and are utilized when possible.

A second way the role of woman as keeper of the family hearth is maintained despite modern pressures is seen in portrayal of men in the kitchen. The impact of men cooking is softened by comedy and an upbeat approach.

In "Guys Prove That the Kitchen Is Not Only A Woman's Domain," men are praised by their wives for entering the kitchen, as in this from Anne Hoffman: "Since my husband, Dave, took early retirement several years ago, he has been spoiling my daughters and me with excellent dinners every night." A mother writes from Luray, Virginia, that preparing recipes with her son allows him to "brush up on his reading and math skills, plus it gives us quality chat time." Thus, women remain primary players in the kitchen. Likewise, two men profiled in "Men Who Run the Range" explain and justify their interest in cooking.

Bryan Cornett, living alone, got sick of fast food and spending money eating out, so he began to make his own meals, a frugal and admirable action. For Rich Murray, it was scouting that taught him to cook-over a campfire. The favourite cooking skill for both men is grilling.

These examples show how the editors have acknowledged the changing role of women, demands on working women, and the incorporation of men into the traditional value system. Two societal changes are notable exceptions: divorce and alternative lifestyles.

In most stories, a contributor's marital status and family are discussed. The approach is different for a divorced woman, as seen in "Her Innovative Renovation Was Simply 'Cent-sational'," an account of Dagmar Kuehn, a "can-do country woman" who "refused to let budget demands derail her dreams of a new kitchen."

Here, we notice what is absent: there is no mention of a husband; we can only assume Kuehn is divorced because whenever a woman is a widow, that fact is noted. Pictured are the daughter and daughter-in-law who helped redo her kitchen, but there is no group family photo as in other stories. Only two instances of divorce were found, one profiling a divorced mother and her son.

No mention is made of the break-up or of the father. Rather, the focus is on the mother's dependence on her parents to impart the same values she was raised with, her effort to provide male role models, and her statement that her son is her number-one priority. Finally, no same-sex couples were pictured in any of the publications examined.

The magazines foreground the relationship between family and religion, two venues of community building heavily laden with traditional values. Reiman positions his publications in opposition to others, calling his company the "good news company," a phrase with overtones of the Gospel. It is specifically the Protestant Christian faith that is a given in the magazines.

In narrating a company film, Reiman asks, if not for his publications, who would portray the "friendly, honest, hardworking people who live in God's country," who would show the "positive side of life," who would provide "uplift every month?"

Ann Kaiser, editor of Country Woman, reveals that the editors view the relationship between family and religion as seamless: "People who are reading it feel that sitting down for a family meal or taking dinner to a potluck at church is a significant part of their lives."

Asked about this taken-for-granted aspect of spirituality in the magazines and whether it was devised by the editors or came from the readership, Ottum deflected the question and framed his response as a critique of contemporary media and culture: A little of both.The magazines have always had that family focus-a strong moral sense.

Nowadays, a lot of people are looking for that.They're feeling dissatisfied with.the bad news they see.There are so many other outlets for people.if they want controversy, if they want hip and trendy.There are few places that they can find the content we provide.Once they do.they find it so refreshing, they stay with it.

The editors' connection of the magazines to religion is realized in the submissions. One woman wrote: the "April/ May issue arrived just in time. A potluck supper loomed at church, and.I wanted to make something I could both share and enjoy."

This assumption of shared Christianity is seen in a letter about her new kitchen from Eve Nasby: "When it came to designing the kitchen, we wanted a place where people could gather. Every Friday night, we host a Bible study with six to 15 people-and lots of good food!"

This matter-of-fact, often celebratory, approach to Christianity is also seen in a cover story of rancher Teri Purdy in Country Woman which notes that "Born on a Kansas ranch, Teri learned early how to ride herd on wayward cattle. And the fact that her mother is a music teacher and her father a minister accounts for the fact that she often gallops into the sunset singing."

The fundamentalist evangelical identity of some readers is captured in "Let's Be Pen Pals" in a letter from a self-described young wife and mother who is "interested in home schooling and simple Christian family living" and who would "like to correspond with women of a similar mind."

Themes of religion and family life are often combined, as in this profile of Martha Pollock: "When she's not busy in the kitchen or looking after the little ones, Martha helps [husband] Doug with his work as a director of a missionary organization. 'I'm a stay-at-home mom because family is important to me,' she explains."

In addition to Christian references in the text, certain sections are expressly devoted to the expression of faith, as in "Our Family's Favourite Grace." In one example, a grandmother shares her three-year-old granddaughter's prayer: "Lord, thank You for the food, bless it and please make it a corn dog!"

The primacy of Christianity and the "otherness" of other religions are clearly seen in "Let's Celebrate Spring" which offers suggestions on making crafts celebrating Easter and St. Patrick's Day. One section introduces Passover by interviewing a rabbi, who explains the meaning of the ritual dinner and who suggests renting the movie "The Ten Commandments" as a way to learn about the holiday.

The Christian spring holidays require no such explanation. We see then, that the narrative structures weave family, religion, and homemaking into a story that asserts a normative ideal.

TASTE CULTIVATION OF A COUNTRY AESTHETIC-AUTHENTIC AND PATRIOTIC

Reiman readers represent a peculiar segment of a large taste public in the United States-the cultivation of the country aesthetic in food and crafts directed to middle-class, middle-aged women who duplicate that aesthetic in their own lives. They are not oriented toward the urban environment and would reject the role of both "high culture" and of Hollywood in defining what holds value in cultural life and production.

The cultivation of taste in the magazines centres on a number of themes: the rural environment, the country style as authentically American, the pastoral way of life represented in food and crafts, and simple handmade food and crafts as expressions of values and lifestyle.

This aesthetic is part of the larger American culture, seen, for example, in restaurants such as Cracker Barrel and in the scrapbooking craze. Positioned as distinct from the avant-garde, as explicitly anti-modern, and as against the fabricated and toward the personally handmade, the adoption of this style becomes both a proud and a defensive strategy.

The term middlebrow describes the country aesthetic that both the readers and the Reiman publications craft, not in the sense of a class moving upward by adopting norms taught to them by professional book reviewers or tastemakers, as this group is not a class per se, but rather as a group coalescing around a set of values made visual in their kitchens and gardens.

Beyond the taste conveyed by the text and by the images, this aesthetic is tied into rural chauvinism with a concomitant association of real Americana. An example of such a presentation is seen in the profile of rancher and veterinarian Teri Purdy, in which the text suggests: "If you'd rather punch cattle than a time clock and swap a salary for a saddle, you might like to give ranch life a try."

Teri concurs, as she adds: "I'm convinced there's a cowgirl lurking in all of us!" Focusing on creating the country home, readers validate their life choices and gain comfort in a world that presents threatening options. This "good news" approach is reinforced by the taste cultivation of an aesthetic of the everyday.

The magazines provide meals that can be made from what's on hand; recipes are quick and easy; pantry staples are simple and common. Self-promotions also stress this quality: "Taste of Home takes a common-sense approach to mouth-watering family-pleasing meals with 75+ down-home, practical recipes per issue."

This middlebrow approach is captured succinctly in "Shortcuts to Share," in which a contributor recommends an easy glaze made from ketchup, baby food, and brown sugar for a glaze that "gives food a wonderful fully fruity boost."

Thus, recipes encourage experimenting with simple, at-hand ingredients with distinctly American flavour, such as ketchup, and reward ingenuity, as in the use of baby food. This positioning of difference, of valorizing the "everyday," defines the style of the magazines' departure from the use of "exotic" ingredients and approaches in other magazines.

CRAFTING THE RHETORIC OF THE "REIMAN FAMILY"

The Reiman publications have been called a "social barometer" of the taste of Middle America. If so, it is a carefully calibrated barometer. Although the construction of content is a collaboration between editors and readers, it is controlled by editors.

They generate a product that appeals to readers, and readers have to find that content compelling enough to submit stories.

Supplying 80% of the content, the readers sustain a social relationship with the editors and with one another. They are joined in a mutual endeavor: to define what the good life is but in a modest and "non-flashy" way. Contributors send in what can only be termed "the Reiman kind of story." The published formulas become a form of emotional tutelage, as the rewards of a stable family life and the presence of church activities are tied to fulfillment.

These become obligatory norms readers must comply with to get stories published. The most telling proof of the editors' ability to involve readers is their dependence on submissions. According to Ottum, each day Reiman receives 400 to 500 e-mail messages and several hundred letters.

The selected 100 or so are edited into a seamless whole. Contributors are "helped along" on how to write their submissions-since the reader who is considering submitting can see by example, the format of the stories becomes "automatic." In sifting through some 32,000 letters to choose 1,200 for any two-month period in which each magazine is published, editorial choices are required.

But based on what? Asked about how choices are made, Ottum deflected the question, stating that the winnowing process involves focusing on people who "love to serve food to their families." However "natural" the editors may claim the process to be, it is deliberate, for as one looks across all the magazines, it seems as if all the titles speak with one voice.

As one commentator wrote: "The most striking element is how seamless it all is, how easy it is to believe that all those folks out there have experiences which happily complement each other, and speak in whole sentences with impeccable grammar."

The concept promoted by the editors-of a community of readers for which Reiman serves as merely a "clearing house"-is nurtured through language, story selection, and shaping of narratives. We can gain insight into the construction of the narratives by identifying common themes in the reader submissions, as seen above, and by analyzing the rhetoric of the editors and of the text.

The editors produce an interactive product that encourages readers to engage with the magazines at a broad and deep level. They ask readers to submit stories and recipes, to participate in contests, to advertise for pen pals, to find a picture of a toothpick hidden in the magazine, to send in a secret ingredient that makes a dish special, to win a prize, to complete polls, to compete for prizes, to send in favourite photos, to share jokes and puns, and to submit a most embarrassing moment or a description of a favourite country character.

The response is impressive: a winning cookie recipe was one of 34,000 entries. The editors marshal a number of rhetorical strategies to craft reader-submitted content into a seamless whole. All work to foster agency on the part of the reader/contributor. First is self-presentation: the editors give credit for their success to readers, portraying themselves as a kind of "receiving and distribution system" rather than the editorial juggernaut they are.

They insist the magazine is merely a conduit that exchanges information among readers, as seen in this letter: "It's not really a magazine. It's a conversation." A second element of the rhetorical style is to distinguish Reiman from other publishing centres, particularly New York City, by characterizing their style as conversational and natural, and others as "exotic," a characterization that ties style to values. Ottum describes other cooking books as publishing "ritzy, entertaining and exotic" copy meant to please advertisers. Ottum furthers this distinction by tying their down-home style to submissions: "Most magazines set themselves apart from the reader-'We're telling you this information and that's it, take it or leave it.'

Our magazines have always been an exchange. They've had a very conversational tone and people have always felt like they are part of a family of readers. And so, they have felt very comfortable writing to us, telling us their stories." This characterization bears fruit in each issue of Taste of Home which introduces a few of the "1,000 editors" who contribute to the magazine this way: "These commonsense cooks aren't 'professionals' who test food in high-rise office buildings.They are probably a lot like you-friendly, down-home, practical, and real."

A third rhetorical strategy, one common to women's magazines in general, is a textual style engineered to establish contact with readers: the insistent use of direct address, active verbs that are emotive, punctuation that exclaims, and nomenclature for subscribers and editors. Direct address is the preferred form.

In Light & Tasty, the table of contents is titled: "Look What's Ahead." Contributors do not tell or say-they "report," "relay," "share," "relate," increasing the sense of sharing a secret or story. Punctuation extends this sense of importance;

exclamation points accentuate many of the stories. Copy is written in a folksy style with a homespun appeal, such as "Have You Herb?"

for a recipe that uses herbs. Contributors are called by their first names, and are identified by hometown, increasing the feeling of participating in an intimate community that spans all of the United States. This sense of community is amplified by the nomenclature used for the home cooks who test recipes: They are referred to as "editors," enhancing the effect that the magazines are written by readers.

A fourth rhetorical strategy is the way "experts" defer to contributors. Here the experts are not admired and looked up to, but rather are presented as helpers to the "real experts"- the homemaker. The magazines are "never preachy," and editors "never try to give the reader the impression that we know more than they do."

The editors forge a link with readers by referring to them as part of the "Reiman family," and by including contributors' names only; except for a few columns, none of the copy carries a byline or is identified as written by staff.

Finally, self-done surveys create a rhetorical tie of reader to magazine. Even conceding the difficulty of ascribing too much import to reader letters, given the self-selection in submissions and in what is printed, these letters are one way to gauge reader response and identify themes the editors wish to promote.

Both can be seen in the editors' report on the "freshening" of Country Woman: "When we included a survey last issue asking you to let us know what you think of Country Woman, we knew we'd get some mail-but never dreamed it would be this much! Our offices were flooded with almost 2,000 responses.

And we're pleased to report that your opinion is resoundingly positive. The most common comment was, 'Keep up the good work!'" In a survey for Quick Cooking, the editors noted that most readers had a hard time finding anything negative: "I've racked my brain to pick my least favourite feature, but I like them all."

The editors chose letters that were most effusive and create a sense of invested readers. However, these are actual sentiments that illustrate the loyalty and affection readers feel toward the magazines. Thus, in interviews, surveys, and the magazines themselves, we find the same rhetorical strategies, all portraying the editors as conduits, supporting the fiction that the magazines exist for the readers and not the company. The reader need look no further than the magazines for authority, as she should view herself as the specialist, not only in die kitchen, but also in proclaiming the value of her life and social position.

Carey regarded journalism as "a form of both cultural production and communal practice."81 His model posits that journalists and readers are engaged in a mutual activity in which published stories form a dialogue. Through such stories, a modern society forms its "constitutive narratives." Kitch called magazines the "most dialogic of all journalistic media" as they nurture a reader identification that fosters their ability to "assess the meaning of American life and to define the 'imagined community of a nation.'"

In asserting that magazines differ from other media forms, Abrahamson makes a case for "magazine exceptionalism" and describes the unique bond magazine editors have with their readers as a "direct community of interest." In the case of Reiman publications, readers not only read and respond to narratives, but supply their own. These narratives tell the story of ideal modern motherhood as rooted in the past, of the assumption of Christianity as the default American identity, and of an authentic country aesthetic, all of which play out more broadly in American culture today.

Appealing to a market largely ignored by other media companies, Reiman editors have been adept at creating community through narrative structures and rhetorical strategies. Their reader-centreed model invites the reader in, asks the reader to contribute, reports on reader interests, appears to foster reader agency, and relies on reader submissions for 80% of the content.

The critical aspect of this model is that it appeals to a

subscriber to join a community mat shares values and beliefs and that places the past and the future within the context of family and religion. The narratives of cooking, crafts, and gardening present these activities as integral to the roles of wife, mother, and grandmother, and at the same time structure these as essential strands to solidifying the family bond and participating in community.

This has been an immensely appealing approach to the Reiman reader as it taps core values in the American cultural landscape, eases tensions between the ideal and the real, provides continuity between the past and the present, and valorizes traditional female activities.

Reiman narratives order experience around family rituals of shared dinners, church potlucks, and the aesthetic of the everyday. They "make the world make sense" by making the world feel comfortable and seemingly familiar. Through a nostalgic lens, the narratives negotiate the tension between contemporary life and traditional values.

Future research might include a study demonstrating how the magazines function as sites for identity formation. Such a study would build on reader response theory, because the reader is not only a reader but a cocreator of the published product. This research might show that the subscriber/contributor turns to the magazines seeking affective experiences that are confirmed in the worldview presented there.

Shared tips, letters, and experiences-they all can be said to nurture a particular orientation toward the world and function as a guide for living. The magazines combine taste, beliefs, and values in a seamless package that valorizes the life the subscriber lives. Reading becomes a connection to others.

Research might show that, like members of the Book-of-the-Month Club, Reiman readers "consolidate their faith in a specific set of values and assumptions about the world." Such a study might demonstrate that the publications provide a site for the same "adjudication, negotiation, and self-reflection" Long found in book clubs.

Within the Reiman pages, values are openly discussed and serve to integrate readers into an imagined community. Given that readers provide the content, this mass-mediated community in some ways prefigured those formed on the Internet. The difference is that editors shape submissions into a seamless whole, one in which readers and contributors share a worldview that seems to be solid and affirming.

A CASE STUDY: DELIBERATIVE DEMOCRACY ON TELEVISION

Research has shown that television contributes to higher levels of political learning. Many have commented that the format of traditional news coverage tends to prevent in-depth thinking. The resulting low level of issues coverage reduces opportunity for public deliberation on television. The problem is further exacerbated by marketplace forces that McManus found drove out enterprise and issue coverage in favour of passive news discovery and high profits.

Since the 1992 presidential election, many scholars have focused on nontraditional news media, primarily television/ radio talk shows, as a more direct conduit for issues discussion between candidates and citizens. However, these scholars have focused primarily on entertainment/candidate driven talk shows on commercial television and radio.

C-SPAN, the cable-satellite public affairs network, is one media organization that has yet to be examined. Relatively unaffected by market forces, C-SPAN's unique minimalist model of content packaging and its potential to create a mediated deliberative space provided a research opportunity to examine the level and quality of citizen dialogue on television.

This study is an exploratory case study focusing on how the content of Washington Journal approximates a deliberative space for civic dialogue. On the surface, C-SPAN would appear to be an ideal place where politically engaged people come together to work through public issues. However, no one has asked if it rises to the ideals both C—SPAN and democratic theorists set forth.

To lay the foundation for this research, we will examine literature on the concepts of television and its role in deliberative, nontraditional news formats, and finally, C-SPAN's civic role and its call-in show, Washington Journal.

MEDIA AND DELIBERATION

Page said public deliberation in today's society must be largely mediated. Since the majority of Americans use television as their primary news source, creating a mediated deliberative space must include television. Still, others argue that the marketplace plays little role in encouraging democratic debate and decision making. Former U.S. Sen. Bill Bradley said, "The market acts blindly to sell and make money, never pausing to ask whether it furthers citizenship or decency."

Faced with challenges of marketplace forces, the question that remains is whether we can imagine political deliberation on television. A number of foundation-funded efforts have imagined the possibility of mediated deliberative dialogue. Friedland's research on The Wisconsin Collaborative Project provided evidence that collaboration among public television stations helped increase the deliberative issues programming.

Civic journalism built on the collaborative model by encouraging newspaper partnerships with commercial and public television and radio stations. One focus of civic journalism was to reframe coverage to create a deliberative space for citizens. One project, Best Practices 2000, funded public and commercial station partnerships to create innovative issue-focused election and political coverage.

These efforts are bound together by the limited creation of civic deliberative space on television and the fragility of the efforts once the funding cycle is completed. Arterton's case studies also showed that telecommunications technologies can improve citizen participation in politics and provide more equality among social groups.

Deliberation

In his most recent work on the public sphere, which

essentially revises and extends all of his previous work on this topic, Habermas reasserts the centrality of a robust and open discourse within the media for a vibrant democracy to be possible in complex societies. Habermas' view of the public sphere is that participants enter with a clean slate.

While this is almost certainly unachievable, it is akin to bringing an open mind to the discussion. Yankelovich connects the democratic deliberative process with dialogue, adding the sharing of feelings and values. However, Yankelovich said, "Television should not seek to reproduce the sprawling, disorganized and repetitive character of real-life dialogue."

Instead, he called television a "proxy dialogue," where those who present views represent other citizens who lack that opportunity. The three requirements for a "proxy dialogue" are equality, listening with empathy, and openly sharing assumptions.

Yankelovich said dialogue is possible when two or more of these elements are present. Further, he argued that mediated dialogue must present issues "from the public perspective rather than from the perspective of a technical expert, partisan political leader, a self-seeking interest group, or current crop of television producers, who insist on staging conflict and confrontation because of their supposedly superior entertainment value."

The purpose of dialogue in public life is for citizens to work through their issues, aspirations, and concerns, and toward resolution. Yankelovich proposed a three-step process for reaching public judgment. The first is consciousness-raising, whereby citizens learn or become more aware of the ideas and concepts surrounding an issue.

Yankelovich says this generally occurs through the media. The second stage is "working through," where citizens "confront the need for change." The final stage is "resolution," in which citizens select among choices developed in the process of working through the issue.

The precursor to dialogue is factual discussion, devoid of values and feelings. Dialogue is achieved when an individual presents his or her own values within a group setting. A more complex level of dialogue is achieved when a person also recognizes the values of others in his or her statements.

The articulation of potential solutions or consequences, without a focus on winning or losing, is the final dialogue element. Underlying this process of coming to public judgment is the notion that people must build on earlier comments and not simply repeat what has already been said. New ideas allow participants in the conversation, both vocal and silent, to assess the worth of a concept within the context of that conversation and provide reaction, feedback, and continued dialogue that might generate additional new ideas. Simply, a new idea furthers the discussion of a public issue or problem with the goal of raising the consciousness of the group on that issue.

In essence, consciousness-raising, as conceived by Yankelovich, seems to be a mediated brainstorm, all of the possible ways of conceptualizing an issue being brought into consideration.

Talk Shows

Both radio and television talk shows play a highly visible role in the American deliberative democratic process. Talk shows are not monolithic and vary widely in content, quality, and professionalism. Still, they share many common characteristics.

Talk shows are distinctive from other information sources, such as newscasts or panel discussion programs, in that they engage directly with the audience regarding political topics. Ordinary citizens are able to become something more than mere spectators, interacting with each other and the host. Munson found that talk shows provide a mediated sense of place, which can be equated with a deliberative space for discussion.

Further, Herbst argued, "Call-in programs provide an excellent, unstructured outlet for public discourse. Unlike voting and participation in opinion polls, call-in programs let callers (those who can get through) express themselves in their own words-sometimes at great length."

Citizens view calling a talk show as real political activity, ,engaging in solving political problems. Pan and Kosicki said, "Exposure to and participation in television and radio talk shows is tantamount to participating in the collective process of constructing public discourse on the issues that are believed to be common concerns of at least some members of the mass public."

This view is supported by survey research. Past research on talk shows has focused either on characteristics of listeners and callers or on the effects of listening to talk shows on political knowledge and attitudes. Only a handful of studies examined the nature of the content of talk shows.

In one such study, Herbst found that the majority of callers fits one of four categories-they were seeking advice, clarification, or information; transmitting opinions; engaging in dialogue; and policing the public sphere. Crittenden analysed the topics of callers and showed that the majority of calls focused on political— governmental concerns, local concerns, and the tendency toward opposition rather than support.

Examining host behaviours, Avery, Ellis, and Glover found a cyclical pattern of host support and reinforcement of callers. In general, the research suggests some people use talk shows as a deliberative space.

None of the studies cited above included C-SPAN call-in shows. C— SPAN does not have advertising and, unlike PBS, does not accept public funding. Instead C-SPAN is funded entirely by cable and satellite distribution fees.

This structure effectively diminishes the impact of market forces, allowing call-in shows structured around viewers' comments and not host personalities. Washington Journal is issue- and caller— driven with guests brought on to help illuminate the issues.

C-SPAN's Civic Value

C-SPAN fulfills three primary roles in our democratic

society. Foremost, it provides the opportunity for citizens to watch government in action through the televising of the U.S. Congress.

Next, it provides an opportunity for citizens to become educated on issues of public debate and importance. Finally, it allows opportunities for citizens, experts, and public policy makers to exchange ideas and to begin working toward a solution or a consensus on an issue.

Call-in programming is a network trademark. Frantzich and Sullivan said, "The call-in format rests at the heart of the C-SPAN mission. The philosophy that engendered it reveals an attitude about the capacity and the capability of the average citizen." Lamb said call-in programming provides a format for citizens to join the public discourse by creating an on-air public space for civic issue political discussions.The opportunities for citizens to interact are not perfect.

Callers often have long waits before they get the opportunity to share their views. There is no way to know how many people with ideas to share did not call or hung up in frustration over the wait. C-SPAN's response to this problem is to limit callers to one call every thirty days.

C-SPAN documents also note the goal of fifteen callers per forty-five-minute programme. Calls are balanced by political persuasion and, except during "open phones" sessions, are focused around a primary topic. C-SPAN guidelines dictate that call-in show hosts promote informed issues discussion and remain on the sidelines of the dialogue.

C-SPAN seems to provide an opportunity for deliberative dialogue. Washington Journal includes many of the elements democratic theorists point to as important to democratic deliberative process. The call-in programme attempts to fulfill these elements through avoiding prescreening of calls and not allowing hosts or guests to dictate the discussion direction.

In many programs, particularly "open phones" programs, citizens help set the agenda. This structure leads to an open forum for exchanging ideas. The hosts, guests, and some callers regularly demonstrate good listening skills and the hosts and callers often point out underlying assumptions. Left unanswered is what the quality of the dialogue created on Washington Journal is, in light of Yankelovich's work.

This research examines the civic nature of the content in Washington Journal, an approximation of a deliberative space for civic dialogue. We examine the connection with citizens through the call-in programs by looking at the range, depth, and context of ideas presented by citizens on C-SPAN call-in shows.

This study seeks to answer the questions: Do C— SPAN call-in segments foster a public space for new ideas to enter the public fray and, once there, how are these ideas treated?The primary issues were: (a) whether callers presented new ideas or repeated someone else's comments and (b) the level of public discourse.

The latter might include sharing core values, recognizing the core values of another person or group, providing a potential solution for consideration, and/or acknowledging the consequences of a solution.

The following sets of research questions were posed. Drawing on Yankelovich, new information is central to consciousness-raising.

This leads to two research questions:

- RQ1: To what extent do callers present new information to the political conversation?
- RQ2: Is there a difference in how long people spend talking about a new idea compared to a repeated one?

Further, based on Yankelovich's work, we wanted to know whether callers to C-SPAN's Washington Journal were likely to address political solutions, the underlying political values of both self and others, and specific consequences of political decisions.

- RQ3: To what extent do people discuss political solutions, their own or others' values, or the consequences of political decisions?
- RQ4: Is there a difference in likelihood of solutions, values, or consequences depending on whether someone presents a new idea?

The last two questions address how the hosts and/or guests react to the callers' comments. If C-SPAN operates as its philosophy suggests, as simply a conduit for people's ideas, there should be no difference in the length of reaction or the type of reaction to a new idea versus an old one.

- RQ5: Do hosts/guests react differently to new political ideas by talking longer?
- RQ6: Is there any difference in the type of response by the hosts/guests to new political ideas?

OPERATIONALIZATIONS AND METHOD

This study used content analysis of C-SPAN call-in shows aired during a three-and-a-half-year period, from June 1997 through December 2000. Specifically, twelve Washington Journal programs were selected for analysis using a purposive method. The individual topics within each call served as the unit of analysis.

The programs were selected based on the following rules: to reflectively capture the formats used by Washington Journal, half of the programs needed to be topic specific (e.g., patients' bill of rights) and half needed to be open phone-line segments (e.g., newspaper roundtable) with no specific predetermined topic focus.

Further, none of the programs could be specifically about the Monica Lewinsky/President Clinton scandal or the 2000 presidential election, as these topics would have skewed the conversation to focus more on conflict and strategy, rather than on problem-solving.

Last, all nondomestic issue discussions were avoided in order to focus on domestic issues, problems with which people are more likely to be engaged and feel are solvable by citizens. The final sample represented a wide range of topics, typical of content on Washington Journal.

The Washington Journal programs varied in length. The shortest programme in the sample was approximately eighteen minutes, and the longest ran one hour. The variations were because of the Congressional schedule rather than topic or caller considerations. Open phone-line segments generally were without a guest and simply had a host in the studio.

There were three different hosts for the various programs.Our analysis is of the calls that were included in the programme and does not include callers left waiting on the phones or who hung up before they were chosen for inclusion in the programme. There is no way to know how many callers with new ideas chose not to call or did not make it on the programme.

However, there is no reason to believe that callers with new ideas were more likely to call or to get frustrated waiting compared to people without new ideas, particularly given C-SPAN's minimalist call screening. Calls were coded for caller demographics (gender, geographic location, and political orientation). The total call length was coded from the caller's hello to the point he or she hung up.

For each topic the caller discussed, we analysed the length of time spent on the topic, whether the topic was a new political idea (in the context of the entire programme), and whether the caller addressed solutions, values, or consequences in the topic. For the purposes of this study, a new idea was considered within the context of the programme, which we treated as a deliberative space.

The call-in programme was treated as if it were a conversation, albeit a mediated one. If an idea was not mentioned previously during this programme, it was considered to be a new idea for this discussion. Programming preceding the Washington Journal was generally unrelated to the focus of the call-in programme.

Comments were only considered a new idea if they made reference to a political or civic issue and offered new information. Thus, a compliment to the show host or an attack on a candidate's personality was not a new idea. Simply, a new idea furthers the discussion of a public issue or problem with the goal of raising the consciousness of the group on that issue.Hosts and/or guests were coded to see their effect on the conversation.

Each response was coded for time and format. Responses were coded according to the following definitions, which were derived from Avery et al.'s code guide: Dismissal, when the guest/host rejected the comments of caller; Elaboration, when the guest/host built on what the caller said; Affirmation and Move on, when the guest/host thanked the caller and either moved to the next call or turned to the guest for comment (if the guest's comment was related to the topic it was also coded as a separate response); Exploratory question, when a guest/host engaged the caller with a question looking for more information (e.g., "So you think Gore is the best at preserving the environment?");

Civic-based question, when the guest/host asked the caller a question based on problem— solving areas: about alternative solutions, values, or consequences (e.g., "So how do we solve this?" or "What do you value in this debate?"); Clarifying comment, when a guest/host limited the response to a correction of something that was said; and No reaction, when the host moved to the next call without comment.

RESULTS

Intercoder Reliability: Two coders analysed a little more than 10 per cent of the calls to ensure intercoder reliability. For the categorical variables, reliability was calculated using Perreault and Leigh's reliability index. The index of reliability values ranged from.80 to 1.00. For ratio-level variables, reliability was examined using Cronbach's alpha. The reliability values for ratio variables ranged from.92 to.99.

Descriptive Statistics: Twelve different episodes of C-SPAN's Washington Journal were examined with a total of 225 callers. Each caller averaged slightly more than two different topics. The average length of time that callers talked, from the moment they said hello to the point they hung up, was 58.77 seconds, with each different topic averaging 24.31 seconds.

The hosts and guests responded to each call for an average of 20.96 seconds, averaging just under two responses per call.Research Question Results: The first research question examined whether callers presented new political ideas in the topics they discussed. Of the 488 different topics from all callers, only 27% of the topics presented new political information.

To examine RQ2, we conducted a one-way analysis of covariance (ANCOVA), comparing the length of time spent on a new idea versus an old idea. The length of the entire call was covaried out to control for the amount of time people talked overall. The results indicated that people were significantly more likely to talk longer when an idea was new rather than old.

The third research question examined the extent to which people used Yankelovich's concepts of solutions, values, and consequences. First, in only 8% of the topics did callers propose specific solutions to political issues. In only 5.6% of the topics did callers explicitly discuss their own values as a basis for their political opinions, and in only 3.6% of the topics did callers discuss the values of other people.

Finally, in 8% of the topics callers specifically addressed the consequences of political solutions.Since these four concepts of civic dialogue were all dichotomous items, a scale was created to see the total number people use for each topic. Eighty-one per cent of all topics contained none of these concepts.

Of those who did discuss at least one of these four aspects, 77% discussed only one, 18% incorporated two of these items, 4% three, and 1% all four (this was actually one topic).Despite this low level of incorporating these key aspects of civic dialogue in the calls, we were interested to see if there were a different pattern of these aspects depending on whether a caller presented a new idea in the topic (RQ4). Chi-square analysis was conducted comparing new ideas to the presence of each of Yankelovich's concepts.

First, callers presenting new ideas were five times more likely to discuss specific solutions. Callers presenting new ideas were more than twelve times as likely to discuss explicitly their own underlying values. As mentioned above, few people acknowledged the values of others. Despite this, people presenting new ideas were four times as likely to discuss the values of others.

Finally, the majority of people discussing the consequences of political solutions were those presenting new ideas. A consequence was discussed almost 18 times as often when the topic was new rather than old.

The last set of analyses examined the reactions of hosts and guests to callers bringing new ideas to the conversation. First, whether the host and guests simply talked longer overall in response to callers who presented a new idea in a topic was examined.

As above, the overall call length was covaried out. There was no difference in overall length of host/guest response for topics with new ideas and for those without new ideas. Next, we compared the amount of time hosts/ guests spent in their first and second reactions.

The first response was most often by the host, while the second response was usually by the guest. The results reveal no difference between new and old ideas in how long the hosts and guests talked in their first response to the callers, or in their second response.

Last, to answer RQ6, we examined whether the format of hosts'/ guests' first and second responses differed depending on whether a new idea was presented. As stated earlier, the reaction of the hosts/guests was coded in one of seven exclusive categories.

A chi-square analysis showed a difference in the pattern of host/guest first response formats to those who presented a new idea and those who did not. To old ideas, hosts and guests responded 42% of the time with "affirmation and move on," followed by an exploratory question (36%), elaboration (12%), and a clarifying comment (10%ro).

To new ideas, hosts and guests responded 49% of the time with "affirmation and move on," followed by an exploratory question (21%), elaboration (18%), and a clarifying comment (12%).

In looking at the second response, no difference existed in the format of the responses to new and old ideas. The most common second response to a caller was either "Affirmation or move on" (43% of the time) or "Exploratory question" (24%

of the time). From our investigation, it seems clear that C-SPAN's call-in programme Washington Journal fulfills some but not all of the elements of a deliberative forum. Citizens do have opportunities to air issues and ideas that had not previously been on the show's agenda and do so at greater length than those who repeat previous discussions.

In almost a third of the topics, callers presented new ideas to the conversation. Further, people were more likely to spend more time on new ideas than old ones. There seemed to be no pattern to who offered new ideas and who did not. Having a large quantity of new ideas does not necessarily result in good quality.

But, as Csikszentmihalyi suggested, presenting as many different ideas as possible is central to problem-solving.41 A sufficient quantity of ideas is a prerequisite to identifying ideas of quality.Another important set of questions focused on how often people incorporated Yankelovich's features of political problem-solving.

While few people incorporated these characteristics in their comments, callers were more likely to explicitly incorporate their own values, the values of others, political solutions and the consequences of these solutions within new ideas than old ones.

Thus, these new ideas tended to be at a higher level of civic discourse than the old ones.This research is the first to show that the structure of a call-in show can help foster a meaningful level of public dialogue as described by Yankelovich.

While Yankelovich provides the theoretical structure, there was no evidence that this structure existed to any meaningful level in a mediated form, such as television. Thus, this study advances Yankelovich's model by advancing his theory into a mediated format.

As suggested in the literature review, C-SPAN hosts try to be a neutral conduit to people's ideas. How the hosts and guests actually responded to new and old ideas was more complicated. There was little difference in how long the hosts and guests talked in reaction to new and old ideas. This supports their neutral conduit notion. Yet, the first reaction by the host/guest (most often the host) was more likely to be a question when the caller did not present a new idea. Perhaps they were trying to move the callers to a more civic point. Further calls were often truncated, since the tendency of the hosts and guests is to affirm and move on more with new than with old ideas, whereas they are more willing to ask exploratory follow-ups with old ideas.

It is interesting to note that the hosts and guests never asked a question that pushed callers to address specifically any of Yankelovich's four aspects of civic dialogue (solutions, one's own values, others' values, and consequences of decisions). So while they often asked questions, political problem solving language was never used.

Callers seem to be describing their own view of what the political issue is, reacting to a disconnected list of anecdotes instead of a conversation. There does not seem to be anyone sitting back and synthesizing these isolated ideas. Because C-SPAN simply reacts to each caller independently, rather than threading the ideas together, the programme does not reach the level of deliberation Yankelovich argued is necessary for problem-solving.

It appears viewers are expected to deduce solutions from the disjointed ideas callers present, without assistance from the hosts or guests. Although one could argue the show's "on the one hand and then the other hand" structure limits the range of opinion, it does tend to prevent any snowballing of opinion that leads to the Spiral of Silence, when individuals perceive they are in the minority on an issue and refuse to voice their opinions.

To the contrary, C-SPAN call-ins seem to prevent this effect. To further civic problem-solving, C-SPAN needs to more fully engage the callers in understanding their own values and the values of others, brainstorming and discussing possible solutions, and helping people recognize the consequences of various solutions. Finally, the hosts and guests should do more to make connections among the various callers, building a thread of continuity throughout the programme. Certainly, the callers to C-SPAN call-in shows are not a representative sample of U.S. citizens, being highly self-selected and extremely interested and engaged in politics.

Still, research on these callers gives us an opportunity to examine how people structure their political ideas in a real context. If the politically engaged are not able to have quality dialogue on issues of public importance, how can we expect the less— engaged populace to do so?

Indeed, the beneficial aspects of such programming for open discussion provide an interesting contradiction to Spiral of Silence. Norris indicated a "virtuous circle," in which the most politically knowledgeable and active citizens are more likely to tune in public affairs coverage and those who attend to public affairs coverage are more likely to become engaged in civic life.

Because this is an exploratory study, future research needs to continue to examine the nature and structure of citizens' political·discussions and to see what people do with this knowledge in context. A similar content analysis should be done on C-SPAN's Web site forums to see how the interaction is different. Perhaps these online ideas are linked together in more meaningful ways that add to the public dialogue because chat rooms and discussion boards allow ideas to be chained together.

Bibliography

Atwan Robert, Barry Orton, and *William Vesterman,* eds. 2000. American Mass Media. New York: Random House.

Bagdikian Ben. 2001. The Effete Conspiracy. New York: Harper and Row.

Dressel Paul L. 2002. Liberal Education and Journalism. New York: Columbia University Press.

Elliott Deni, ed. 2004. Responsible Journalism. Beverly Hills, Calif.: SAGE Publications.

Glasser, T. (2003) Press responsibility and First Amendment values. In D. Eliott (ed.), Responsible Journalism. London and Newbury Park, CA: Sage.

Hamelink, C.J. (2000) Information imbalance across the globe. In J. Downing, A. Mohammadi and A. Sreberny-Mohammadi (eds) Questioning the Media: A Critical Introduction, second edn. London: Sage.

Hamelink, C. (2004) International communication: global market and morality. In A. Mohammadi (ed.) International Communication and Globalisation. London: Sage.

Melody, W.H. (2000) 'Communications policy in the global information economy', in Ferguson, M.F. (ed) (2000) Public Communication: The New Imperatives, London: Sage.

Olasky Marvin. 2003. Prodigal Press: The Anti-Christian Bias of the American News Media. Westchester, Ill.: Crossway Books.

Ward Walter J. and *Associates.* 2002. The Nature of News in Three Dimensions. Stillwater: Oklahoma State University, Bureau of Media Research, School of Journalism and Broadcasting.

Willis Jim. 1990. Journalism: State of the Art. Westport, Conn.: Praeger Publishers.

Index

O

P

R

S

T

V

W